BRITISH BROADCASTING AND THE DANISH RESISTANCE MOVEMENT

1940–1945

BRITISH BROADCASTING AND THE DANISH RESISTANCE MOVEMENT 1940-1945

A STUDY OF THE WARTIME BROADCASTS OF THE B.B.C. DANISH SERVICE

BY

JEREMY BENNETT

Formerly Churchill Fellow
University of Copenhagen

CAMBRIDGE
AT THE UNIVERSITY PRESS
1966

CAMBRIDGE UNIVERSITY PRESS
Cambridge, New York, Melbourne, Madrid, Cape Town, Singapore,
São Paulo, Delhi, Dubai, Tokyo, Mexico City

Cambridge University Press
The Edinburgh Building, Cambridge CB2 8RU, UK

Published in the United States of America by Cambridge University Press, New York

www.cambridge.org
Information on this title: www.cambridge.org/9780521158442

First published 1996
First paperback edition 2010

A catalogue record for this publication is available from the British Library

Library of Congress Catalogue Card Number: 66-17533

ISBN 978-0-521-04161-4 Hardback
ISBN 978-0-521-15844-2 Paperback

For

T. L. B.

CONTENTS

PLATES

FOREWORD

BY ALAN BULLOCK

British broadcasting to Europe during the Second World War has not hitherto attracted much attention from historians. This is a pity for, quite apart from the intrinsic interest of the problems of wartime propaganda, Mr Bennett shows in this pioneer study that here is a subject which throws a good deal of light on British policy towards Europe on the one hand and on the character of the German occupation and the attitudes of the different resistance groups on the other. Mr Bennett's book in fact has a double interest: it examines in detail the particular case of Denmark and at the same time provides a model of what could be done in a dozen further cases ranging from the B.B.C.'s broadcasts to other occupied countries (France, Holland, Norway, Poland, each with special features of its own), to the very different problems of broadcasting to countries like Spain, Finland and the enemy peoples themselves.

One half of Mr Bennett's story was already partly familiar to me. I joined the embryonic European Service at the beginning of 1940 when its editorial staff was accommodated in a couple of rooms at Broadcasting House and remained with it to the end of the war, by which time it had not only grown into one of the world's major broadcasting services but had won a standing in Europe which none of its competitors—American, Russian or German—could rival. To have been one of the foundation members of this team is still a matter of pride to me and I was at least aware of, even if I did not take much part in, the divisions of opinion and disputes on the British side which Mr Bennett describes. I have found it fascinating to watch an historian take up and examine these issues with a detachment which was difficult for anyone to achieve at the time. Even more interesting is the correspondence (or lack of it) which he establishes between events in occupied Denmark and the lines the British were trying to follow in their broadcasts. This is the other half of the picture which was so difficult to visualize with any confidence during the war and much of which is told here for the first time, at least in English.

Denmark is a small country and the B.B.C.'s Danish broadcasts were only a small part of its European Service. The problems which emerged, however, on both sides of the North Sea were typical of those which beset broadcasting to all the occupied countries, and Mr Bennett's account of them opens up the whole field of wartime broadcasting to Europe. I hope that it will be followed by studies of a similar nature for other parts of the B.B.C.'s European Service and that these will match the high standards set in the present volume.

St Catherine's College
Oxford
August 1966

FOREWORD

BY JØRGEN HÆSTRUP

It is hardly possible to overestimate the importance the B.B.C. broadcasts had for occupied Denmark. It was impossible after 1945 fully to explain to the world and to new generations what fundamental meaning the broadcasts had for the imprisoned country, for its information and guidance, for its feelings and its attitudes. The ordinary and, until 1940, largely unknown letters B.B.C. acquired in the course of a few weeks almost magical qualities. For the imprisoned they came to stand for freedom, truth and hope. The voices from London and the institution behind those voices became close and trusted friends.

A personal experience can perhaps contribute something to describe conditions. On 22 June 1941, the day of the German attack on the Soviet Union, the first sensational B.B.C. announcements of the invasion were received in my home during the morning. The summer holiday began on just that day, and the next few weeks were to be spent in a little fishing village where we had rented a couple of rooms for our holiday. In these rooms there was no radio, and the thought of being cut off from the B.B.C. on just that day was more than unbearable. All worries on this occasion proved, however, to be unnecessary. When it was time for the evening broadcast from the B.B.C., the well-known voices from London rang out from the open windows of a long row of fishermen's cottages. Like eavesdroppers we edged a little nearer to one of the houses, and a few minutes later we found ourselves hauled into a strange room. We were part of a listening group of fishermen, farmers and holiday-makers—different professions, different ages, but one ear only. The group lasted out the holiday, and started up again during the following holidays. Acquaintances from here later became useful in resistance work. This is a random example amongst thousands.

This group did not confine itself just to listening in to the radio. After listening sessions followed prolonged discussions, and encouragement from the B.B.C. became an important basis for the lively political debate which during the war and occupation flared up over the whole of Denmark. It is a peculiar fact that, when German censorship attempted to suppress information and prevent free discussion, occupied Denmark was better and more widely informed than at any time previously. A widespread debate began and gradually shook itself free from all direction from above. The Danish Resistance movement, and its fight against the Germans and the official Danish policy, was born from the initiative of the ordinary man and began in his home or place of work; it was born from impulses brought to this anonymous miniature battlefield to a great degree by the B.B.C.'s closely listened-to and keenly discussed bulletins and commentaries. Censorship created ideal conditions for the words from London.

In Jeremy Bennett's thorough and clear study of the B.B.C.'s Danish Service we have a long-wanted account of attitudes and aims in London, but no account, however detailed, could completely attest to the vital significance for Denmark of the broadcasts from London. The personal evidence of this could only be brought out by the ten thousands of Danes still living who, in the five years of the occupation, became thankful victims of a countrywide B.B.C. addiction.

Sct. Klemens
August 1966

ACKNOWLEDGEMENTS

A Churchill Fellowship to the University of Copenhagen in 1962 enabled me to carry out the necessary research work in Denmark for this book. I am deeply indebted to the Trustees of the Churchill Endowment Fund for this award.

I would like to express my thanks to Dr Jørgen Hæstrup for spending so much of his time in helping and guiding me—his three books on the history of the Danish Resistance movement provided the basis for this work: to Mr Alan Bullock, Master of St Catherine's College, Oxford, for kindly agreeing to write a foreword to this book: to Dr G. R. Elton, of Clare College, Cambridge, for his continual encouragement: to Dr Elias Bredsdorff, Reader in Scandinavian Studies at Cambridge University, for reading and commenting on the manuscript: to the members of the Institute for Contemporary Danish History (D.N.H.), Copenhagen: to the Royal Archives, Copenhagen: to the Royal Institute of International Affairs and the Wiener Library in London, and to many people both British and Danish, who have put papers at my disposal: and to my wife for her help and her patience.

I am very grateful to the B.B.C. for the help that I have received. I would particularly like to mention Miss Margaret Sampson of the European Service and Miss Mary Hodgson of the Archives Section who, by sorting out relevant material, made my research into B.B.C. documents much easier than it might otherwise have been. I was not appointed to the staff of the B.B.C. European Service until after this book was written. The views expressed in it are entirely my own, and should not be regarded in any way as being official.

Finally I acknowledge with thanks the assistance given to me by the Danish Freedom Foundation, whose generous support has made this book possible.

Hampstead J. B.
August 1966

The essential difference between totalitarian and democratic, between autocratic and liberal, propaganda (is this). The former appeals to mass emotion, whereas the latter relies upon the free mind. Thus, whereas the totalitarian method is essentially a short-term method—being a smash-and-grab raid upon the emotions of the uneducated—the democratic method should be a long-term method seeking gradually to fortify the intelligence of the individual. In other words, the 'passionate idea' which is at the root of all totalitarian propaganda cannot be maintained indefinitely, since the emotions of man cannot remain permanently strained. By contrast democratic propaganda, although its effects are less immediate and far less sensational, does aim at creating a durable state of common sense.

Harold Nicolson, M.P., formerly Parliamentary Secretary to the Ministry of Information and Governor of the B.B.C., writing in the *B.B.C. Handbook* for 1941.

To the Fascists the purpose of propaganda is to create a uniform opinion, docility without independent thinking. The means to the end is to appeal to the lowest mass-instincts; fear, hatred, greed, and national vanity. And the method adopted generally consists of insults, slander, lies which are repeated with ever growing violence. This is propaganda for lies, in contrast with the B.B.C.'s propaganda for truth.

From *De Hører B.B.C.*

LIST OF ABBREVIATIONS

A.B.S.I.E.	American Broadcasting Station in Europe.
A.R.P.	Air Raid Precautions.
B.B.C.	British Broadcasting Corporation.
D.P.T.	Dansk Presse Tjeneste (Danish Press Service).
O.K.W.	Oberkommando der Wehrmacht (German High Command).
P.I.D.	Political Intelligence Department.
P.W.E.	Political Warfare Executive.
S.H.A.E.F.	Supreme Headquarters Allied Expeditionary Force.
S.O.E.	Special Operations Executive.
T.T.	Tidningarnas Telegram Bureau.

CHAPTER I

THE FIRST BROADCAST[1]

Denmark has been brutally invaded.

Sven Tillge-Rasmussen in a B.B.C. broadcast on 9 April 1940

The first B.B.C. broadcast in Danish was on 9 April 1940—the day of the German invasion of Denmark. At 18.30 hours the Home Service was interrupted for fifteen minutes, and ten minutes of Norwegian and five minutes of Danish were transmitted. The first Danish speaker was Sven Tillge-Rasmussen and he read the following message:

> The British Broadcasting Corporation brings in its first announcement in Danish a special message to the Danish people. Here it is.
>
> For the second time Denmark has been brutally invaded by Germany. The British people have received the news with deep indignation and wish to send to the Danish people a message of warm sympathy. This event has strengthened the British resolve to pursue the war until the nations of Europe are liberated from the menace of Prussian aggression.

This was followed by a short news summary, also in Danish.

The news of the German invasion of Denmark had come through to London during the morning of 9 April. Sven Tillge-Rasmussen, who was the London correspondent of *Politiken*, thought that some form of message should be broadcast by the B.B.C. the same day to express the sympathy of the British people. He had telephoned the Ministry of Information which he had visited frequently for press conferences in his normal capacity as a foreign news correspondent. He and Charles Peake of the Ministry of Information composed the first message between them. This was then passed on to the

[1] This chapter is based on material provided by the B.B.C., and in particular on *Some Notes on the B.B.C. Danish Service*, compiled by the European Service of the B.B.C.

Foreign Office for the approval of Lord Halifax, the foreign secretary, before being broadcast later in the day.[1]

The message to shipping calling on Danish ships to seek allied ports was not broadcast on the same day, as is commonly thought.[2] This message went out on 10 April and was broadcast in a number of B.B.C. services. It read:

Here is a message to all masters of Danish and Norwegian ships telling them that the order to proceed to Italy, Spain and other neutral ports was made under German dictation and should be disregarded.[3]

In view of the forcible occupation of Denmark and parts of Norway, the masters and crews of Danish and Norwegian vessels which proceed to Allied ports will be treated as friends, not enemies. Every protection will be afforded by the British Admiralty to such vessels and they will receive welcome and compensation for their service.

This broadcast was read by Jørgen Edsberg who represented B.T. and *Pressens Radioavis* in London.[4]

A further appeal to Danish shipping was made by a Danish merchant seaman, Captain H. C. Røder.[5]

[1] This account was given to me in an interview with Sven Tillge-Rasmussen.

[2] It was later thought that the message from the B.B.C. to Danish shipping was the first broadcast to Denmark on 9 April. It was not. The message to shipping was broadcast on 10 April. This is confirmed by (*a*) *Some Notes on the B.B.C. Danish Service* and (*b*) correspondence from Roy Duffel, who was the Danish section Programme Organizer 1946–57, published in the magazine *Denmark* for December 1957. Here it is stated that the message to shipping was definitely not the first broadcast to Denmark.

In this magazine it is also stated that Lord Halifax was thought to have composed the first message to the Danish people, broadcast on 9 April. This conflicts with the evidence of Sven Tillge-Rasmussen that he and Charles Peake of the Ministry of Information composed the words. It is probable that Lord Halifax approved the message before it was broadcast.

[3] This referred to instructions sent out from Denmark by radio soon after the German invasion on the morning of 9 April 1940, to Danish ships telling them to proceed to neutral ports.

[4] B.T. is the name of a Danish newspaper, and *Pressens Radioavis* refers to the Danish radio news.

[5] In his book, *De Seljede Bare*, Captain Røder seems to have confused the dates (*a*) of the first B.B.C. broadcast to shipping, (*b*) of his arrival in London, and (*c*) of his own broadcast over the B.B.C. They are all one day too early.

It is probable that his broadcast to Danish shipping was on 12 April, not on the 11th as he states. This, however, cannot be proved beyond doubt as there appears to be no record of his broadcast in the B.B.C. archives.

On 26 May, fifteen minutes instead of five were allowed for Danish broadcasting. This marks the real beginning of the Danish section of the B.B.C. European Service.

The first Danish transmissions were prepared in the Council Chamber at Broadcasting House, the headquarters of the B.B.C. Later, operations were transferred to the greater safety of the basement, but after Broadcasting House had been bombed twice, there was a hurried move in December 1940 to Maida Vale, where shelter was so slight that no more than half the section was allowed to assemble at one time. The amount of time allowed to the section for broadcasting grew steadily. From fifteen minutes per day, the amount was increased later in the war to four fifteen-minute transmissions daily. In February 1945 the first half-hour transmissions began.[1]

Despite German interference Danish listeners were on the whole able to hear the B.B.C. broadcasts. The Germans made frequent attempts at jamming the B.B.C. broadcasts, but their jamming apparatus was made largely ineffective by Danish sabotage actions.[2] This was one indication that Denmark felt that it was worth undergoing considerable risk to prevent German jamming of the broadcasts from London. Reuter reported in January 1944 that 'one of the biggest German radio interference transmitters has been put out of action by saboteurs'.[3]

The B.B.C. had earlier in the war given instructions to Danish listeners on how to avoid German jamming. They were told to construct aerials of a special type which would defeat German counter-measures. It was reported that as a result 'thousands of Danes can now hear every word'.[4]

By the end of 1944 sabotage actions against German jamming transmitters were a regular feature of resistance warfare. An

[1] This information is from *Some Notes on the B.B.C. Danish Service*. The Danish section of the B.B.C. introduced its first half-hour broadcast on the evening of 4 February 1945 (B.B.C. archives).

[2] *The Citizen* newspaper (Gloucester), 31 January 1944; also stressed in *Some Notes on the B.B.C. Danish Service*: 'In spite of German jamming, wartime listening to the B.B.C. was probably more intensive in Denmark than in any other country.'

[3] *The Citizen*.

[4] The *Daily Sketch*, 17 September 1943.

attack in December against jamming apparatus in Amager, south of Copenhagen, was described as 'one of the most daring coups of the war'.[1] Every German attempt to set up jamming apparatus was sooner or later followed by a sabotage attack. As a result, for most of the war, the B.B.C. was audible in Copenhagen and throughout the rest of the country.

It was not forbidden in Denmark to listen to foreign broadcasts as it was in Norway and other German-occupied countries. This was one of the real benefits of Hitler's moderate policy towards Denmark. A large percentage of the Danish population were also radio owners. This was a very important factor in the dissemination of news and propaganda, for a high percentage of radio owners meant that sets were more likely to be spread over a wider area. Figures produced during the early part of the war put Denmark second only to Sweden in the list of European radio owners. There were 863,400 registered sets in Denmark, which meant that for every thousand people there were approximately 225 radio sets. This was a higher proportion than in any other German-occupied country.[2]

From the beginning the B.B.C. had therefore an advantage. The number of sets in Denmark was considerable, and radios were not forbidden. In addition Danish sabotage effectively countered German jamming, at least in the latter part of the war.

The objectives of the B.B.C. were twofold. First and foremost the broadcasts aimed to provide a comprehensive news service for Danish listeners. Talks and news commentaries from London provided the main alternative to the German-censored news-

[1] *Evening News*, 13 December 1944.

[2] Figures for August 1941 quoted in *Voices in the Darkness*, by E. Tangye Lean. Denmark was second highest in the list of European radio owners. Figures quoted were:

	Radio owners (thousands)	Radio owners per 1,000 people
Sweden	1,470·4	230·8
Denmark	863·4	224·6
Britain	9,132·2	190·3
Holland	1,440·6	160·8
Norway	429·4	145·2

papers, and the German-controlled radio in Denmark. The B.B.C. became, and remained throughout the war, Denmark's main contact with the free world. News was what the Danish listeners needed to hear, to keep hope alive in 1940. It was during 1940 that the B.B.C. began to build up its great reputation in Denmark for objectivity, because it did not attempt to disguise the seriousness of the situation in Europe.

The second objective of the B.B.C. broadcasts to Denmark was political. The B.B.C. broadcasts to Denmark were aimed at influencing the ideas of the Danish people. Throughout the war the Danish section of the B.B.C. European Service was effectively the major instrument of British political propaganda in Denmark. Through broadcasting, Britain could reach the majority of the Danish population easily and quickly. The B.B.C. therefore gave prominence to the British view on events, and this at times conflicted with other views. Should the B.B.C., for example, be primarily a supplier of local news to Denmark, of news of events in Denmark itself which because of German restrictions could not be circulated quickly? Or should the B.B.C. give most of its attention to the general war effort of the Allies, and particularly to projecting British policy and ideas into Denmark? This was a question which caused open conflict in 1944 between Danes and Britons.[1]

Britain did not indulge in the same kind of propaganda as Goebbels. Although the B.B.C. was responsible for projecting British ideas and actions in Denmark, in doing so it never sacrificed its reputation for truth and consistency. In 1940 and throughout the war, reliability and accuracy were considered more valuable than extravagant promises.[2] Because of this reputation for objective broadcasting, the B.B.C. had an advantage. It attempted to influence Danish opinion, to ask

[1] Discussed in chapter 14.

[2] The aims of propaganda from a non-totalitarian state were discussed in an essay by Harold Nicolson, M.P., parliamentary secretary to the Ministry of Information, in the *B.B.C. Handbook* for 1941. Accuracy was of prime importance in broadcasting from Britain, and this was stressed by Sir Robert Bruce Lockhart in his book *Comes the Reckoning*.

questions, to provoke discussions, and then to provide answers which suited the purposes of both the Allies and the Danish Resistance. This subtle type of propaganda, incorporated in news commentaries and talks, given mainly by Danish journalists in London, was far more effective in Denmark than the German form of propaganda. It was moderate and to a certain extent disguised, and for this reason was more likely to be accepted by Danish people. The European Service of the B.B.C., of which the Danish section was a part, earned not only the respect of the peoples of the German-occupied countries, but also of the enemy. The German authorities described the broadcasts from London as 'more deadly than steel'.[1]

Danish became the twenty-second foreign language of the B.B.C. European Service. In April 1940, when the Germans overran Denmark, the B.B.C. European Services were only in an embryonic stage. Foreign broadcasts from London were relatively new and untried. Early in 1938 it had become clear that radio was becoming more and more important in world politics. The establishment of a service in Arabic to oppose the vicious anti-British propaganda carried out by the Fascists in the Near East and North Africa can be said to have been the beginning of the B.B.C.'s broadcasts in a foreign tongue. In March 1938 services had been established in Spanish and Portuguese for listeners in Latin America, and these were followed by the first services to Europe, in September 1938 at the height of the Munich crisis, in French, German and Italian.[2]

The new Danish Service was therefore part of a larger but still as yet inexperienced European Service. However, the importance of the services to Europe had been recognized, and their general principles evolved. These were to be truth, news and objectivity. The latter was important, for after Dunkirk

[1] Quoted in *British Broadcasting* by T. O. Beachcroft. This was the description given to the B.B.C.'s European broadcasts by the German authorities in 1942.

[2] Accounts of the B.B.C.'s early external broadcasts can be found in the *B.B.C. Handbooks* for 1938–41, and also in *Propaganda* by Lindley Fraser, ch. 6.

the main difference between German and British propaganda became strikingly evident. The British principle in the darkest days of the war was, and could only be, an attitude of waiting. In answer to Goebbels' attacks, the British could only reply—'the more you win now, the longer it will take us to beat you finally, and the greater will be the losses on both sides'. As a general rule the B.B.C. did not attempt to enter into polemics with Goebbels' propaganda, or to try to equal his claims. In 1940 the broadcasts from London in the European Services of the B.B.C. were in character with the 'blood, toil, tears and sweat' attitude of Winston Churchill.

In contrast, German propaganda promised an early victory, and the longer it took the Germans to win the war, the less convincing became their protestations. For Britain this was essentially a better position from which to work. Obviously from the allied side there could be no rash promises of an early British victory, when most of Europe was occupied by the enemy, and Britain itself faced invasion.[1] Although the B.B.C.'s objective approach was a policy, it was also a necessity.

It was a policy which paid dividends. E. Tangye Lean[2] wrote in *Voices in the Darkness*:

> On the German radio, ships, unless they had the inescapable solidity of the *Graf Spee* or the *Bismarck*, never sank; they only faded away. No U-boat met its end; retreats were merely 'readjustments of an unstable line'. What thoughts must have awakened in minds used to such denials on hearing London give the loss of a cruiser its fair prominence, or begin—'The news from the Pacific is grave'—when the Afrika Korps was decimated and Moscow was out of danger? The stray listener was probably tempted to come again.

Because of this frankness, broadcasts from Britain were taken to be more reliable than the German, especially as a German victory became less and less likely.

The reason for the B.B.C.'s large European audience was that

[1] *Propaganda* by Lindley Fraser, ch. 6.
[2] E. Tangye Lean is at present director of the B.B.C.'s External Broadcasting.

the broadcasts provided a reliable and accurate news service.[1] It was news above all that the European audiences wanted to hear. The desire for news explained the great wartime popularity of the B.B.C., and it also demonstrated the deep psychological need of the peoples in the German-occupied countries. Danish as well as other European listeners had to hear the B.B.C. broadcasts to convince themselves that all hope was not lost, and that events were not really as bad as they often appeared to be from the German-controlled state radio and from the censored newspapers. London was the last remaining stronghold which had not fallen to the Germans, and therefore its voice carried great prestige. Perhaps the most important general contribution of the B.B.C.'s wartime broadcasts was that they were encouraging, and that they never allowed their listeners to give up hope. When in 1948, Lt.-Colonel Højland Christensen,[2] who had fought with the Danish Resistance, presented the B.B.C. with a table on the top of which was a map of the area known to the Resistance as Region III South Jutland, it was the 'encouraging voice' of the B.B.C. which was remembered in the inscription.

[1] The importance of an accurate news service was emphasized in an essay 'How does the Danish section function?' written by Robert Jørgensen for a B.B.C. pamphlet published in Danish and called *De Hører B.B.C.* Here it is stated: 'The news is the fundamental factor of the Danish transmissions.'

[2] Lt.-Colonel Aage Højland Christensen was an officer in the Danish army who took an active part in the Resistance and was from October 1944 leader of Region III.

CHAPTER 2

DENMARK SEEN FROM LONDON

The nonchalance of the Danes.

The Times, 15 April 1940

On 28 May 1940 Robert Jørgensen was appointed editor of the Danish section of the B.B.C.[1] Editor was B.B.C. terminology for the leader of one of the regional sections of the European Service. He remained at the head of the Danish section until the end of the war. Jørgensen was a Danish-born British subject who before the war had established a press service in London which specialized in Anglo-Scandinavian affairs. He had enlisted as a press officer with the British Expeditionary Force after the invasion of Denmark and Norway. He was released and he then joined the B.B.C.[2]

Until Robert Jørgensen's appointment, the Danish section had been led by Ronald Turnbull, previously Press Attaché at the British Legation in Copenhagen.[3] After his release from the B.B.C., Turnbull went to the British Legation in Stockholm, where he played a vital part, particularly in relaying information back to Britain from German-occupied Denmark.

During April and May when the section was being organized, British public opinion on Denmark was not favourable. Jørgensen noted that his references, when he had volunteered to join the British Expeditionary Force to Norway, were obtained, not from his own Legation, but from the Norwegian.[4] The British public and the British press were not sympathetic to Denmark's fate, and there was little understanding of why Denmark had not resisted the German invasion. An article in *The Times* just after the invasion of Denmark was typical of the attitude of the British press throughout the spring and early summer of 1940.

[1] *London Kalder* by Robert Jørgensen, ch. 1.

[2] *Ibid.*

[3] *Ibid.*

[4] *Ibid.*

It read:

The impression uppermost in the minds of every member of the party (the group of diplomats who left Denmark by train on the 13th April) seemed to be the extreme lightheartedness with which the Danes had seen their country pass out of their possession. They contrasted the obvious alertness with which the Dutch were standing on guard with the nonchalance of the Danes. The only resistance offered was that of one or two attachments at the frontier, the sentries at the Palace in Copenhagen, and one or two airmen. Cases occurred in which soldiers were ordered by their officers at the revolver's point to stop firing on the Germans.[1]

Unfavourable comparisons with Norway were immediately made in most of the newspapers. During April there was much written of the heroic resistance of the Norwegians, but little about Denmark. 'Norwegian Courage and Skill' was a headline of *The Times* on 19 April. This attitude towards Denmark was not improved when it was reported in the British press that Germany was successfully obtaining large amounts of food and livestock from Denmark.[2]

During the spring and summer of 1940 the British press did not know whether to treat Denmark as a friend or an enemy. There was some sympathy at the violation of Danish territory, but none for the policy of the Danish military and political leaders.[3] The continuation after the invasion of a constitutional government in Denmark under the king made the situation far from clear. Few in Britain in April 1940 showed much optimism about the fate of Denmark when it became known that Danish political leaders had agreed to form a government, despite the fact that the Germans were the real rulers of Denmark. It was known that Denmark had signed a non-aggression pact with Germany, but the reasons that prompted this were not understood in Britain.[4] No British commentator

[1] *The Times*, 15 April 1940.

[2] E.g. *Daily Telegraph*, 26 April 1940.

[3] For example, *The Times* reported on 20 July 1940 that the Danish government had yielded to German proposals and had withdrawn from the League of Nations.

[4] The non-aggression pact was signed, on German initiative, in May 1939. For a brief and concise summary of the attitude of the Danish government at the time

or journalist pointed out that the Danish policy of neutralism and low expenditure on armaments which had been followed during the previous decade was partly responsible for the lack of resistance in April 1940.

It had also been made clear to Denmark by Britain before April 1940 that, in the event of a German invasion, Denmark could not expect direct military help from Britain.[1] This in itself was a reason why Britain was not in a position to criticize Denmark for lack of armed resistance, as by its refusal to offer assistance in the event of invasion, Britain must have accepted that, without that support, Denmark was likely to yield to German pressure. At the time, however, Denmark was only compared with Norway, and received little British sympathy. Later, when it was seen how easily the German armies swept through France and the Low Countries, Denmark's surrender seemed more understandable.

It was at this inauspicious time that the B.B.C. began its broadcasts in Danish. The failure of the British expedition in Norway and the successful invasion of the Low Countries by the Germans created a backwash from Scandinavia. People became more interested in Holland, Belgium and France. The Danish Legation in London under Count Reventlow was of little assistance to those concerned with the Danish section of the B.B.C. There was no Danish exile government in London, as there was from Norway, to give its support. There was only the Danish Minister in London, who now represented an enemy-occupied country and whose position was of necessity ambiguous. His legation staff could not help with recruitment of journalists for broadcasting, and least of all could his legation give advice on the policy to be followed in the broadcasts to Denmark.[2]

The B.B.C. managed to recruit the nucleus of the section mainly from Danish journalists in London. The first members

of the invasion, see *Panorama Denmark*, published by the Danish Ministry of Foreign Affairs, 1963, text by Jørgen Hæstrup.

[1] Churchill had made this clear at a meeting with Scandinavian war correspondents on 2 February 1940; mentioned in ch. 1, p. 42, of *Kontakt med England* by Jørgen Hæstrup.

[2] *London Kalder*, ch. 1.

of the section were Ragna and Paul Palmér, Jørgen Edsberg, Ole Mouritzen and Leif Gundel.[1] With this skeleton staff, and with the help of outside commentaries from London representatives of Danish newspapers, transmissions to Denmark were able to continue.

The vital question for the newly formed Danish section during the latter part of 1940 was what policy the broadcasts should follow. Policy making was a more difficult problem for the Danish section than for any other foreign section of the B.B.C., because of the complex status of Denmark after the invasion. This problem was not faced by other sections of the European Service, with the exception of the French, simply because the status of their countries was clear-cut. Only in Denmark and France was the situation in doubt. France was involved in this problem to a lesser degree because of the presence in London of De Gaulle and the Free French and because a state of war between France and Germany had existed and was maintained from London. Denmark in contrast had never declared war on Germany. In the case of Norway, Holland, Belgium, Poland and Czechoslovakia there was no doubt that these countries were at war with Germany. They had been occupied, and in all cases representatives of the governments, and in some cases royalty of these countries, had escaped to London where they had declared themselves free and had set up exile governments. The sections broadcasting to these countries had the official backing of these representatives in London, and a clearly defined policy of broadcasting to enemy-occupied countries where there was no form of constitutional government.

The situation in Denmark was different, as a Danish government was in office, and the Danish king remained in Denmark, after the German occupation. The problem was a very real one for those who had to decide what policy to follow in the Danish broadcasts. It provided government officials in Britain with extreme difficulties which led to doubt and indecision later in the war. It was equally difficult for the Danish section of the

[1] *London Kalder*, ch. 1.

B.B.C. to make its broadcasts to Denmark effective, when during 1940 it appeared that the Danish people were satisfied with the position of their government under the occupation.

The speakers of the Danish section could not follow the example of most of the other sections of the B.B.C. European Service. They could not from the beginning openly encourage the Danish people to resist the enemy, because of the position of the government, at first under Thorvald Stauning and then under Vilhelm Buhl, acting as a barrier between the Germans and the Danish people.[1] The Danish section had at first to broadcast to a country with a national government which had undertaken to govern democratically in spite of the presence of the Germans. The government had the support of Parliament. The king had appointed the *statsminister* and had asked the population to preserve peace and quiet. The greater part of the Danish population felt, at least until November 1942 when Scavenius became prime minister, that the continued existence of the Danish government was the best possible means of protection from the Germans. Those who criticized the Danish section of the B.B.C. for having no clear policy for the first two years of the war, tended to forget this fundamental problem.

The existence of the Danish government until August 1943 caused a number of difficulties both for the Foreign Office and for the B.B.C. Because of present British restriction on official documents less than fifty years old, it is not possible to examine in great detail Foreign Office policy towards Denmark in the first three years of the war However, the B.B.C. broadcasts give as good a picture as it is possible to get of British official thinking on Denmark during this period. They show that policy throughout the five years of the German occupation of Denmark was not consistent, and that it was subject to fluctuation. They show that Britain's view of Denmark changed

[1] Thorvald Stauning, Danish prime minister and leader of the Social Democrats, died in May 1942, and was succeeded as prime minister by Vilhelm Buhl. Buhl was replaced as prime minister in November 1942 by Erik Scavenius, the foreign minister, as a result of German pressure. Scavenius remained as prime minister until 29 August 1943, when the government ceased to function.

radically between 1940–3, that although at times sabotage was discouraged from London, the B.B.C. was throughout wholeheartedly behind Denmark in its fight for freedom.

In the difficult task of planning broadcasting policy towards Denmark the B.B.C. was able to turn for advice to the government propaganda departments. However, it took nearly two years to achieve effective co-ordination.

CHAPTER 3

THE ORGANIZATION OF THE BRITISH PROPAGANDA DEPARTMENTS[1]

Foreign propaganda must be in line with Foreign Policy.
The Lord President of the Council in the House of Commons, 3 July 1941

Now that the B.B.C. European Service had begun broadcasting in Danish, the British propaganda departments became increasingly interested in Denmark. Denmark had become one of the growing number of German-occupied countries in Europe which Britain had to penetrate by radio and other forms of propaganda, to counter German censorship. From mid 1940 onwards the various British propaganda departments played an important part in Britain's effort to counteract the oppressive effect of the German occupation in Denmark, by advising the B.B.C. on broadcasting policy.

At the beginning of the war three separate organizations in Britain were engaged in propaganda work—the Ministry of Information, the Department of Propaganda to Enemy and Enemy-Occupied Countries, and the European Service of the B.B.C. The Ministry of Information was in Bloomsbury, the Department of Propaganda was housed at Woburn Abbey, the home of the Duke of Bedford, and the European Service of the B.B.C., after being shunted around, finally settled at Bush House, which became its headquarters and is where it remains today. As the Germans steadily overran the whole of Europe, the Department of Propaganda became responsible for advising on

[1] The organization of the British Propaganda departments, and their work, is not described in great detail in any published works. The best account, although it is very general and highly personal, can be found in Sir Robert Bruce Lockhart's book, *Comes the Reckoning*. Bruce Lockhart was director-general of the Political Warfare Executive.

The references to Hansard are quoted in *Warfare by Words*, by Ivor Thomas.

the policy to be adopted in the broadcasts to the newly invaded countries. The European Services of the B.B.C. were engaged throughout the whole war in broadcasting to enemy countries and those occupied by the enemy. The Department of Propaganda and the B.B.C. European Services were now involved with Denmark.

The B.B.C. was the mouthpiece of British propaganda but in status it was not a government department, as were the Ministry of Information and the Department of Propaganda. It was, as it is today, an independent public body with its own governors and executive officers. In a White Paper the government summed up the position of the B.B.C: 'In short, the B.B.C. enjoys independence of programme content. In the Government's view the impartiality and objectivity of the B.B.C. is a national asset of great value, and the independence which the Corporation now enjoys should be maintained.'[1]

This was the status of the B.B.C. in wartime, but it was obvious that if the European Services were the major arm of British propaganda abroad, some co-ordination between the various British groups which were engaged in propaganda work was essential.

'As far as policy was concerned the Foreign Office had the last word on foreign propaganda,' wrote Sir Robert Bruce Lockhart in his book.[2] This applied too to radio propaganda, and the ultimate responsibility for the policy of foreign broadcasting lay with the Foreign Office. The methods of carrying out the policy were the responsibility of the Ministry of Information, and of the B.B.C. itself.

This was confirmed by the lord president of the Council, Sir John Anderson, in the House of Commons on 3 July 1941, when he said, 'In regard to foreign policy, the dominant position must be occupied by my Right Hon. friend (the

[1] Quoted in *The European Service of the B.B.C.—Two Decades of Broadcasting to Europe 1938–1959* published 1959 by the B.B.C. The White Paper referred to was published in 1957.

[2] Ch. 6, part 2, in *Comes the Reckoning*. Bruce Lockhart admits later in his book (ch. 3, part 2) that there was a tendency in P.W.E. 'to try to make foreign policy by means of propaganda instead of being content to support policy by propaganda'.

1 (*a*). Broadcasting House, London, the headquarters of the B.B.C. This photograph was taken in 1945, and bomb damage can be seen at the top of the building.

1 (*b*). One of the meetings, held twice daily, of the editors of the B.B.C. European Services, November 1943. At the head of the table is N. F. Newsome, director of European Broadcasts. To his immediate left is Alan Bullock, to his right is D. E. Ritchie, better known as Colonel Britton, and seated sixth to his right at the table is E. Tangye Lean, now director of the B.B.C.'s External Services. Robert Jørgensen, editor of the Danish Service, is seated fourth from left in the photograph (second row).

2 (*a*). Robert Jørgensen, editor of the B.B.C. Danish Service, 1940–5.

2 (*b*). Rodney Gallop of the Foreign Office wh[o] broadcast in the Danish Service as 'a goo[d] English friend of Denmark'.

2 (*c*). John Christmas Møller speaking in the Danish Service from London in October 1942.

Foreign Secretary), subject as always to the War Cabinet. Therefore it must continue to be the duty of the Foreign Secretary to indicate the target at which our foreign propaganda is to be aimed. The means by which that target should be reached are primarily a matter for the Ministry of Information.'

In effect, responsibility for the policy of broadcasting was divided at the beginning of the war between the B.B.C. itself and the Department of Propaganda to Enemy and Enemy-Occupied Countries. This department was in close contact with the Political Intelligence Department (P.I.D.), which was itself a branch of the Foreign Office and was also housed on the Woburn estate in Bedfordshire. The co-ordination of propaganda was, however, not at first satisfactory for several reasons.

First, there were too many separate departments concerned with propaganda and they were frequently at loggerheads with one another. Inter-departmental jealousy was common, for as the Germans overran Europe, responsibility for propaganda to the countries under enemy occupation passed automatically from the Ministry of Information to the Department of Propaganda and the Ministry found itself almost entirely excluded from the European scene. Further, for their respective countries, the Ministry and the Department of Propaganda were supposed to provide advice for the foreign broadcasts of the B.B.C. However, physical separation made effective control of the B.B.C. almost impossible. As the Department of Propaganda was in Bedfordshire and the B.B.C. in London, the B.B.C. was able to assert its virtual independence. Chaos and bitterness was inevitable and Bruce Lockhart relates that at this point 'there was more political warfare on the home front than against the enemy'.[1] When Churchill became prime minister in May 1940, certain changes were made. The Department of Propaganda was put under the control of Hugh Dalton who had been newly created minister of Economic Warfare in the Churchill govern-

[1] *Ibid.* ch. 6, part 2. A good account of the early problems of the propaganda departments is given in this chapter of Bruce Lockhart's book.

ment. Dalton appointed Reginald Leeper as official in charge of the Department of Propaganda, but as Leeper was also head of the Foreign Office Political Intelligence Department, this meant that the two departments were in effect one. This the Political Intelligence Department did not like, as it was the smaller of the two, and the resignation of one of its leading experts as a protest did not help restore tranquillity. Dalton tried to remedy this state of affairs by bringing most of the Department of Propaganda to London, where he hoped that it would be in a better position to control the B.B.C. However, friction continued with the Ministry of Information, and when the new plans were ready to be put into operation, the German air raids on London had started. As a result of bomb damage, the Department of Propaganda returned again to Woburn after only one month in London, leaving behind only a small group of military experts. So the original difficulties of the separation of the B.B.C. from its propaganda advisers remained.[1]

The ministerial control of propaganda was equally confused. Until February 1942 propaganda to enemy and enemy-occupied countries was in theory the responsibility of three ministers.[2] Anthony Eden the foreign secretary had the final word on policy, Hugh Dalton the minister of Economic Warfare controlled the Department of Propaganda, and Brendan Bracken the minister of Information was responsible to Parliament for all broadcasting. During August 1941 the problem was simplified by the three ministers agreeing to act together. Under them an executive committee was established under the leadership of Robert Bruce Lockhart, Reginald Leeper, Brigadier Dallas Brooks and Ivone Kirkpatrick, who was Controller of the

[1] This problem was raised in a question to the prime minister in the House of Commons on 11 September 1941 (*Hansard*, vol. 374, no. 100):

Mr Noel Baker: 'Will this new executive [P.W.E.] be able to deal with the housing and staffing of the foreign broadcasting service, the inadequacy of which has long been a scandal?'

Prime minister: 'I think the answer is that the small anonymous executive will probably concentrate some of their earliest attention on this point.'

[2] 'responsibility of three ministers', cf. *Hansard*, 11 September 1941, vol. 374, no. 100.

B.B.C. European Services.[1] Bruce Lockhart was the chairman responsible for the co-ordination of foreign policy and propaganda. His was a Foreign Office appointment.

This new organization was given the title of Political Warfare Executive (P.W.E.), and the Executive Committee, or Advisory Propaganda Policy Committee as it was later called, from then on until the end of the war virtually controlled and administered British propaganda. The committee received guidance and approval from weekly meetings with the three ministers. Its formation was announced in the House of Commons on 11 September 1941.[2] This body was vital to the organization of British propaganda. From September 1941 onwards, all previously divided departments were united under the new executive committee. The two main tasks, which had been approved by the Foreign Office and the chiefs of staff, were clearly defined—(i) to undermine and to destroy the morale of the enemy and (ii) to sustain and foster the spirit of resistance in enemy-occupied countries.[3] The next problem was how to get the organizations as physically close to one another as possible to ensure smooth co-operation.

With a ministerial change in early 1942 the ministers responsible for P.W.E. were reduced to two.[4] Dalton was moved from the Ministry of Economic Warfare, and at this point P.W.E. was given a new charter by the prime minister. Anthony Eden, as foreign secretary, was made responsible for policy and Brendan Bracken, as minister of Information, for administration. Bruce Lockhart was made director-general.[5] The accommodation problem was settled in February 1942 when the skilled propagandists were moved from Woburn to London and placed in Bush House, where the B.B.C. European Service was stationed. Symbolically, P.W.E. occupied the part

[1] Their names were not openly announced in the Commons until 15 April 1942 (*Hansard*, vol. 379, no. 53).

[2] *Hansard*, vol. 374, no. 100.

[3] As stated by Bruce Lockhart, *Comes the Reckoning*, ch. 1, part 3.

[4] Cf. *Hansard*, 18 March 1942, vol. 378, no. 46.

[5] It was announced in the Commons that a director-general had been appointed, but no name was given (*Hansard*, 25 March 1942, vol. 378, no. 49).

of Bush House immediately over the European Service. The machine now ran smoothly and P.W.E. was able to effect the control of policy over the European broadcasts which was its by right. The organization and liaison was now complete, but it had taken nearly two years.[1]

These developments in the organization of propaganda radically affected the broadcasts to Denmark. It was this committee, P.W.E., which fixed its sights on Denmark and other countries, and provided guidance, information and directives for the Danish broadcasts. Furthermore, the liaison that took place between P.W.E. and the B.B.C. at higher levels, also took place between P.W.E. and the Danish section of the B.B.C. From February 1942 weekly meetings were held to decide upon the policy of the broadcasts to Denmark.

These weekly directive meetings were held in Bush House between members of the Northern Department of P.W.E., the Political Intelligence Department of the Foreign Office, and the Danish section of the B.B.C. Frequently Rodney Gallop of the Foreign Office, who broadcast over the B.B.C. as *en god engelsk ven af Danmark*, attended these meetings. Sometimes, too, a member of the Danish section of the Special Operations Executive (S.O.E.) was present. At the meeting the week's news in relation to Denmark was discussed, and the policy to be pursued by the Danish section of the B.B.C. was decided upon. The editor, Robert Jørgensen, was always present. Brinley Thomas, director of the Northern Department of P.W.E., or Dr J. W. Varley, his deputy, usually represented P.W.E., and Thomas Barman, P.I.D. In addition T.M.Terkelsen, who had been in London on 9 April 1940 as a newspaper correspondent, was usually present at these meetings as a member of the staff of P.W.E. Since the early stages of the war Terkelsen had been at Woburn, where he had been engaged in Danish intelligence work. When P.W.E. was formed he joined its northern department. It was in this capacity that he wrote most of the weekly directives for P.W.E. to the Danish section of the B.B.C.

[1] Bruce Lockhart, *Comes the Reckoning*, ch. 3, part 3.

These directives were the result of the weekly meetings, and showed how various items of news could be used effectively for propaganda in the B.B.C. broadcasts to Denmark. It was these weekly directives from P.W.E. which provided the basis of the propaganda, as distinct from the routine news, in the B.B.C. broadcasts.[1]

These directive meetings were important because they represented a weekly collaboration of departments dealing with Danish affairs. The presence of Rodney Gallop at most of the meetings was not unimportant. He was called by the Danish Minister in London, Count Reventlow, 'a truly active supporter of Denmark in England', and it was in this role, as an active supporter, that he took part in policy discussions with the B.B.C. Danish section. He was a member of the British Foreign Service, had been in the British Legation in Copenhagen, and had travelled from Denmark in the diplomatic train on 13 April 1940. He had been posted to the South American Department of the Foreign Office on his return to London. Although he was officially dealing with South American affairs, he spent much of his time working for Denmark, and he broadcast over sixty talks to Denmark during the war. He was perhaps the most effective contact that the Danish section of the B.B.C. could have had with the Foreign Office, and Robert Jørgensen collaborated continuously with him from the summer of 1940.

The directive meetings were a wise precaution against conflicting policies. This was why an S.O.E. representative was often present, or was at least kept informed of the decisions taken by this weekly meeting. For example, these meetings prevented broadcasts encouraging sabotage over the B.B.C. during the summer of 1942, when it was clear that S.O.E. was not ready to begin full-scale operations in Denmark.[2] Had B.B.C. broadcasts encouraged Danish Resistance groups to increase the number of sabotage actions at a time when S.O.E.

[1] T. M. Terkelsen and Robert Jørgensen both gave information about the weekly directive meetings in interviews.

[2] Cf. chapter 6.

was suspending operations and could not supply necessary help, many Danish lives might have been lost. Therefore the weekly directive meetings had the beneficial effect of co-ordinating propaganda with operational policy.

However, most of the directive meetings were concerned simply with news and how the most could be made of it. As an example, political murder by the Germans provided the Danish section of the B.B.C. with good reason to arouse the feelings of Danes in Denmark. In 1944, there were at least two murders of clergymen. The news of the first murder, that of Pastor Kaj Munk, was first received over the B.B.C. monitoring service. The B.B.C. continuously monitored the broadcasts of Kalundborg Radio. The important news was transcribed and kept for reference and use by the Danish section of the B.B.C. The director of the monitoring service recalled the absolute horror on the faces of the girls as they listened in to Kalundborg Radio when the news of Kaj Munk's death was received.[1] On 5 January 1944, the B.B.C. announced 'that four unknown, armed men yesterday entered Kaj Munk's home, took him forcibly away in a motor car and shot him in a plantation near Silkeborg, where his body was found this morning. The killing of Kaj Munk would seem to indicate that the Germans are setting no limits to their terror, and to the provocation carried out by their henchmen.'[2]

Then came the murder of another Danish clergyman, and the weekly directive to the Danish section of the B.B.C. read as follows (for the week 2–8 December 1944):[3]

The Murder of a Clergyman—the young clergyman Egon Johannesen, aged 26, has been murdered in his home at Husum near Copenhagen by the Gestapo or Danish Nazis. The murder is regarded as revenge for an attempt on the life of a Nazi clergyman Pastor Strøbech, who, however, managed to escape. The murder is known to have made a deep impression on Danish minds, particularly as the Rev. Johannesen, in spite of his youth, had come to be regarded as a

[1] F. A. Rush, in an interview.
[2] B.B.C. news commentary, 5 January 1944 (Danish Archives).
[3] P.W.E. directive to the Danish section of the B.B.C., 2–8 December 1944, (*ibid.*).

coming leader in Danish church life as well as an authority on the Old Testament.

Treatment. The Germans began their campaign to terrorize the Danish Church by the shooting of Kaj Munk and, by shooting the young clergyman Johannesen, they hoped to be able to silence the clergy, which has taken an uncompromising attitude towards the Germans. We should quote articles from the Swedish press and other sources in order to let the Danish clergy know that their fight is being appreciated.

The treatment of this news of a political murder was deliberately intended to raise the anger of the Danish people, who, although perhaps not the most frequent churchgoers as a nation, could nevertheless be expected to react strongly to German terrorization of their own national church.

Other directives upon which the B.B.C. Danish section acted were intended to do more than raise anger amongst the listeners. In November 1944, when extensive sabotage of railways in Jutland was being carried out, the B.B.C., as a result of its P.W.E. directives, had the task of encouraging action and sabotage against the Germans, while at the same time showing British appreciation of what was already being done in Denmark as an active contribution to the allied war effort.

The weekly directive for 25 November until 1 December 1944 read as follows:[1]

Transport Sabotage

The sabotage against railways in Jutland continues to be the outstanding feature of the Danish resistance. During the period from the 8th–15th November inclusive, there were 25 sabotage attacks against Danish railways, mainly in North Jutland. In addition to the important junctions already sabotaged, Viborg has now been subjected to a successful attack. The Danish State Railways are finding it increasingly difficult to replace the destroyed material and it is no exaggeration to say that railway transport in Jutland is in a state of chaos. German troop transport through Jutland is being delayed for as much as five days and goods are accumulating on railway stations.

[1] P.W.E. directive to the Danish section of the B.B.C., 25 November–1 December 1944 (*ibid.*).

Treatment

Our policy must still be to pay attention to railway sabotage as a particularly effective contribution to the war effort. Draw attention to the German nervousness in Norway which has led the German military authorities to intern several hundred railwaymen in the North. Give news of the railway strike in Holland which continues in spite of the heavy suffering which the disruption of transport must necessarily impose on a country which is already a theatre of war. We should, on a suitable occasion, review the change which Danish sabotage has undergone during the last couple of years, having been transformed from industrial sabotage to almost exclusively transport sabotage. Use this to pay tribute to the Danish patriots for their keen understanding of the war situation in its changing phases.

This directive suggested that the B.B.C. should encourage and appreciate Danish sabotage activity, while at the same time making the Danes feel they were playing a part in the allied fight against Germany. This explains the wider perspective given in the directive with reference to both Norway and Holland, the two occupied countries besides Denmark for which there was strong Danish sympathy and interest.

CHAPTER 4

POLICY 1941

> In the case of Denmark it is necessary to encourage more real resistance.
>
> B.B.C. Intelligence report, August 1941

From April 1940 until February 1942, when the Political Warfare Executive (P.W.E.) began exercising some control over the Danish broadcasts, policy was decided very largely by the Danish section of the B.B.C. itself. During this period the only regular control over the Danish broadcasts was that exercised by the B.B.C. Central Desk. Occasionally, propaganda guidance filtered through to the section in the form of letters or memoranda from members of the Political Intelligence Department, or alternatively from the Department of Propaganda. These letters were usually addressed directly to the Editor, Danish section, or to the Central Desk of the B.B.C. This advice, when it came, had to be followed, as it usually spoke with the authority of the Foreign Office. However, such propaganda guidance was relatively rare in the first year of the war, and the Danish section was for most of this period independent of outside control.[1]

The effect of this freedom from control in policy matters took some time to show itself, but it was nevertheless important. The forming of any consistent policy takes time, and it took time for the Danish section of the B.B.C. to decide what policy to follow in its broadcasts. After a period of apparent indecision[2] until approximately the middle of 1941, the broadcasts began to

[1] Confirmed by Robert Jørgensen in an interview.

[2] This 'apparent indecision' was caused largely by lack of information on events in Denmark. Sten Gudme, the Danish journalist who came to London in May 1941 to help with propaganda work to Denmark, said in his account (deposited in the Danish Archives) that the first request of the British authorities on his arrival in Britain was that he should write a comprehensive report on the situation in Denmark. This report went to both the Foreign Office and the Ministry of Information, from where any information useful for broadcasting would have been

crystallize into an attack against certain Danish personalities, followed by an attempt to create dissatisfaction in Denmark with the policy of the Danish government. The aim of the section was to force a break between the Danes and the Germans by showing on all possible occasions that the Danish government could not, and did not, act in Danish interests because it was continually under heavy German pressure. As more and more concessions were made to the demands of the Germans, the Danes eventually came to realize that they could no longer trust their government to protect their interests. The B.B.C. tried to show Denmark how impotent its government really was under German occupation.

The B.B.C.'s method was to attack the Danish government's policy of negotiation with the Germans.[1] The Danish section, however, had to exercise some restraint in its broadcasts until about November 1941. The section was slow in mounting its propaganda offensive against the policy of the government, but this was not the fault of the members of the section. Although the editor remained largely independent of outside control, he still had to find out what the official British view on Denmark was, so that the broadcasts did not pursue an entirely different policy. For example, Robert Jørgensen decided to allow attacks on certain Danish personalities, such as the broadcast

passed on to the B.B.C. This was the first full account of the situation in Denmark that the British Government had received.

This lack of information on Danish affairs made it very difficult for the early broadcasts of the Danish section of the B.B.C. to have any definite 'policy' beyond the general aim of encouraging Denmark not to give up hope.

[1] Most Danish people believed after the invasion that the hardships of the German occupation would be alleviated if the Danish government remained in office. The government would, they hoped, be able to some extent to resist German demands by a policy of 'negotiation'. Serious concessions, however, were soon made, particularly after the German invasion of Russia. The government had to agree to the banning of the Communist party, imprisonment of certain Danish Communists, the establishment of a Danish Free Corps for service on the Eastern Front, and adherence to the anti-Comintern Pact. By the time the former foreign minister Erik Scavenius became prime minister in November 1942, the policy of negotiation had become largely a policy of concession to German demands.

During 1940 the obvious comparison was made abroad between the governments of Stauning and Marshal Pétain. There was little sympathy for the attitude of either outside his own country.

by Gundel entitled 'Perfidious Scavenius' in February 1941. He could not, however, allow broadcasts intended to encourage sabotage in Denmark. Several of the Danish section speakers wished to give broadcasts that would encourage unrest in Denmark, but they had to co-ordinate with the policy of the director of the B.B.C.'s European Broadcasts, and with the policy of Special Operations Executive (S.O.E.).

The central direction of the B.B.C. European Service was immediately responsible for everything broadcast by every section of the European Service and was in close contact with the Foreign Office. To maintain contact with all the regional sections, the director of European Broadcasts, N.F. Newsome,[1] held meetings twice daily, morning and evening, in his office, where all the editors of the various sections were present. As a result of these meetings, a general directive was issued each day to the editors, giving news of general importance and showing how the news should be treated. This directive was normally common to all sections and material contained in it would form a large part of the broadcasts sent out by each section. Furthermore, editors would receive notes from the director suggesting lines of propaganda to be followed by their various sections. Newsome also spent a great deal of time in his office, so that he should be available to the editors for discussion on policy concerning individual countries. The general directives were based partly on news coming into the B.B.C. Central News Desk from all conceivable sources, press agencies and newspaper correspondents providing most, and partly as a result of discussions held regularly at a high level between the Foreign Office, the Ministry of Information and the B.B.C.

Clearly, the policy of the Danish section could not conflict with the views of the Director of European Broadcasts. Agreement was usually reached at the frequent meetings between Robert Jørgensen and N. F. Newsome. For the first year and a half of the war, the general attitude was that of waiting.

[1] N. F. Newsome, as director of European Broadcasts, was responsible to the controller of the European Services, Ivone Kirkpatrick.

The director could not help or encourage Jørgensen to follow an active policy from the beginning as he wished, because he himself received no encouragement from the Foreign Office.

The other organization with which the broadcasts had to co-ordinate was Special Operations Executive (S.O.E.).[1] Special Operations had been set up secretly in the summer of 1940 as a result of the recommendations of a committee which had met to consider the battle between Britain and Germany for the control of vital strategic war materials. Under Hugh Dalton, the minister of Economic Warfare, it dealt with subversive activities in the German-occupied countries, and was intended, in the words of Churchill, 'to set Europe ablaze'. The activities of S.O.E. in Denmark have been described authoritatively and in great detail by Dr Jørgen Hæstrup in his three books.

Special Operations Executive was throughout the whole war the only British group which carried out direct action on Danish territory. S.O.E. officers went into the field to lead or to help train saboteurs. All these operations were carried out in the strictest secrecy, both in their planning stage in London and in their execution in Denmark. As far as British military action was concerned, Denmark was only on the subversive list. In fact, during the winter and spring of 1943–4 there were negotiations for co-ordination of plans between S.H.A.E.F., S.O.E., and the Danish underground army,[2] as there was always a possibility that Denmark might become a major combat area over which armies would fight and march. This however never happened. It meant that the Danish section of the B.B.C. had to co-ordinate its policy with only one executive group, the

[1] For a description of the formation of the Danish section of S.O.E. (Special Operations Executive) see *Kontakt med England* by Jørgen Hæstrup, ch. 3, and particularly the footnotes to chs. 3 and 4, which give the sources of information in both published and unpublished works on the setting up of the Danish section of S.O.E.

For a general description of the beginnings of S.O.E. see *The Fateful Years* by Hugh Dalton.

[2] See *Hemmelig Alliance* by Jørgen Hæstrup, vol. 2, particularly ch. 4, and also *Panorama Denmark*, by Hæstrup, p. 35.

Danish section of S.O.E. In the case of France or Holland the B.B.C. had to co-ordinate both with the subversive S.O.E. and, after June 1944, with S.H.A.E.F. controlling the policy of allied military operations.

The policies of S.O.E. and the B.B.C. Danish section were similar—to force a break between the Germans and the Danish government, and to bring Denmark into line with the rest of enemy-occupied Europe. The Danish section of the B.B.C. had, however, to wait until S.O.E. was ready for operations in Denmark. There was no possible use in encouraging premature revolt. S.O.E., in turn, had to wait for the Foreign Office to decide upon action, and this explains the lack of consistent aggressive policy in the broadcasts of the Danish section of the B.B.C. in the first two years of the war.

Could it have been that the echo of the Duke of Wellington's famous words was still resounding in British departments: 'I always had a horror of revolutionising any country for a political object. I always said that, if they rise of themselves, well and good, but do not stir them up; it is a fearful responsibility'?

There is an element of truth in the application of the Duke of Wellington's words to the British attitude to Denmark in the summer of 1940. British policy towards Denmark rested fairly and squarely with the Foreign Office. From April until October 1940, there is a certain amount of evidence that the Foreign Office did not know what to think about the new situation in Denmark. Certainly, very little information about Danish affairs reached Britain, and this did not make decisions easy to reach.[1] The vague position allowed to the Danish Minister in London, Count Reventlow, by the Foreign Office confirms this view. He was allowed to continue his work in Great Britain, representing 'Danish interests', which was a practical arrangement which left formal questions open.[2] His position was very

[1] See Sten Gudme's account in the Danish Archives. This is also confirmed by Robert Jørgensen.

[2] See Hæstrup's essay, *Denmark and Britain*, for the Oxford Conference on European Resistance Movements, December 1962.

different from that of the Danish Minister in Washington, Henrik Kauffmann, who declared that he would no longer accept orders from Copenhagen. This action in Washington was only possible because it represented American wishes. The Americans wanted Greenland and needed Kauffmann to sign an agreement,[1] but as far as the British were concerned, there was no similar incentive to encourage Reventlow to take a similar independent stand. His vague position in Britain was in accordance with the wishes of the Foreign Office. The British government was as yet unwilling to commit itself on Danish affairs.[2]

The Foreign Office wish to remain uncommitted affected the B.B.C. The Danish section received little propaganda guidance during the first year of the war from the departments concerned because they were disorganized, and because there was almost no information on Denmark available. The other channel of advice, the Director of European Broadcasts and the Controller of the European Services, received guidance from the Foreign Office and the Ministry of Information. The Foreign Office was, however, without a policy, and S.O.E., the only other group which could perhaps have influenced the Danish broadcasts in this early period, only began recruiting its staff in October.

Until October 1940 the Danish section of the B.B.C. had therefore no real policy in its broadcasts to Denmark.[3] The Foreign

[1] The U.S. government considered Greenland to be in the area embraced by the Monroe Doctrine, and as a precautionary measure decided to send troops there. To give this an air of legality, the U.S. government signed an agreement in April 1941 with the Danish Minister in Washington, Henrik Kauffmann, who immediately after the German occupation of Denmark had declared himself a 'free' Danish Minister. This agreement provided for the establishment of bases in Greenland required for the transfer of American troops to Europe. Full Danish sovereignty over Greenland, both during and after the war, was affirmed.

[2] In the absence of any detailed information from Denmark the policy of the British government of necessity remained non-committal.

[3] The purpose of the broadcasts at this time was simply to keep the Danish people informed of events outside Denmark, and that they should be as encouraging as circumstances permitted. Apart from this, no real policy had been decided upon. This was the case until October 1940 when the formation of the Danish Council in London gave the Danish section of the B.B.C. its first opportunity to pursue a

Office and the propaganda departments at this stage of the war could only wait and see what would happen in Denmark, before deciding what British broadcasts should try and achieve. The broadcasts from Britain during the first months after the German occupation of Denmark were therefore deliberately uncontroversial and were based mainly on general war news. The most that the section could do, in the absence both of any news coming out of Denmark and propaganda guidance, was to probe the possibility of Denmark eventually taking an active line against the Germans. This was done discreetly by emphasizing the pro-allied activities of Danes abroad, particularly of Danish seamen,[1] and by broadcasting accounts of other European Resistance movements.[2]

This policy of broadcasting news of Danish activity in Britain took definite shape during October 1940 with the announcement on 9 October of the formation of the Danish Council in London. In the Danish Council the B.B.C. found its first propaganda weapon, and upon it built its first policy.[3]

This was to show, as much as possible by broadcasting, what Free Danes outside Denmark were doing for the allied cause. It

broadcasting policy. This was to tell Denmark that there were Danes abroad who were willing, even at this black stage of the war, to throw in their lot with the Allies, and to give all their support to the allied cause.

[1] 'Danish seamen'—of whom it was estimated that there were, by the end of the war, 5,000–6,000 in allied service. (Figures quoted in *Survey of International Affairs 1939–1946,—Hitler's Europe*, p. 522, in the section on Denmark.)

[2] Stories about other European Resistance movements were frequently broadcast in the first years of the war. Henning Krabbe, a member of the Danish section of the B.B.C. and author of *Voices from Britain*, told me in an interview that one of his main tasks in 1940–1 was to assemble material on the activities of other European Resistance movements, so that stories about them could be broadcast in Danish.

Other sections of the B.B.C. European Service also told the countries to which they were broadcasting, stories about Danish Resistance. This spreading of news about Resistance movements in the foreign language services remained B.B.C. policy throughout the war. A quotation from the general directive of the director of European Broadcasts (N. F. Newsome) for 9 April 1942 illustrates this: 'Naturally resistance stories will centre on Norway today, but don't forget the Danes. The Free Danes' gift to the Royal Air Force is a good item. Considering the effort made by the Hun to secure the docile collaboration of at least one little nation, his failure in Denmark is pretty notable.'

The general directive was received by all editors of the B.B.C. European Service, and much of the news content of the foreign broadcasts was based upon it.

[3] Confirmed by Robert Jørgensen in an interview.

was, as one B.B.C. commentator said, 'to stir the consciences of Danes at home by telling them what Danes abroad were doing towards the common fight'.[1] For this purpose the Danish Council was perfect. Its formation in October 1940 and also that of the Danish section of S.O.E. can be said to have coincided with the first signs that British official circles thought the Danes should be helped to regain their freedom, and should be regarded as friends.

Rodney Gallop and Robert Jørgensen tested the opinion of the Foreign Office about the Danish Council, and obtained official support on certain conditions.[2] These conditions were worked out in the Northern Department of the Foreign Office under Sir John Dashwood, and were approved by the foreign secretary, Lord Halifax. The conditions for recognition were that the Free Danish movement should be supported by the majority of Danes in Britain, that the British would not become involved in Free Danish affairs, that the Free Danes should be economically independent, and that they should guarantee not to set up a national council or government.[3]

The announcement by a Danish commentator of the formation of the Danish Council, over the B.B.C., contained the following:

> The formation of the Danish Council is being gratefully received amongst our countrymen. The English press has given us extremely encouraging views, and the representatives of the American press are also extremely interested in us. We are specially thankful to the B.B.C. which has not only given our members the opportunity to talk in Danish to Denmark about our work and our plans, but also has several times talked about the formation of our Council in Danish and Scandinavian broadcasts, and has given information about it in many other languages.[4]

Relations were of necessity close between the Danish section of the B.B.C. and the Danish Council, as the one needed the other for its work—the B.B.C. needed the council to show Denmark that Danes abroad were behind Britain, and the council needed the B.B.C. to enable its members to speak to

[1] Leif Gundel, in an interview.
[2] Interview with Robert Jørgensen.
[3] R. Jørgensen, *London Kalder*, ch. 2.
[4] *Ibid.*

3 (*a*). King Christian X on one of his daily rides through Copenhagen during the German occupation.

3 (*b*). A derailed train in Jutland. Danish sabotage of German transport became particularly effective in 1944.

4 (*a*). The R.A.F. attack against the Gestapo headquarters in Jutland, 31 October 1944. Mosquitoe of the R.A.F. Second Tactical Air Force can be seen bombing the University of Aarhus where th Gestapo had its headquarters. The B.B.C. Danish Service relayed news of this attack back t Denmark with great speed and effect.

4 (*b*). A closer view of the bomb damage, showing the shattered buildings and German staff ca parked in front. Both photographs were taken by one of the attacking aircraft.

Denmark. The special liaison officer between the council and the Foreign Office was T. M. Terkelsen, and between the council and the B.B.C., Robert Jørgensen.[1]

Leif Gundel, secretary of the Danish Council and a regular commentator over the B.B.C., described the council's main purposes as threefold. To present Denmark in a favourable light towards Britain was, he thought, the most important function. Secondly, the council was a centre of information for those who were interested in Danish affairs, particularly journalists. Thirdly, as representatives of the Free Danish community, the council became a liaison body between the community as a whole and other British departments.[2]

Both Gundel and Jørgensen have since stated that news of the council and the activities of the Free Danes abroad, particularly the Danish seamen, of whom over 3,000 were in allied service at this time, provided the mainstay of the broadcasting from October 1940 until the end of 1941. Although the policy of the Danish section of the B.B.C. was still far from moving into an active line, the effect of its propaganda was soon felt in Denmark.

The Danish journalist Emil Blytgen-Petersen was the main commentator over the B.B.C. about the activities of the council. On 23 January 1941 he stated the position of the Free Danes abroad, unequivocally: 'We free Danes believe—as you no doubt do yourself—that the liberation of Denmark depends on the victory of the Allies, and that it is our duty to aid Great Britain in her struggle, and we believe that by doing so, we shall also be saving Denmark.'[3] On 18 February 1941 Blytgen-Petersen was able to announce that the council had received public and official support from the British Government by the presence of two members of the government, R. A. Butler, M.P., from the Foreign Office, and Captain H. Crookshank, M.P., from the Treasury, at a reception held by the council at the Dorchester Hotel.[4]

[1] Confirmed by Robert Jørgensen in an interview.

[2] Interview with Leif Gundel.

[3] B.B.C. Archives.

[4] *Ibid.* This luncheon was held on 18, not 19, February as stated in *London Kalder*.

German reaction was not long forthcoming. It was clearly seen by the Germans in Denmark that the emphasis on the Danish Council in the broadcasts could have the effect of turning Danish opinion at home against the government and its policy of negotiation with the Germans. This was what the Danish section of the B.B.C. was directly trying to achieve. The German reaction was to brand the Danish Council as an exile government, run by traitors to the Danish king, the Danish government and the Danish people. 'How', Kalundborg Radio demanded, 'could there be a Danish government in London, when Count Reventlow was already there representing the interests of the legal Danish Government and the Danish King?'

Then ensued a running propaganda battle between the B.B.C. and the German-controlled Danish radio. Blytgen-Petersen declared on 22 February 1941:

> The German Radio always tries to pave the way with lies. Such was the case with the German lies about the Danish Council in London. When the lunch [18 February 1941] had taken place, and even before, it was of course asserted that the Danish Council had been officially recognized as a Danish government, while the truth is that the Danish Council on the said occasion got material proof of official support. It is evidently the Germans who, at the present time, consider it to their purpose to stamp the Danish Council as a revolt directed against our King and his Government.[1]

On the same day Leif Gundel attacked the Danish foreign minister Scavenius over the B.B.C. for supporting the German view of the Danish Council. This was an indication of a further step forward in policy. After emphasizing the activities of the Free Danes abroad, the B.B.C. now attempted to invite criticism in Denmark of leading Danish personalities, and questioned the policy of the Danish government, not least that of the Danish foreign minister. This was characteristic of the way the B.B.C. gradually built up a firm anti-German and anti-collaborationist policy in its Danish broadcasts. By the summer of 1941, the step towards criticism of leading Danish personalities who were not firm enough in their attitude towards the

[1] B.B.C. Archives.

Germans had been deliberately taken, and names such as Scavenius were more frequently mentioned. However, by August it was definitely felt in the B.B.C. that the Danish section had reached saturation point in the first stage of its policy, that of emphasizing the activities and views of the Danish Council and the Free Danish movement.

This is evident from a report produced every month by the B.B.C. Intelligence section intended as a survey of the European audiences.[1]

The August Intelligence report[2] stated that, in several cases, Danish people had said that they were hearing too much over the radio about the Free Danish movement and that the continual emphasis on Free Danish activities was causing not only resentment but the idea that the Danish section of the B.B.C. was 'controlled' by the Free Danish movement. As such, it did not speak with the authority of Britain, but was merely the mouthpiece of a minority group of Danes abroad. So the criticism in Denmark ran, and it is difficult to judge whether this was inspired by German propaganda, or was genuine. Probably, it was a mixture of both. Certainly in 1940 the policy of concentrating for propaganda purposes on the Danish Council was the only possibility. By August 1941 it had died a natural death, and criticism from Denmark caused a change in the policy of the B.B.C., and a sharpening of its attitude.

The events that led up to this change were as follows. The B.B.C. Intelligence report for August 1941 also mentioned that a Danish-born American, who had left Denmark at the end of May 1941, had written 'to inform us that amongst the intellectual classes in Copenhagen, our broadcasts in English for

[1] The B.B.C. Intelligence section's main task was to deal with all the incoming news from the services, agencies, and other sources, and to test it for accuracy and for its news and propaganda value. The Intelligence section then handed the news on in the form of finished stories to the section editors, and they in turn added local detail and gave policy slants according to the instructions of their directives. The regional heads of the Intelligence section kept in close contact with the editors of the European Service and gave them guidance and advice. Naturally there were at times differences of opinion between the editors and their colleagues in Intelligence.

[2] B.B.C. monthly *Survey of European Audiences* for August 1941 (Danish Archives).

Europe were highly thought of, while our Danish service was dismissed in those circles as being no more that the mouthpiece of the Danish Council (a body, it is implied, which commands little respect inside Denmark)'. The report continued that

a number of Danish citizens now in England and also several Danish-Canadian troops, who have been interviewed, have observed that they listened to our Danish broadcasts and judged from their colouring that they must be managed by the Danish Council. This false impression, conveyed apparently by the broadcasts themselves as well as encouraged intentionally by spokesmen of the Danish Council in an effort to magnify the importance of their organization, may explain why Danes in Denmark tend to listen to B.B.C. transmissions in English, Norwegian or Swedish. It seems desirable that the independent nature of the service should be made clear by means of a revised attitude, if not by explicit explanations (to which there may be objections). It is safe to say that the Danes in Denmark, so far as they place their trust in Liberation in other hands than those of their King, place it in Britain's promise rather than in the activities of the Danish Council.

The report, under a heading 'General Policy', concluded with the following:

While in the case of Norway most of our efforts must be devoted to holding patriots in check so as to avoid premature and useless bloodshed, in the case of Denmark it is necessary to encourage more real resistance and in fact it might be advisable to provide so much resistance that the Germans would take complete charge of the country, thus finally assuring us of the wholehearted support of the Danes. Denmark's position is unique and the fact that she is treated relatively leniently as a model state of the new order, and as an example to other countries, is inhibiting her powers of resistance.[1]

[1] This of course was only the opinion of the Scandinavian Intelligence officer, and cannot be regarded in any way as representative of the B.B.C.'s policy. In fact, as is explained later in this chapter, although the B.B.C. wanted to take an active line in its broadcasts to Denmark, it still had to co-ordinate with the policy of S.O.E. At this stage of the war, S.O.E. could not have given sufficient material support to the Danish Resistance to justify an all-out propaganda offensive over the B.B.C. The strength of propaganda attacks had always to depend on the extent to which S.O.E. was prepared to send material support to the Resistance. Words were no use without weapons.

However, the Intelligence section was probably right to suggest a stiffer tone in the Danish broadcasts, which were at this time becoming too involved in Free Danish activities.

Two important points stand out from this Intelligence report. First, that there was clearly dissatisfaction in the Intelligence section of the B.B.C. with the Danish section's policy of laying great emphasis on the activities of the Free Danish movement in its broadcasts. Secondly, that it was clear from the paragraph, under the heading 'General Policy', that a more positive and activist line was, from the summer of 1941, demanded from the Danish section of the B.B.C.

First, the dissatisfaction with the policy of emphasizing the activities of free Danes. It was clear that the B.B.C.'s report was based only upon a small number of interviews with people who had travelled from Denmark. Therefore, although these interviews could be taken as reasonable grounds for criticism of the Danish broadcasts, they could not be taken as generally representative of Danish public opinion. This leads to speculation as to whether there was in fact some ulterior motive in the criticism of the Danish Council. Certainly, the Controller of the European Services wanted to hear what the Danish section had to say in reply to these criticisms. The most probable solution was that the B.B.C. Intelligence section felt the time had now come for putting less emphasis on the Free Danish movement, and more emphasis on British activities. In addition, the B.B.C., proud of its professionalism, would not have liked it thought that one of its European sections was considered to be controlled, not by the B.B.C. itself, but by the Danish Council.

Robert Jørgensen's reply to these criticisms confirmed that the emphasis on the activities of the Danish Council and the Free Danes was decided upon by him, but with the approval of the various authorities concerned. His reply, in a letter to Ivone Kirkpatrick, controller of the B.B.C. European Services, dated 17 August 1941 was:

The position (re—the Danish Council) as far as I am personally concerned is quite clear. I have with Mr Barker's[1] consent, with Mr Newsome's and Mr Ritchie's[2] full knowledge and approval, used the Council as a weapon in our propaganda to Denmark. It is in

[1] A. Barker, overseas news editor in the B.B.C. [2] D. E. Ritchie; see p. 40 n. 1.

accordance with the policy laid down by the Foreign Office and the Ministry of Information that I look upon the Council as a useful instrument in our war effort, representing, as it does, Danes who are willing to stake all on a British victory—thus voicing Denmark's desire to fight for her freedom.

There are, it seems, unfortunately still some Danes both in and outside Denmark who are not as yet convinced as to the certainty of a British victory. These people are consequently not interested in any effective Free Danish movement because, as they say, 'its activities might cause trouble for the Danish Government with the Germans'. This is of course precisely what makes it useful to us. Whilst we have faithfully reported the activities of the Danish Council, nothing has ever been said in any of our transmissions which might have given listeners the impression that the B.B.C. Danish Service is in any way managed or influenced by the Danish Council.

The general policy suggested in the survey is of course what we have been aiming at, and also conforms with the activities of the Danish Council, but the execution of this policy would in fact be greatly hampered were it not for the existence of an organized Danish opinion outside Denmark such as that expressed by the Free Danish movement.

In a further minute on this problem the Editor of the Danish section described the Danish Council as 'one of our most powerful weapons to counter German propaganda in Denmark, and for this reason, the Danish Council enjoys the confidence and active support of the highest British authorities'.[1]

It was clear that there was to be less emphasis on the activities of the Free Danes in the Danish broadcasts from the summer of 1941. The council had been a useful weapon of propaganda, as the Editor of the Danish section had said in defence of his policy. From the summer of 1941 the broadcasts to Denmark became stiffer in tone and followed a more openly active policy. Against a background of increasing attacks from Britain against the Danish government, the Danish *V* campaign was launched.[2]

[1] Minute on the position of the Danish Council re the B.B.C., August 1941 (Danish Archives).

[2] This description of the *V* campaign is based on the B.B.C. pamphlet *De Hører B.B.C.*

The famous *V* sign was first thought up by the Belgian section of the B.B.C. European Service. By the end of 1940 the B.B.C. had begun to think seriously how it could balance the advantages which the Germans had gained by their propaganda in the countries they had invaded. The Germans had the advantage of occupying these countries, and their propaganda filled the newspapers and the hoardings. As a result there was little chance of British propaganda infiltrating or circulating.

It was an attempt to find some concrete expression of the will of the German-occupied countries to free themselves which led to the start of the *V* campaign. The speakers of the Belgian section of the B.B.C. had heard how Belgian boys had covered walls with the letters 'R.A.F.'. They realized that the German soldiers throughout Europe were getting more and more on the nerves of the national populations. They could see that there was an increasing desire to mock and irritate the Germans by wearing forbidden emblems. The German soldier was annoyed, or simply ignored, on all possible occasions. In Denmark the attitude of the population was shown by the wearing of R.A.F. roundel caps, and by the practice of shunning the Germans whenever possible. This was known as the 'Cold Shoulder'.[1]

The Belgian section decided to tell the Belgian people to draw *V*'s wherever possible. The *V* was a single letter, quick and easy to draw. The speed with which it could be chalked on a wall, or scribbled on a piece of paper, made the risk of being caught by the Germans considerably less. The *V* was chosen purposely. It was the first letter of the French word '*Victoire*', and the Flemish word '*Vrijheid*'. On 14 January 1941 the campaign was launched over the B.B.C.'s Belgian service. It was later to spread over the whole of Europe. It was not until

[1] *The Times* reported on the 'Cold Shoulder' on 24 July 1941: 'To the Danes belongs the credit of inventing another badge, insignificant in appearance but, like the already famous *V* sign, deeply significant of a state of mind. It represents a new order, unthought of by Hitler—the Order of the Cold Shoulder, D.K.S., standing for *Den Kolde Skulder*, and it expresses the feelings towards the Germans of about 90% of the Danish population.'

some time after the mysterious Colonel Britton,[1] on 6 January 1941, had begun to give his regular talks to 'Europe's Underground *V* Army' that the Danish section of the B.B.C. took up the idea. It was something of a problem to find a suitable word or expression in Danish which was short, easy to say, and kept the letter *V*. The solution was found by Leif Gundel, one of the B.B.C.'s Danish speakers. On 12 June 1941 Gundel launched the *V* campaign in Denmark. He closed his talk with these words:

> Vi har *V*'et, det gode, gamle, danske *V*, der staar for *Viljen til at Vinde*—for *Vejen til Sejr*—for *Varslet* om arvefjendens endelige sammenbrud—for den gamle *Vikingeaand*—V'et der betyder at
>
> VI VIL VINDE![2]

This campaign caught the imagination of the whole of Europe, and the *V* became a symbol of unity and solidarity. It was aimed at breaking the morale of the German soldier. The effect was described in a broadcast to Denmark on 12 June 1941.

> Wherever a German soldier turns, his eyes meet the *V* sign. It is an ever present sign that he is surrounded by enemies, by people who hate and despise him, by men who wait only for a suitable chance to attack him. These men are united in one purpose only—to throw him out and become free again.

On 27 June 1941 Colonel Britton introduced the *V* campaign in sound. C. E. Stevens, Oxford don, lecturer in Ancient

[1] Colonel Britton was the mysterious speaker over the European Services of the B.B.C., who broadcast regularly to Europe's underground armies of resisters and saboteurs. His aim was to encourage them in their fight against the Nazis, and occasionally he gave them instructions so that their actions would co-ordinate with allied strategy.

The first *V* campaign lasted from early 1941 until May 1942, when Colonel Britton announced that he would not speak again 'until the moment comes to indicate a particular line of action which is needed' (*Daily Telegraph*, 2 June 1945).

Colonel Britton broadcast again just before D-Day when he gave important messages to the Resistance movements. On this occasion he spoke anonymously, and was introduced simply as a member of General Eisenhower's staff.

It was not until June 1945 that it was revealed that the anonymous Colonel Britton was in fact D. E. Ritchie, director of the European News Department of the B.B.C.

[2] (We have the *V*, the good old Danish *V*, which stands for the Will to Win, for the Way to Victory, for the Warning of the enemy's final collapse, for the old Viking spirit, the *V* that means—WE WILL WIN.)

History and a member of the Ministry of Economic Warfare, discovered that the Morse code for the letter *V*—dot, dot, dot, dash—fitted perfectly the opening bars of Beethoven's Fifth Symphony. This naturally opened up new opportunities for annoying the Germans, and the *V* sign played on a kettle drum was from that time forward used as the interval signal for the B.B.C.'s European Services.

The *V* sign caught on quickly in Denmark.[1] One of the pamphlets sent from Britain to Denmark took the title *Vi Vil Vinde*, and even the announcers of the Danish state radio put special emphasis on the letter *V* whenever it occurred. It also caught on in Norway, where the Resistance on one occasion drew *Vi Vil Vinde* in the dirt on a Norwegian road. This was then photographed by the R.A.F., and the picture was used on a 20 *øre* stamp issued by the Norwegian government in London.

Despite Goebbels' instructions that the *V* campaign was to be counteracted by the announcement that the *V* in future would stand for the German word *Viktoria*, its success was undeniable. The *V* campaign in Denmark came at a very suitable moment, when the Danish section of the B.B.C. was about to take a much firmer line towards Denmark and when, as a weapon of propaganda, the Danish Council was being used less. The *V* sign was important in Denmark, as in the rest of German-occupied Europe, as a symbol of unity and purpose. A *V* chalked on a wall made one Dane feel that there were others who felt as he did. The *V* became a visible bond for the army of the Resistance. As a later broadcast to Denmark emphasized: 'The Nazis are completely clear how ominous a sign this is of the spirit of the oppressed peoples. They know that the *V* sign is the first ripple in the sea of Resistance which will gradually become a deluge, and which will wash the last Nazi up on the shore of defeat, like a dead body.'

[1] On 14 July 1941 it was reported in the *Daily Telegraph* that the Germans were taking stern measures in Denmark to repress the *V* sign. One Dane had been sent to prison for 40 days for writing 'Victory' on an office occupied by the German military authorities.

The Danish section of the B.B.C. at this time suggested that listeners in Denmark should organize themselves in groups for illegal listening if a German ban on radios should be imposed. It may well have been these early warnings from Britain which stopped the Germans from taking this precaution. It was better for the Germans, and in accordance with their policy towards Denmark, to allow open listening to the B.B.C. rather than to find that more clandestine groups had been formed, whose purpose was likely to be more than simple radio listening.

The *V* campaign, launched in the summer of 1941, was Britain's first concrete contribution to the rise of the Danish Resistance movement. It gave the newly formed resistance groups a symbol as important to fighters for freedom as the sign of the fish was to early Christians in Roman times. Perhaps the British had learnt from the Nazi swastika that a symbol was an essential psychological weapon. The *V* began to appear everywhere, in paint, on walls, on coins, and in the dirt on German cars. The *V* became the sign of the 'unofficial Denmark' which, against the orders of its government, treated the Germans as enemies. The sign became the symbol of an attitude, and this in turn led it to become a symbol of action. In this lay the beginnings of the Danish Resistance movement. 'The earliest sources of the Danish Resistance', wrote Dr Hæstrup,[1] 'are untraceable and vanish into a fine network of innumerable, long since dissipated, moods, deliberations, resolutions and —eventually—actions. A remark, a confidential talk, an arrangement, a demonstrative act. Later, or perhaps at the same time, a leaflet, a private meeting, a *V* sign, an attempt to raise fire, or steal weapons.'

Why had the Danish section of the B.B.C. waited until late 1941 to begin its first concentrated attack on the policies of the Danish government? To help stir up the Danish people so that they would force the collapse of their government and start resistance against the Germans had been the policy of the Danish section since the beginning. This was 'of course what we have

[1] Hæstrup, *Panorama Denmark*, p. 20.

been aiming at' was the reply of the Editor of the Danish section to his critics. Why then had it taken nearly one and a half years before the B.B.C. began to show its real colours?

The answer to this concerned both S.O.E. and the Foreign Office. The B.B.C. Intelligence report of August 1941 had contained the following words: 'While in the case of Norway most of our efforts must be devoted to holding patriots in check so as to avoid premature and useless bloodshed, in the case of Denmark it is necessary to encourage more real resistance.' This indicates that the B.B.C. was fully aware of the possible operational effects of its broadcasts. If sabotage was called for too early over the radio, before either S.O.E. was ready to send in equipment and men to help with such operations, or before resistance groups on the Home Front were well organized for sabotage operations, then pointless bloodshed and the death of patriots would be the result. There is evidence that the B.B.C. was fully aware of this possible danger, and of the necessity for co-ordinating its broadcasting policy with that of S.O.E. It was this need that led to an S.O.E. representative being present at the directive meetings of P.W.E., or if this was not possible, to S.O.E. being informed of the proceedings. Co-ordination between S.O.E. and the B.B.C. was necessary, and it was to be expected that a stiffening of B.B.C. policy meant that S.O.E. was ready for action in Denmark. This was the case in the autumn and winter of 1941.

The years of 1940–1 were years of preparation for the Danish section of S.O.E. Commander Hollingworth, the leader of the Danish section of S.O.E., was given little support in the early months. In his account given to the International Conference on European Resistance Movements at Oxford in 1962,[1] Dr Hæstrup summarized the position of S.O.E. at the end of 1940 and the beginning of 1941 as follows:

> It is obvious from Danish sources that the British authorities had no settled political decision regarding the complications which a Danish section [of S.O.E.] would have to face. Some light was

[1] An essay entitled *Denmark and Britain* prepared for this conference.

thrown on British intentions when in late autumn [1940] Charles Hambro [head of S.O.E.'s Western European section] came to Stockholm and got an opportunity to talk things over with Munck. He pointed out that the British were grateful for the forthcoming intelligence and it was arranged that this service should continue and expand. At the same time Hambro expressed the necessity for Danish sabotage. It was, however, realized in Great Britain that circumstances did not at present allow any such sabotage *and that S.O.E. was not yet prepared to sustain it.* To quote Hambro—'I made it clear at that time that it would not be in the interests of Denmark or Great Britain if unnecessary sabotage was to break out in Denmark at the moment.'[1]

At the end of 1940 the position, as far as S.O.E. was concerned, was clearly that Britain expected sabotage to take place eventually in Denmark, but at that stage was not prepared to encourage it because S.O.E. was not prepared to sustain it. The policy of the B.B.C. during this period was accordingly not to encourage action in Denmark. Instead the B.B.C. concentrated on giving information to Danish listeners, predominantly news about other Resistance movements, and news of conditions in Britain. Danish Council activities were also reported.

The winter of 1940–1 saw the first positive development in S.O.E. activities.[2] Commander Hollingworth[3] had been given an office in Baker Street and had begun recruiting his staff. In January 1941 Reginald Spink[4] joined the staff of the head-

[1] Hæstrup goes into the question of Intelligence material sent from Denmark to Britain, and the British desire for sabotage in Denmark, in great detail in *Table Top*.

[2] S.O.E.'s policy towards Denmark was described by General Sir Colin Gubbins in an essay for the Oxford Conference, 1962: 'S.O.E.'s planning in regard to Denmark at this stage (early 1941) was concerned with preparing its primary role of stimulating provocation and sabotage against the Germans within Denmark. This concept of the "New Order" in Europe must be shown to be what in reality it was—German hegemony—and it must be for the Danish people ultimately to revolt against it themselves.'

[3] Commander R. C. Hollingworth, R. N., was head of the Danish section of S.O.E. from October 1940 until May 1945. Previously he had been in Copenhagen as assistant to the naval attaché at the British Legation.

[4] Reginald Spink was, from January 1941, Hollingworth's chief assistant in S.O.E.'s headquarters in London. Before the outbreak of war Spink had been in Denmark first as a student at the International People's College at Elsinore, and then as a teacher of English.

quarters, and Albert Christensen[1] was sent as British Consul to Gothenburg, to be a channel of information from Denmark. In February Ronald Turnbull[2] arrived at the British Legation in Stockholm to act as S.O.E.'s representative. Contact was now established, and S.O.E. was technically ready to start operations in Denmark. The training of parachutists continued throughout the summer. On 27 December 1941, the first two S.O.E. parachutists were dropped into Denmark. C. J. Bruhn,[3] one of the parachutists, was tragically killed when his parachute failed to open.

The year 1941 saw the building up of the Danish section of S.O.E. and the first attempt at infiltrating S.O.E. men and equipment into the field. This in itself represented a further development of policy. It showed that the British government was now prepared to encourage active resistance in Denmark.

When this decision was taken is not easy to determine. It must have been a Foreign Office, as well as a military, decision which led to the starting of operations in Denmark. There is no doubt that events in February 1941, when the Danish naval torpedo boats in Copenhagen were seized by the Germans, were of major importance in showing the Foreign Office the necessity for stronger action against Denmark. Two telegrams from the Foreign Office which were passed on by Ronald Turnbull to Ebbe Munck, a Danish journalist and a leading resistance figure in Stockholm, illustrate this.[4]

[1] Albert Christensen, who was in Denmark as a business man before the outbreak of war, came out with Hollingworth, Spink and others who were later concerned with Danish Resistance, in the diplomatic train which was allowed by the Germans to leave Denmark on 13 April 1940. For an account of this see Hæstrup, *Kontakt med England*, ch. 1.

[2] Before the invasion of Denmark, Ronald Turnbull was press attaché at the British Legation in Copenhagen.

[3] At the outbreak of war Bruhn was studying in England to be a doctor. In the summer of 1940 he was a member of the A.R.P. Soon after, he joined S.O.E., and he began training in January 1941. For an account of the first operations carried out by S.O.E. in Denmark, and of Bruhn's tragic death, see *Kontakt med England*, ch. 7.

[4] Quoted in *Kontakt med England*, ch. 7. Copies of the telegrams are in the Danish Archives.

The first telegram was dated 11 February 1941 and read:

> In light of present information there is public contempt for lack of guts in Danish Navy, for allowing T.B.s to be handed over to Germans. The only way to partially redeem their honour is to make quite certain that submarines are not also allowed to fall a prey to Germany.

The second was dated 28 February 1941:

> His Majesty's Government are unable to accept reason advanced by Danish Government for their inability to sabotage or scuttle torpedo boats, particularly as they must have had prior warning of German intentions. It must now be expected that Germans will demand Danish submarines. If Danish Government do not scuttle these, His Majesty's Government must regard them as acting voluntarily in German interests and H.M. Government must adapt their policy accordingly both now and when peace comes to be made.

This was a very strongly worded telegram, and the threat in the last sentence was unmistakable. It was a threat, too, which was repeated no less clearly over the B.B.C. Rodney Gallop of the Foreign Office came to the microphone on 24 March 1941 with one of the best broadcasts of the war.[1]

He began by quoting Hitler's *Mein Kampf*: 'A shrewd conqueror will always enforce his exactions on the conquered only by stages. Then he may expect that a people who have lost all strength of character, which is always the case with every nation that voluntarily submits to the threats of an opponent, will not find in any of these acts of oppression sufficient grounds for taking up arms again.' Gallop pointed out that Hitler was depending on the success of this theory in Denmark. He contrasted the firm defence of the Danish king and people against the Germans, with the weakness in conceding to German demands shown by the government. He then listed the concessions of the government to date—the removal of the two government ministers Hedtoft-Hansen[2] and Christmas Møller[3] from office and the handing over of the torpedo boats to the Germans

[1] B.B.C. Archives.

[2] Hedtoft-Hansen, leading Social Democrat.

[3] See chapter 5 and notes.

were only two examples of many. Then came the unmistakable warning to the Danish people, which had been in sharper terms expressed in the telegram about the torpedo boats. 'When the oppressed nations of Europe are freed, and are gathered round the table of a new peace conference, the part which will fall to each one will inevitably depend on the contribution which that country has brought to the common cause.' Gallop then urged the Danish people to press the government to resist further demands. In this broadcast, he was probably following Foreign Office advice to draw attention to the firm attitude of the king and people, as opposed to the weakness of the government.

This speech, besides containing an unmistakable threat, marked a further advance in British policy towards Denmark. The threat was that if the Danes remained inactive throughout the occupation, the support that Denmark would receive after peace was declared would be little. Gallop's statement, however, also implied a firmer British commitment in Danish affairs. The commitment was clearly this: if Denmark resisted the Germans then she would be rewarded by British support throughout and after the war. The phrase, 'there is a chair waiting for Denmark at the allied council table', used over the B.B.C., was indicative of the promise of British support if Denmark helped herself. Gallop's speech can be seen both as a threat in the event of inaction, and also as a reflection of the firmer British commitment, at a time when S.O.E. was preparing to mount operations in Denmark.

The policy of attacking the Danish government and individual members by name was clearly shown in the broadcasts throughout 1941. Leif Gundel, in a talk entitled 'The Velvet Glove is Off', in January 1941, attacked the supplement to the criminal law which had been rushed through both houses of the Danish parliament.

It is only this new criminal law which has brought conclusive evidence for all the world to see that the Danish Government is hopelessly compelled to allow the Nazis to interfere with Danish politics and not only that, but also with the daily life of the man in the street. Never before in the history of modern civilization has a democratic government dared to make a criminal law retrospective so that sentences can be passed for offences committed long before the law became public.[1]

He exposed the government for what it was—completely under the domination of the Germans. In February, Gundel made a personal attack in a talk called 'Perfidious Scavenius', blaming Scavenius for the lies that were circulating about the Danish Council.

In March, Stauning was attacked, and his name linked with Scavenius. In a broadcast entitled 'Stauning's Surrender', Stauning was attacked by Blytgen-Petersen for his speech in the Students' Club in Copenhagen. The whole spirit of his speech 'was only too clearly Mr Scavenius's'. The broadcast ridiculed Stauning's acceptance of German domination because 'nearly in the same hour as he spoke in the Students' Club in Copenhagen, the American Senate passed a Bill providing unlimited material support from U.S.A. to England for her fight against the Nazi dictatorship'. In conclusion Stauning was compared very unfavourably with the Norwegian prime minister, Nygaardsvold. 'Most pitiful it is to hear Stauning say that Denmark must trust the German promises when only a few weeks ago the German robbery of the torpedo boats represented the most flagrant German breach of promise to date, the most shocking violation of Denmark's sovereignty.'[2]

In these attacks, the Danish section was following its own declared policy, but because contact was maintained with the Foreign Office through the Director of European Broadcasts, it was clearly also in line with British foreign policy. A directive from the Political Intelligence Department to the Editor of the Danish section for the week 18–24 June 1941 stated:

The time has come to stiffen the tone of our broadcasts to Denmark. All the evidence available in this country tends to show that the Danes are well satisfied with the reputation they have established

[1] B.B.C. Archives. [2] *Ibid.*

for themselves as 'cold shoulderers' of the Germans. They should be told discreetly that this is not enough. There is a chair waiting for Denmark at the Allied Council table in London but it has to be earned. It can be earned only by deeds. Without directly encouraging the Danes to commit sabotage, they should be told, as often as possible, of what the Norwegians, the Dutch and the Czechs are doing to resist and to defeat the oppressor.[1]

A general directive to the B.B.C. European Services from the Political Intelligence Department, dated 13 August 1941, gave further indication of the official British attitude towards sabotage in mid 1941. It was headed 'Sabotage', and read:

The Pan-Slav Conference in Moscow has ended with a rousing call to the whole of Europe to indulge in widespread sabotage. Our policy for the moment, about appeals for sabotage, might be summed up as follows. We ourselves are not making appeals for sabotage (news talks should be watched to see that we do not). We should be extremely discreet in using anyone else's appeals for sabotage. We should report any event like the Pan-Slav Conference quite objectively and not in a rousing manner. We should report, with discretion, sabotage that is actually taking place. Much hangs on the word 'discretion', but the foregoing will perhaps indicate what is meant. It is important too that we should not give too many details of sabotage that is being carried out.[2]

It is interesting to note that in both directives it was emphasized that there was to be no direct encouragement of sabotage. S.O.E. was not yet in a position to support sabotage in occupied countries. As far as Denmark was concerned, it was clear that in the summer of 1941 the Danish section of the B.B.C. was trying to turn Danish public opinion against the government's policy of negotiation with the Germans, without directly encouraging sabotage. Anti-German feeling was to be nourished in the hope that the Danes themselves would demonstrate. This in turn would produce fiercer attacks over the radio from Britain against the policy of compromise and negotiation, and also greater encouragement to take up active resistance. This was the B.B.C.'s policy in the summer of 1941.

In June 1941, the Russians entered the war and this provided

[1] Danish Archives. [2] *Ibid.*

the British propaganda departments with food for thought. A warning of the possible consequences of German propaganda in Denmark about the Russians was clearly needed. Instructions went to the Danish section of the B.B.C. in a directive dated 18–24 June 1941. 'Russo-German relations, whatever the final outcome, will loom large in this week's news. It is well to bear in mind, if Russo-German relations become acute, that German propaganda to Denmark, and indeed to most other countries, is bound to take a violently anti-Communist line in order to play upon such anti-Communist prejudices as still exist among the middle classes.'[1]

Advice on the policy to be followed by the B.B.C. in its Danish broadcasts for the period 25 June–1 July was received in a note from Thomas Barman of the Policial Intelligence Department. The main interest was the Russian-German war, and the Danish listener was to be warned by the B.B.C. that this was a Baltic war which could have profound effect on the Danes. The regional aspect, from the Danish point of view, was to be stressed.

> The Germans have started their propaganda that this is a war to eradicate Communism and they will continue to urge the Danes to join in a war which they will say is a war to defend western civilization against Communism. This argument worked in Finland, Sweden shows signs of being affected by it and it will no doubt have certain effects in Denmark. Therefore, the B.B.C. must emphasize that the Russians are only fighting in defence of their soil and because they love their country.[2]

During this period the B.B.C. was trying to improve its Danish broadcasts. An output monitoring service was already in existence. These monitoring groups listened into all the broadcasts of the various sections of the B.B.C. European Service, and then sent back a critical report on them. For example, there were comments on the B.B.C. Danish section announcers. In the report for the end of September 1941, the Danish announcers were said to pronounce clearly and deliberately.

[1] Danish Archives. [2] *Ibid.*

'Blytgen-Petersen sounded rather like a very tired Danish preacher on Tuesday, but was much more spirited when dealing with the outcome of the Moscow Conference.' Sven Tillge-Rasmussen had an 'excellent voice for bitter declamation'. Rodney Gallop's Danish accent was 'far from perfect but every word could be clearly understood, and the authenticity value of his voice from England must have been considerable'.[1]

Reports too began to come in from Stockholm on the effect the B.B.C. broadcasts were having in Denmark. These indicated that, in many cases, Danes who understood English listened to the B.B.C. Home Service, as they felt it was less biased and less exaggerated. However, 'the popularity of the B.B.C. broadcasts is such that in the Summer it is possible to walk along roads in the suburbs and hear loudspeakers from many houses, all tuned into the B.B.C. news service'. It was also reported that the total number of registered radio owners in the whole of Denmark was at the end of September 1941 896,137, compared with 860,372 at the same time in 1940. An interesting observation was also made by engineers in the control room of the Copenhagen electricity supply. Every evening at 18.15 the consumption of electric current rose steeply, indicating that some 150,000 radio sets were being switched on and tuned in to the Danish news bulletin from London.[2]

This was encouraging news for the B.B.C. Danish section as, in the autumn of 1941, it continued its attack on the policy of the Danish government. In October, the output monitoring service reported that there had been a very skilful attempt at rousing Danish apathy. 'The Danish attitude of "sitting on the fence" while the Germans were in occupation of their country was shown up by the commentator.'[3] However, at the end of October 1941, the service had to report that 'the

[1] Output Monitoring Scheme report, 29 September–5 October 1941 (Danish Archives).

[2] Report from Stockholm on the effect of the B.B.C. broadcasts, October 1941 (Danish Archives).

[3] Report on the B.B.C.'s Danish broadcasts, 19–26 October 1941 (Danish Archives).

demand for strong emphasis on the failure of official Denmark to contribute to the allied victory does not seem to have born fruit yet'.[1]

During the month of November events in Denmark gave the Danish section of the B.B.C. the opportunity for which it had been looking to attack the Danish government for continually acting under German pressure.

A more aggressive attitude from the B.B.C. was demanded. A letter from Thomas Barman to Robert Jørgensen dated 1 November 1941 set the tone for the November broadcasts. It read:

> Your appeals to Danes to resist the Germans seem to be drawing blood. You will note that the L.S.[2] people openly attacked the B.B.C. for doing it. As usual, they maintained that your policy is contrary to the King's request. So now is the time to plug your catalogue of German violations of the April 9th agreement. Don't you agree?[3]

This was done, and the report on the B.B.C. Danish broadcasts for the week 2–9 November 1941 emphasized this.

> The news talk of the 3rd November, 'The Broken Promise', was an excellently worded appeal to the good sense and love of liberty of the Danes. It threw light on the L.S. and their treacherous strivings to twist the King's words round to suit their own purposes. The speaker reminded the Danes at home of the falseness of the German promises made to them at the invasion of their country. The speaker in forcible terms pointed out the folly of trusting any further in the Government, that had let them down so badly. They were told to consult their own consciences in future.[4]

The report added that a news commentary of 4 November had effectively attacked Stauning and his political associates, such as L.S. Møller and Valdemar Thomsen. A good point was made in this commentary when it was suggested that the Danish king, flag and language would become merely a symbol of everything which the Germans had taken from Denmark, if the present government was allowed to continue. The report,

[1] Report on the B.B.C.'s Danish broadcasts, 26–28 October (Danish Archives).
[2] L.S. = *Landbrugernes Sammenslutning*, the Danish Farmers' and Peasants' party.
[3] Danish Archives.
[4] *Ibid.*

however, complained that there seemed to have been no further attempt to follow the directive previously issued about Stauning and Scavenius. 'Stauning's age, for instance, might be stressed to good effect. He might be compared with Pétain in his obvious failure to grasp realities.'

On 25 November 1941 Erik Scavenius, the Danish foreign minister, signed the Anti-Comintern Pact,[1] thus placing official Denmark squarely on the side of Germany against the Russians and therefore the Allies. This gave the Danish section of the B.B.C. its first real opportunity since the occupation of exploiting a dangerous situation in Denmark. The broadcasts about the signing of this pact were a fitting conclusion to the November policy, as laid down by Barman in his letter of 1 November.

K. G. Anker-Petersen of the Danish Council came to the microphone and expressed the indignation of the whole Danish community abroad.

> The Danish Council in London learnt with the greatest indignation and sorrow that Foreign Minister Erik Scavenius yesterday gave Denmark's approval to the so-called Anti-Comintern Pact. It is clear to Free Danes abroad that Denmark's participation in the conference in Berlin puts Denmark in the eyes of the world, not so much as an enemy-occupied country, but as a country which has now accepted what Hitler aims at, the New Order in Europe.[2]

The Danish section of the B.B.C. was now able to exploit an action of the Danish government to real effect. This was the most dangerous realignment in foreign policy which the Danish government had made since the occupation, as it now brought Denmark still closer to German policy. For large sections of the population it was clearly a move in the wrong direction, and their indignation was shown by serious rioting in Copenhagen. There were demonstrations both against Scavenius personally, and against the signing of the pact.

[1] This was the greatest concession which the Danish government had made to the Germans since the occupation, and was part of the anti-Communist policy forced on the government. In June 1941 the government was forced to ban the Danish Communist party, and many Danish Communists were unlawfully imprisoned.

[2] B.B.C. Archives.

This was not unnoticed abroad. On 28 November *The Times* reported in detail the rioting in Copenhagen, in an article entitled, 'Danish Crowds Defy Police—Mass Demonstration In Copenhagen'.

The Danish Police have had a very trying time curbing disorders in Copenhagen which began on Tuesday while the Foreign Minister Hr. Scavenius was joining the Anti-Comintern fraternity in Berlin. A few hundred students began it by assembling at 2 o'clock at Amalienborg—the Royal Palace.

A theological student who read a draft resolution was restrained and detained by the Police, but the crowd grew rapidly and the Police began an energetic attack. They stopped their attack when the whole crowd began singing the National Anthem—it was scarcely reasonable to object to their singing that outside the Palace. The students, walking ten abreast, led the way from the Palace to the premises of the Danish Nazi newspaper *Fædrelandet*. They demonstrated there and also outside the Parliament House and the Foreign Office in spite of Police efforts to disperse them.

By this time the crowd numbered several thousands. They swept the Police aside at Højbro and demonstrated in many other parts of the town with cries of 'Down with Scavenius' and 'Down with the traitors'. They sang patriotic songs, including *Ja vi elsker* (the Norwegian national anthem), and carried Danish, Norwegian, Swedish, Finnish, and Icelandic national flags. The demonstration continued after darkness had fallen. The Police used searchlights, charged the crowd with truncheons and fired a number of blank shots, successfully barring the way to the Hotel d'Angleterre, where the German headquarters are established.

Windows were broken and other minor damage was done, particularly to German property. In one building a solitary German, apparently thinking it was an anti-Comintern demonstration, came to the balcony and gave the Nazi salute, but he retired when the crowd began pelting him with relatively harmless but unpleasant missiles. The sole reference to the disorders in Wednesday's Copenhagen newspapers was that the tram-car service was interrupted for a short time in several places.

This was the spontaneous outburst for which the Danish section of the B.B.C. had been hoping and working since the early summer of 1941. To what extent the rioting was directly or indirectly influenced by the B.B.C. broadcasts cannot of course be assessed. However, it is probable that the feelings of the population on this sensitive issue were inflamed by the B.B.C. broadcasts. At least the Intelligence section of the B.B.C. considered that the riots following the signing of the pact were 'the most striking single proof yet received of the power of the B.B.C.'.[1] Radio propaganda was not the direct cause of the outburst, but in giving wide publicity to events at this time, the B.B.C. showed the Danish population that its spontaneous outburst was encouraged from Britain, and that this was the kind of reaction to German pressure which Britain expected of the Danish people as a whole.

The view that the B.B.C. Danish broadcasts had influenced events in Denmark during November was later supported by a report on propaganda, which was formulated as a result of discussions between Christmas Møller and T. M. Terkelsen in the early summer of 1942. The report dated 20 May 1942 spoke of the events in November as follows:

> At the time of the Anti-Comintern Pact when active propaganda was directed to Denmark from London, the broadcasts may have increased the weight of the demonstrations but they would almost certainly have occurred even if the B.B.C. had been non-existent. But asked whether the transmissions were useful, the reply must be—very much so. They supplied the demonstrating youth with a background and an encouragement because the youth felt that their actions were being appreciated.[2]

An important result of the events in Denmark in November 1941 was the declaration of Count Reventlow, the Danish Minister in London. On 2 December 1941 he resigned, stating that he could no longer accept instructions from the Danish Foreign Ministry, as he considered the Danish government's adherence to the Anti-Comintern Pact was likely to damage Denmark's good name in Great Britain. He remained, however, in London to continue 'Free Denmark's diplomatic relations with the British Government'.[3] His telegram of resignation was

[1] Report, January 1942. [2] Danish Archives.
[3] Reported in the *Manchester Guardian*, 3 December 1941.

sent to the Danish Legation in Stockholm, which was requested to inform Copenhagen. There was no immediate reference to Reventlow's decision in the Danish press and radio, as German censors prohibited it. Denmark was first informed by the B.B.C. news in Danish.[1]

Reventlow's declaration was only possible because the British government agreed to it, as was Kauffmann's earlier action in Washington with the approval of the U.S. government. It was announced that 'His Majesty's Government have decided to recognize Count Reventlow as continuing to be responsible for the protection of such Danish interests as are not under enemy control'.[2] With Reventlow's resignation doubts about Denmark in Britain diminished. The Danish government had openly approved German foreign policy; sections of the Danish population immediately showed their indignation by the first open riots since the occupation; the Danish Minister resigned with British approval.

Reventlow's declaration came at a convenient time for S.O.E., although this was probably a coincidence. S.O.E. was now ready to mount and sustain operations in Denmark. The first parachutists went in during December,[3] and the Danish section of the B.B.C. was now allowed considerably more freedom to attack Scavenius and other Danish people suspected of collaborating. The rioting in Copenhagen had the important effect of showing Britain that sections of the Danish population were now prepared to show their anti-German feelings. Popular demonstrations were an important factor in deciding British policy. The Danish section of the B.B.C. was now able, with less restraint than before, to generalize its attack on the Danish government as a whole. Its chief aim was to show that the government could not serve Danish interests as it was so heavily under German pressure. This was the policy which the Danish section of the B.B.C. now followed and which

[1] *Sunday Times*, 14 December 1941.
[2] Reported in *The Times*, 12 March 1942.
[3] See Hæstrup, *Kontakt med England*, ch. 7.

was eventually proved right by the events of August 1943,[1] when German pressure became so extreme, in the face of Danish unrest, that the government was no longer able to function.

Further, a plan of action which had been discussed earlier in 1941 was now put under way. A well-known Danish political figure was to be brought to England to lead the attack against Scavenius' policy over the radio.

[1] The Danish government under Erik Scavenius finally ceased to function on 29 August 1943.

CHAPTER 5

CHRISTMAS MØLLER IN LONDON

Christmas Møller's arrival in Great Britain
is described as an historic event.

B.B.C. broadcast, 14 May 1942

John Christmas Møller arrived in England on 14 May 1942, with his wife and son.

The reasons for the British government's decision to invite Christmas Møller to Britain were given by Major-General Sir Colin Gubbins, of S.O.E.[1]

The Danish section of S.O.E. was still trying to establish a stronger and more influential body than the existing Danish Council to rouse public opinion within Denmark against the German occupation, and to appeal to Danes throughout the world. For this purpose invitations were sent to Christmas Møller, leader of the Conservatives, and to Hedtoft-Hansen, leader of the Social Democrats, to come to Britain.

Christmas Møller first heard of this invitation from Mrs Erik Seidenfaden[2] on 9 August 1941.[3] She had just returned from Sweden where she had met Ronald Turnbull, S.O.E.'s representative in the British Legation in Stockholm. Turnbull had shown her a letter from Hugh Dalton, minister of Economic Warfare,[4] to the Danish Social Democrat, Hedtoft-Hansen. She had memorized this letter, and its contents were that Dalton and other British government ministers wanted some Danish politicians to come to England. In this connection three names were mentioned—Hedtoft-Hansen, Christmas Møller

[1] Essay *Britain and Denmark* written for the Oxford Conference, December 1962.

[2] Wife of Erik Seidenfaden, who was one of the founder members of the Danish Press Service.

[3] The decision of Christmas Møller to escape to England and the events that led up to this were described by Christmas Møller himself in a report now in the Danish Archives.

[4] The minister of Economic Warfare, Hugh Dalton, was responsible for S.O.E.

and Nicolai Blædel, a newspaper editor of extreme anti-German views. It was natural that Hedtoft-Hansen was mentioned first, as he and Dalton had met personally at an international socialist conference shortly before the outbreak of war.

Hedtoft-Hansen refused the invitation to go to England mainly because he felt that loyalty to his party and to Stauning required him to stay in Denmark. He felt his duty was to help the Danish government in its difficult task, and not to go to England to support a different policy, which would inevitably make the government's position even more precarious in Denmark.

Christmas Møller's views were different. After he had been told of Dalton's letter, he wrote to Victor Mallet, the British Minister in Stockholm. On 29 November 1941, he received final confirmation from the British Minister.[1]

Dear C.M.,

All your letters and messages have been received. Your presence is urgently needed in England.

You are needed, and all the more so now, to help lead those Danes who are free now in their work for the common cause of freedom for our country as well as your own. With conditions in Denmark becoming daily more critical, it is vitally important that at least one well known Danish patriot should come out of Denmark to help lead the free Danes, who are at present in great need of leadership. It has always been felt that you, and a leading socialist whose name has already been put to you, were ideally suited to lead the Danish forces of liberation. At this moment when the fate of the Stauning Government and even perhaps of the King is in the balance, there must be a representative body of Danes, ready to take over the responsibility of speaking and acting for Denmark in the present great conflict. You are needed to play a most prominent part in the work of liberation.

It is impossible in a short space to go into too many details. It is sufficient to say that your presence in England is desired by his Majesty's Government and also by individual members of the war cabinet. It would be understood, from the financial point of view, that you and any members of your family who also left Denmark

[1] Quoted in Christmas Møller's report (Danish Archives).

would be properly provided for. You are assured of a warm welcome in England from the Government and from many others who appreciate the courage and leadership which you have shown in Denmark, particularly in recent months.

It is wisest for me not to sign my name but you can be sure that I have the authority to make the above statements. Come here as soon as you possibly can. If you can bring your socialist colleague, so much the better. Above all, come soon.

Christmas Møller also received a letter of invitation from Michael Kroyer-Kielberg, chairman of the Danish Council. However, he was not able to go immediately. Ice held him up until the following April, and he arrived in Britain during May.

On 14 May 1942 his arrival was reported by the Danish section of the B.B.C.

In the big conference room of the Ministry of Information, Mr Christmas Møller was introduced by the Parliamentary Secretary to the Ministry of Information. Over a hundred journalists representing England, the British Empire, America and the rest of the Free World were present and greeted Mr Møller with enthusiastic applause, as the first Danish politician who has arrived in England since the German occupation. The journalists were favourably impressed by Mr Møller's charming personality. At the entrance to the Ministry of Information, Christmas Møller had to force his way through a battery of press photographers. He willingly showed his famous Danish smile. Christmas Møller's arrival in London is a great and happy event for the Free Danes.[1]

Christmas Møller was clearly an obvious choice amongst Danish politicians to lead the assault from the Danish section of the B.B.C. In the months after the German occupation he had shown himself openly anti-German in his activities and speeches. While minister of Commerce in the Stauning government he had openly called the Germans 'enemies within our walls'.[2] He was soon forced to resign as minister. The German papers were jubilant. *Berliner Börsen Zeitung* wrote: 'From the very beginning Christmas Møller placed obstacles in the path of Sca-

[1] Danish Service news bulletin, 14 May 1942 (B.B.C. Archives).
[2] Quoted in *Denmark—Hitler's Model Protectorate*, by Sten Gudme.

venius' efforts to bring about a favourable Danish attitude towards Germany.' Møller was then forced to give up his seat in Parliament in January 1941 as a result of further German pressure.[1] This did not prevent him campaigning round the country trying to unite Denmark against the Germans. At the Forum in Copenhagen on one Sunday evening Møller spoke to a crowd of 12,000. The normal capacity was 8,000.

It was this reputation, and his obvious popular appeal, which decided the British government to invite Christmas Møller to Britain. S.O.E. needed the support of a well-known Danish personality, for the reason that its operations, by their very nature, needed a friendly population for success. Agents parachuted into an occupied country had of necessity to depend on local help, and the more co-operative the people were, the easier was the agents' job. The risk of informers was less, and a sympathetic population was of assistance in providing information. Christmas Møller's job was therefore to use his considerable powers of persuasion over the B.B.C. to turn the Danish population against the Germans, and therefore indirectly against the government. Rumours at about this time had been circulating in Britain that some allied airmen, shot down over Denmark, had been handed over to the Germans by Danish people.

At his first press conference,[2] Christmas Møller stated publicly that the decision to come to Britain was made entirely on his own responsibility. He had come to give truthful information about conditions in Denmark, and he hoped to be able to tell Danish people at home about British ideas and what was going on in the free world. For him, this visit to Britain was of dual purpose—to explain and describe Danish attitudes and conditions, and to be free to say over the B.B.C. what he wanted, to Danes in Denmark. The former he later achieved to a great degree, by a vast number of articles, speeches and broadcasts. He began the

[1] Christmas Møller was forced to resign as minister of Commerce on 3 October 1940. On 10 January 1941 he resigned as a member of Parliament.

[2] 14 May 1942.

work of speaking for Denmark in Britain soon after his arrival. An example was given by Blytgen-Petersen on 14 August 1942 over the B.B.C.:

Just as we journalists at home learnt to catch him on the phone when the train made a stop, so the English journalists have learnt to catch him for a lightning interview at the railway stations, as was the case when he travelled through Leeds the other day. For this journey had given Christmas Møller a chance to explain Denmark's position in influential provincial papers over here, and to speak of the Free Danish movement of which he is the Leader. In this way he contributed to the solving of one of the greatest duties and tasks of the free Danes, namely to spread knowledge of Denmark's real position under the German occupation.[1]

He was also sufficiently well known to make contacts with British and other allied circles in London. He continually put forward his ideas on Denmark at dinner parties, in speeches and in personal meetings. His energy, judged by a typical day's work, was inexhaustible. He was able to meet British politicians on a more equal footing than, for example, members of the Danish Council could. On 21 August 1942 he broadcast to Denmark: 'I have talked to the Foreign Secretary, Anthony Eden, about Denmark, and received a strong impression of the sympathy of the British Government for us. I have explained to the Russian Ambassador, Maiski, that the Danish people were not behind the persecution of the Communists, and the ban on their party, but that it took place under German pressure.' He had also met King Haakon: 'I have a very strong impression of Norway's formidable position here and in the rest of the free world, and I am very happy to be able to say to you that there are the best of relations between Norway and the Free Danish movement.'[2] Denmark now had a voice of authority to speak for it in the free world.

The other purpose of Christmas Møller's coming to Britain was that he should be free to urge active resistance and sabotage over the B.B.C., and that he should take a major part in

[1] Talk by E. Blytgen-Petersen in the Danish Service on 14 August 1942 (B.B.C. Archives).
[2] B.B.C. Archives.

supporting Danish resistance from Britain. In this he was less successful than he wished, because of restrictions imposed upon him by British authorities. He was neither taken into the confidence of S.O.E., which because of security reasons had to be very reticent in all its dealings, nor did he have a free rein over the radio as he had expected.

The story of Christmas Møller's disappointment over the restrictions placed on him in London went back to the time of his original invitation to Britain, when he was led to believe from Victor Mallet's letter that he would play a major part in London in Danish matters.

His reputation, and the fact that he had been a minister in the Danish government, meant that he mixed with senior British officials on terms of equality. His attitude was undeniably anti-German—in fact he held ideas which it seemed would only have met with approval from the British government. He was ready to help the Allies in whatever way he could. To Anthony Eden, British foreign secretary, he wrote on 24 June, soon after his arrival: 'My main point is that whatever Britain asks of us for the war effort, we Danes must accede to, whatever sacrifice it entails.'[1]

Yet Christmas Møller was not taken into the confidence of British officials responsible for Danish affairs.

On 19 July 1942, he wrote to Commander Hollingworth, leader of the Danish section of S.O.E.[2]

It is absolutely impossible for me to work under the conditions which have ruled through the last two months, and I therefore think we should stop taking up one another's time.

You know that I left Denmark by request and that a Danish politician was very badly needed as a leader. I have since been kept in complete ignorance concerning all that has occurred. Now and then I learn casually that Sneum[3] is in prison, that there is money

[1] Danish Archives. [2] *Ibid.*

[3] Thomas Sneum had flown a small plane across the North Sea from Denmark to England in June 1941, bringing with him valuable information about German radar work in Denmark. He was then sent back to Denmark by the British Intelligence service to gather more information. He returned to Britain in the summer of 1942, and was for a short time, owing to a misunderstanding, held in prison.

now in Denmark, that the Prince is going to Stockholm in a few days,[1] that three new men are going to Denmark[2] and so on—but it is quite outside your thoughts that these three are to speak with me, let alone that it is quite certain that my advice will not be asked as to whether they ought to be sent.

I neither can, nor will, work in this way. At home in Denmark they naturally believe that my advice is taken and that immediately I came over, I was brought into consultation concerning everything, and at home in Denmark they follow your requests because they believe that I back them up.

His anger was understandable. He had been requested by the British government to come over and lead the Free Danish movement from London. He had been identified in Denmark with extreme anti-German views, and the British government knew this when they invited him. In London he was expected to remain in a backwater. He was not given information on events in Denmark, nor was he consulted about the planning of S.O.E. operations. Soon after his arrival the influence that Christmas Møller had over policy towards Denmark was nil.

This was because the most unexpected switch in British policy towards Denmark was occurring in the spring of 1942. Christmas Møller was brought out of Denmark to encourage active resistance over the B.B.C. When the plans for bringing him out were made in the autumn of 1941, British policy, as expressed in the B.B.C. broadcasts, was still the same—to make the Danes realize that their government was acting under heavy German pressure, and that it could therefore not act in Danish interests. By following this policy, the Danish section of the B.B.C. hoped that pressure within Denmark itself would force the collapse of the government. The B.B.C.'s task was to increase that pressure.

Christmas Møller remained over the winter of 1941–2 in Denmark, and still the policy of the Danish section of the B.B.C. remained the same. Terkelsen continued to attack collaborators

[1] 'The Prince.' This refers to a member of the organization known as the 'Princes'.

[2] The three referred to were S.O.E. men, Hans Hansen, Peter Nielsen, and Knud Petersen, who were parachuted in at Farsø, Jutland, on 1 August 1942.

in Denmark. On 10 January 1942 he broadcast his talk 'Quisling Rats'. 'Danes who last night listened to the European broadcasts from London heard Colonel Britton mention the names of certain Danish Quislings like Knutzen, Director of the State Railways, and Gunnar Larsen.'[1] He warned that the Allies were now considering in London what steps were to be taken after the war to deal with Quislings. This was no moderate broadcast designed not to aggravate the situation in Denmark.

Sometime after this broadcast, British policy had begun to change, before Christmas Møller had even left Denmark. In the week before his departure for Britain, he had been in contact with some of the leading advocates of Danish Resistance.[2] He had met the two editors Seidenfaden and Kiilerich,[3] and had taken part in the discussions which led to the publication of Denmark's greatest illegal newspaper *Frit Danmark*. He had also met the agents parachuted into Denmark from Britain, and on 23 April 1942 the majority of the parachutists were in his home.[4] Before leaving Denmark he had given his support to the growing resistance and had identified himself with illegal activities. It was clear in his mind that this was the kind of activity he was going to encourage over the B.B.C. from Britain.

Unknown to Christmas Møller, Ronald Turnbull, S.O.E.'s representative in Stockholm, had written on 11 April to the leaders of the Intelligence section of the Danish army, who were referred to in all correspondence as the 'League' or alternatively the 'Princes'.[5] Not long after the occupation of Denmark, the League began to exfiltrate intelligence material to Britain, via the Danish journalist Ebbe Munck and the British Legation in Stockholm. This intelligence material represented the main, sometimes the only, contact between Britain and Denmark during 1940 and 1941. The Danish army was not disbanded after the German invasion, and the

[1] B.B.C. Archives.

[2] See Hæstrup, *Table Top*.

[3] Ole Kiilerich, newspaper editor, and leading member of the Committee for Free Denmark.

[4] *Table Top*, p. 385.

[5] *Ibid.* pp. 363–77.

Intelligence section was able tocontinue its work, with the difference that it now provided material for the British government.

The letter of 11 April was sent by Ronald Turnbull via Ebbe Munck to the League. It gave London's answer to a proposal known as the *P*-plan[1] which had been put forward by the Danish army officers. Their idea was, broadly speaking, that the *status quo* should be respected in Denmark while they put the *P*-plan into operation. This was to form illegal military groups of trained personnel throughout the country, so that they could be mobilized at any given moment. While these groups were being formed, the vital intelligence information which Danish Army Intelligence had been sending regularly to Britain by way of Sweden was to be continued, and if possible increased. Sabotage was to be avoided at all cost, as any action which might disturb the *status quo*, and therefore the position of the Danish army, would only serve to make the task of the League more difficult.

This proposal was accepted by the British departments concerned with Denmark. S.O.E. now had to curb its activities. It was not a complete surrender to the demands of the League, because S.O.E. insisted on sending in more parachutists, although they were not wanted by the army officers. No unnecessary sabotage was to be undertaken, but the parachutists would, under the direction of Eigil Borch Johansen,[2] S.O.E.'s chief contact in Denmark, undertake certain actions against transport and communications.

S.O.E. now reduced activities in Denmark in favour of the plan proposed by the Danish army officers. For the Danish section of the B.B.C. it meant, however, a complete reversal. In Turnbull's letter to the Danish army officers of 11 April, it was stated that 'London will modify its radio propaganda to avoid upsetting the *status quo* inside your country, and steps are being taken to bring American propaganda into line. In future all

[1] See Hæstrup, *Kontakt med England*, ch. 10.

[2] Eigil Borch Johansen had been involved in resistance activities since 1940. From January until June 1942 he was S.O.E.'s chief contact in Denmark, and was largely responsible for Christmas Møller's successful escape in May. From October 1942 he was at S.O.E.'s headquarters in London.

unnecessary incitement to sabotage will be avoided and unnecessary attacks will not be made upon the present Government.' Turnbull, towards the end of the letter, also wrote:

With regard to propaganda, as I say above, this is now to be co-ordinated so that nothing will be said or done to create unsuitable conditions for the effective development of the *P*-plan. *London radio have abandoned the policy of attempting to form a split in your Government and agrees that nothing must be done which might cause a change in the status quo.* It is realised that the present Quisling Government must remain for the time being, if we are to preserve the organization which the League has under its control.[1]

The policy of the Danish section of the B.B.C. was thus by one letter forced to a standstill, and the success which it had achieved in November 1941 could not now be consolidated with further attacks against the Danish government.

During May the original *V* campaign was also abandoned. Colonel Britton explained that he would not speak again 'until the moment comes to indicate a particular line of action which is needed. I cannot tell you what that line will be. Until that moment comes', he said, 'I shall be working with my colleagues and advisers on the plans.'[2]

Colonel Britton had clearly found himself on the horns of a dilemma. While he had, during the preceding year, been always cautious in his advice to the underground *V* army of Europe, there had always been groups of resistance fighters who had ignored his warnings. The work of the German firing squads had increased.

It was clear that in May 1942, at the time of Christmas Møller's arrival in Britain, the underground armies of Europe were being discouraged from any actions, particularly sabotage, which would endanger them. The end of the war was not in sight, nor, apparently, was the allied invasion of Europe. Colonel Britton and his advisers thought that now was the time for the European Resistance groups to hold their hands, to wait, and to strengthen their positions, until that moment came for

[1] Quoted *Table Top*, p. 378. [2] E. Tangye Lean, *Voices in the Darkness*.

'the particular line of action that is needed'. The decision to end the *V* campaign, and to 'freeze' the situation temporarily in Europe, was almost certainly influenced, if not directed, by P.W.E. and the Allied General Staff. While the Allies were waiting and planning, it was clearly the time for resistance groups to save their members from the firing squads and strengthen their numbers, until the time came when the Allies could support them with more than words.

Christmas Møller was of course unaware of the decisions that led to this change of policy. He arrived from Denmark expecting to call for increased resistance over the B.B.C. His letter to Hollingworth of 19 July 1942 suggests that he was not even offered an explanation of why he could not go to the microphone to ask Denmark to sabotage whenever possible.

He was, it seems, deliberately kept in the dark about policy towards Europe, and Denmark in particular, during the early summer of 1942. He might, despite the top secrecy which necessarily had to surround the activities of S.O.E., have been informed, simply, that considerable discussions on policy towards Europe were being carried on at the time, and that pending some decision the *V* campaign and calls for sabotage to European Resistance groups were to be suspended, in the hope that these groups would take fewer risks and strengthen their positions. He could perhaps have been warned that this was likely to be only a temporary measure, to cease when allied strategy required more action in Europe.

The position of Denmark, within this policy, was not made clear to him. There is probably one overriding reason for this. Christmas Møller did not trust the League. On his way out from Denmark, he had told Turnbull in Stockholm to build up the organization of resistance in Denmark on Eigil Borch Johansen, and upon no others. *He had indicated his complete lack of confidence in the policy of the League.*[1]

[1] On 4 May Christmas Møller wrote to Borch Johansen from Sweden on his way to Britain: 'I am having a talk this afternoon with the Captain (Turnbull) and I have already told him that the organization must be built up round you' (see *Table Top*, pp. 385–6).

It is therefore evident that Christmas Møller was not taken into the confidence of S.O.E. after his arrival in May 1942, when ideas to which he would have violently objected had he known about them were being followed. To accept the plan of the League was, from about 11 April, British policy. Christmas Møller was forced to accept the restrictions placed on him. He was not allowed to make any provocative speeches over the radio. The subjects and dates of some of his speeches were as follows:

Talk about the Danes Abroad	7 June 1942
What England thinks of Denmark	21 June 1942
Opinion in England	28 June 1942
The Danish Seamen	5 July 1942
Tribute to King Haakon	2 August 1942
Co-operation amongst the Northern Countries	July/August 1942
Finland	August 1942
A Visit to a Machine Gun Factory	16 August 1942
Miner's Life	23 August 1942
Visit to a Fighter Station	30 August 1942

These talks were more fitting to an afternoon Home Service broadcast and many of them could well have been peacetime talks. They were not the fighting speeches which the Danish people expected of Christmas Møller, nor, clearly, were they the type he wished to give.[1]

A letter of 25 May from the League to Turnbull indicated

[1] *The Survey of International Affairs 1939–1946—Hitler's Europe*, published by the Royal Institute of International Affairs (1954), is inaccurate on the subject of Christmas Møller's radio talks. It states: 'Once in England it was natural, therefore, that Møller should take the lead in the Danish Council; he became its President and at once began a vigorous campaign on the radio exhorting his compatriots at home to resist and to sabotage the German war machine', and again: 'In the Summer of 1942 with the ebbing of the tide of the German military successes and the vigorous direction of Møller from London, it (sabotage) took on a more serious aspect.'

The survey is inaccurate on two points. (1) Møller did not at once begin to make provocative speeches over the radio, as my list of the subjects of his talks during the summer of 1942 indicates. He was not allowed to make provocative speeches, and his first really aggressive speech was not made until September, some four months after his arrival in London. (2) Møller was not vigorously directing sabotage over the radio from London during the summer of 1942, and did not do so even after September 1942. Sabotage only really became serious in the years 1943–5.

that the army officers were pleased with the quiet way in which Christmas Møller's broadcasts had begun. They wished him to continue 'in the quiet way which had been adopted in the first broadcast'. They expressly stated: 'It is of the utmost importance that Christmas Møller maintains the present policy. He must under no circumstances let himself use his broadcasts for propaganda purposes, nor must he at any time let himself be carried away in front of the microphone.'[1] The army officers were clearly nervous of the possible consequences of Christmas Møller's speaking his mind over the radio. In fact they probably did not realize that it was impossible for a speaker of any of the sections in the B.B.C. European Service to depart from the prepared text. All radio broadcasts were submitted for translation and censorship. The speeches were then read over the radio while a switch censor followed the text. Any departure from the prepared text would have meant that the speaker was switched instantaneously off the air.[2]

[1] *Table Top*, p. 393.

[2] There is a description of the responsibilities of the switch censor in E. Tangye Lean, *Voices in the Darkness*.

CHAPTER 6

A TEMPORARY HALT

Raising local forces in Europe.

General Sir Alan Brooke, January 1942

By May 1942 the views of the League had been accepted in Britain. The Danish Army Intelligence officers had extracted the promise, made in Turnbull's letter of 11 April,[1] that unnecessary sabotage would be discontinued, that radio propaganda would be greatly modified, and above all that the British would do nothing to upset the *status quo* in Denmark. British foreign policy at this point clearly accepted that it was in the best interest to allow the League to build up local forces according to the *P*-plan, and for them to continue to transmit intelligence material to Britain. The intelligence work was to continue while secret mobilization, aimed at building up a force within Denmark, to act at a 'suitable' moment, was to be increased. It was argued that the effectiveness ofboth the intelligence work and the forming of local military groups depended on the continued existence of the Danish government and, consequently, the Danish army. 'Sabotage might only endanger a political situation in Denmark of equal value to both Denmark and Great Britain.'[2]

It is likely that one of two main reasons led to the decision on the part of the British authorities to accept the argument of the League. The first and most probable was that the intelligence material coming from the League, via Stockholm, was of such value that the British wished to do nothing which might endanger its continuation.[3] During the spring and summer of 1942

[1] Referred to in chapter 5.

[2] *Denmark and Britain* by Jørgen Hæstrup. Essay prepared for the Oxford Conference on European Resistance Movements, December 1962.

[3] The papers of Ebbe Munck in the Danish Archives show that a great deal of intelligence material was being sent to Britain via Stockholm during this period. The reports themselves can be seen in the Danish Archives.

Ebbe Munck's supplementary papers (Danish Archives) show also that these intelligence reports were highly praised by the British authorities.

the Danish Intelligence officers were transmitting intelligence material of great value to British government departments.

During this period a definite guarantee was given from London that no British Intelligence service activity would take place in Denmark.[1] Turnbull further stated to the League: 'The Joint Chiefs of Staff Committee and the War Cabinet have agreed that absolutely no work of any kind will be done in your country without your knowledge and without being agreed between you and the Captain.'[2]

Intelligence was given top priority and it seems that Admiralty influence was the most important in deciding this policy.[3] Certainly, information about German fleet movements, numbers and names of ships in Danish ports and information about north German ports would have been of great value to Naval Intelligence. Naval information seems to have been the most valuable that came from Denmark. It was of more interest to the Allies to know about fleet movements in the Baltic and North Sea than about military installations in Denmark itself, which were only intended for defensive purposes. It is probable that the Admiralty requested S.O.E. to reduce its activities in Denmark in the summer of 1942, to ensure that the flow of intelligence material from the League to Britain would continue. However, until the British records are opened, the answer to this and similar problems vital to the history of wartime Denmark will not definitely be known.[4]

[1] See Hæstrup, *Table Top*. This was clearly an important guarantee as far as the Danish officers were concerned. They evidently did not want their excellent Intelligence service interfered with by British Intelligence agents operating from London. Intelligence operations were to remain entirely under Danish control.

[2] Code name for Ronald Turnbull. This passage is quoted in *Table Top*.

[3] This view was given support by an article of Ebbe Munck's in the Danish paper *Jyllandsposten* on 25 November 1954.

[4] Although from Danish sources it is possible to see what kind of intelligence material was being sent to Britain, it is still not possible to see what use the British made of these reports, and what arguments were used, and by which British ministries, in favour of increasing the Intelligence service from Denmark, and decreasing sabotage operations. This vital question will not be answered until the British government decides to release the documents concerned. If the present Public Records Act remains unchanged the answer will not be known definitely until 1992.

The second reason for the Foreign Office's general acceptance of the views put forward by the League in the summer of 1942 was that allied strategy did not demand action in Denmark. British policy at this point was not to undertake further commitments, particularly in North Europe, unless they were vital, when victory was in the balance in another theatre of war—North Africa. During the period of preparation, before the North Africa campaign began in earnest, British policy was one of consolidation and not one of increased action.

The summer of 1942 was the beginning of a particularly critical period of the war. The balance was about to be regained, but there had been no major British or allied victories which could justify the view that Britain was now on the offensive. It was the beginning of the period of planning and waiting which culminated in the D-day landings.

In the autumn of 1942, the crisis was reached. On 23 October 1942, the British 8th Army attacked the German lines at El Alamein, and after twelve days' heavy fighting, victory went to Montgomery. On the night of 7–8 November, British and American troops landed in Morocco and Algeria and within a few days occupied the whole of French North Africa as far as the Tunisian frontier. Lastly, on 19 and 20 November, three Russian army groups attacked on a front north and south of Stalingrad and within five days succeeded in encircling twenty-two German divisions between the Volga and the Don. Alan Bullock wrote that 'taken together, these three operations marked the turning point in the war and the seizure of the initiative by the Allies. Henceforward, Hitler was forced to stand on the defensive.'[1]

This eventful period in the autumn of 1942 was marked by several months of waiting, perhaps of indecision. In July 1942 the tide had not turned, and clearly a great deal of new thinking was done in British government circles. The natural tendency during a period such as this was to wait and see what happened. It was a period of summing up, the first time in which the

[1] *Hitler—A Study in Tyranny* by Alan Bullock, book 3, ch. 12.

Allies had had a chance to plan and think. Hitherto, the entire battle had been to stem the German advance.

The more specific problems of the Danish Resistance were affected by the beginning of this new phase of the war. Why was the *P*-plan and the continued sending of intelligence material considered more important than increased sabotage in Denmark during the summer of 1942?

A quotation from the diary of General Sir Alan Brooke, dated 6 January 1942, is perhaps illuminating.

> Dined with Dalton and discussed with him his sabotage activities in Europe. . . *and also the question of raising local forces in Europe to be armed and equipped at the last moment. There is a great deal to be done in this direction at present, and I don't feel we are doing anything like enough.*

This conversation between General Brooke, chief of the Imperial General Staff, and Dalton, the minister responsible for S.O.E. activities in Europe, took place some two months before Turnbull sent his letter to the League outlining the acceptance of their *P*-plan. The Danish *P*-plan was precisely 'the raising of local forces in Europe to be aimed and equipped at the last moment' which General Brooke discussed with Dalton in January 1942. It may be a coincidence that precisely what was suggested then became policy in Denmark only two months later, but it was not coincidence that the two men who discussed these points were on the one hand the man responsible for co-ordinating all British military operations and on the other the minister in charge of S.O.E. It can certainly be assumed from this discussion that the idea of building up local military forces throughout Europe was discussed during the spring and summer of 1942. General Brooke was primarily interested in these forces as a means of support when the inevitable allied landing in Europe came.

This was also confirmed by Robert Bruce Lockhart, director-general of P.W.E.

> At the end of May, Brooks[1] and I had a useful meeting with the British Chiefs of Staff, at which the whole problem of resistance in

[1] Brigadier Dallas Brooks, a member of the Executive Committee of P.W.E.

> the occupied countries had been fully discussed. In reporting on the state of morale in the various countries, I made the point that some considerable measure of Anglo-American military success was a necessary condition to any stronger action by the oppressed peoples. General Sir Alan Brooke gave us what we badly needed: a clear and concise directive. What the Chiefs of Staff wanted from a military point of view was (i) *the formation and support of organizations in the occupied countries which could take charge at the moment of Germany's collapse.* (ii) Sabotage activities by these organizations in connection with our military operations. (iii) A continuous sabotage of a go-slow nature by all possible means of passive resistance.[1]

Sabotage was requested, but first in importance was the formation of resistance organizations, as planned by the League in Denmark.

The change of policy towards Denmark in the spring of 1942 may well have been the result of this and other discussions between the minister responsible for S.O.E. and the Chief of the Imperial General Staff. At this particular phase of the war the League came forward with a plan which fitted perfectly with General Brooke's ideas about European resistance groups. It was immaterial that the allied landings came, not in Denmark, but in Normandy. As the fortifications on the west coast of Jutland indicate, the Germans, and in particular von Hanneken, the German military commander in Denmark, feared that the allied invasion might take place there during 1943 or 1944.[2] Further, nobody was to know into what countries open battle might later spread, so that there was a good argument for the setting up of these local military groups 'to be armed and equipped', wherever possible.

However, British support for the *P*-plan was one thing, but Britain's agreement to reduce sabotage activity had more significance. The League's argument that sabotage would only make their position, and therefore their work, more difficult had been accepted in principle by the British authorities, but it is

[1] *Comes the Reckoning*, pp. 182–3.

[2] General von Hanneken, the German military commander in Denmark, showed some concern that the allied landings might be in Jutland. His reports to O.K.W. in Berlin show this.

doubtful if this request alone would have been enough to make S.O.E. suspend active operations in Denmark. S.O.E. was clearly determined to send the three parachutists into Denmark on 16 April 1942,[1] although the League did not want them. Three more men were also sent in in August.[2] S.O.E. did not agree to suspend all operations but stated that no active work would be carried out without prior consultation with the League.[3] Further, the presence of S.O.E. parachutists in Denmark with strict instructions to lie low makes it seem likely that there was a general directive issued by the Foreign Office during 1942 concerning S.O.E. encouragement of sabotage in German-occupied countries. In Denmark, the men and the apparatus were ready but had instructions not to operate, except in cases of immediate importance.

It was thought in the B.B.C. at this time that the halt of sabotage actions by S.O.E. agents in certain enemy-occupied countries was connected with events in Yugoslavia, where the situation was confused.[4] S.O.E. had sent in a British officer, Captain Hudson, in September 1941 'to contact, investigate, and report on all groups offering resistance to the enemy, regardless of race, creed or political persuasion'.[5] He had first contacted Tito's Communist guerilla bands,[6] and then he

[1] These three were Christian Rottbøll, Paul Johannesen, and Max Mikkelsen, and they landed in a large field at Aggersvold near Jyderup.

[2] This was the group that landed at Farsø, Jutland, on 1 August.

[3] Plans for strategic sabotage were continued. The three men parachuted into Denmark on 1 August had instructions to sabotage ferries but they were not in fact able to do this because their equipment fell into German hands, and because S.O.E.'s position in Denmark deteriorated badly. Rottbøll, the leader of S.O.E.'s parachutists in Denmark, was shot in August. Johannesen was also killed, while operating a wireless transmitter, and three of the remaining S.O.E. men were arrested. By September the whole S.O.E. organization in Denmark had collapsed.

[4] For a description of events in Yugoslavia see F. W. Deakin's essay, *Britain and Yugoslavia*, written for the Oxford Conference, 1962; also *Eastern Approaches* by Fitzroy Maclean, ch. 3, part 3.

There is also a chapter (17) in *British Foreign Policy in the Second World War* by Sir Llewellyn Woodward on British policy towards Yugoslavia.

[5] See *Britain and Yugoslavia* by F. W. Deakin.

[6] Also referred to as the Partisans. They were led by Josip Broz Tito, who was secretary general of the clandestine Yugoslav Communist party.

moved over to Colonel Mihailović, leader of the Četniks,[1] the other major group offering resistance in Yugoslavia.

Hudson's reports to London indicated that conflict between the Communists and the Četniks was growing, and he recommended that no official support should be given by Britain to Mihailović until the breach was healed with Tito. However, in London it was apparent that Mihailović was considered not only the leader of Resistance in Yugoslavia but also the first great Resistance leader to emerge from German-occupied Europe.

The B.B.C. played a major part in building up the Resistance image of Mihailović in its overseas broadcasts.[2] Mihailović also had the support of the Royal Yugoslav government in London, which had appointed him minister of War. This appointment was recognized by the British authorities, and the result was that Mihailović received complete support as far as propaganda was concerned.

During the period December 1941 until June 1942 all direct radio contact between Hudson and S.O.E. was lost. It was clear from his reports before radio contact was lost, that the situation could become explosive if Četniks and Communists turned against each other. In this period there were eight attempts at parachuting men into Yugoslavia, all of which failed. This indicated how anxious London was to know the real situation in Yugoslavia. Eventually British support was switched from the Četniks to Tito, but in the spring of 1942 there was clearly

[1] The Četniks were formed largely by officers and non-commissioned officers of the Royal Yugoslav army who had escaped internment. They were led by an army staff colonel, Draza Mihailović.

The word Četnik is derived from the Yugoslav word *Četa* meaning a company.

[2] See Maclean, *Eastern Approaches*, ch. 9, part 3: 'with the help of our propaganda we had in our imagination built up Mihailović into something that he never seriously claimed to be.'

Also see F. W. Deakin, *Britain and Yugoslavia*: 'It was therefore decided to concentrate on building up the resistance figure of Mihailović, the first in Axis-occupied Europe, and this in effect was the main effort of the British at this early stage and largely the work of the British Broadcasting Corporation.'

The idea of building up the image of Mihailović is mentioned also in the directive for the setting up of Radio Denmark, quoted in chapter 16.

doubt about the best course of action. Mihailović, as the first great leader of European Resistance, was largely the B.B.C.'s own creation. Doubt about the wisdom of this propaganda offensive on his behalf must have been felt during early 1942, and the B.B.C. was, as a result, reluctant to press ahead with propaganda broadcasts in other countries at this point, when events in Yugoslavia were becoming potentially explosive. A certain reluctance to be provocative in foreign broadcasts became evident at this time,[1] as the B.B.C. had no wish to be accused after the war of being involved in internal politics abroad. The result was a more cautious approach. This complex period in British-Yugoslav relations coincided with the period when S.O.E. agreed to the demands of the League and promised for the present that Britain would not press for action in Denmark. The demands of the Danish army officers for a freezing of the situation in Denmark came at a time of British caution and hesitation towards European Resistance movements generally.

From the available evidence it seems probable that the decision not to call for sabotage in Denmark during the summer of 1942 depended on four factors. First, the express wish of the League that it should not take place. Secondly, that the *P*-plan was in accordance with official British policy towards enemy-occupied countries at this time. Thirdly, that the B.B.C., on Foreign Office instructions, was clearly cautious about calling openly for sabotage because the Allies were not yet ready for an offensive. Lastly, in Yugoslavia, it was very doubtful what the result of British propaganda would be. An outbreak of armed conflict between Partisans and Četniks would have been very damaging to the reputation of the B.B.C. in the whole of Europe, especially as it had committed itself to such an extent in building up the image of one of the leaders. Had this occurred on a large scale, the reactions of other European Resistance movements might well have been to mistrust B.B.C.

[1] Christmas Møller's broadcasts during the summer of 1942 are evidence of this.

motives. If calls for sabotage were to produce bloodshed and perhaps civil war in Yugoslavia, they might well then be ignored by other Resistance movements, and S.O.E., through the fault of the B.B.C., would have lost much of the initiative on the European scene. It was evident that in the summer of 1942 calls to sabotage over the B.B.C. were not to be lightly made.

In August the situation began to change. The first indication of a reversal to the more aggressive policy of pre-April 1942 was a talk on the B.B.C. entitled 'Danish Sabotage Exhortation'.[1] This gave the information that Danish patriots were circulating letters within Denmark exhorting the population to sabotage. One such letter was quoted. Two Danish children had died from undernourishment. This was because Danish children suffered from the war at the same time as German and Finnish children were being brought in numbers to Denmark. The answer was that the war must be finished soon.

'Help our children. Damage the Germans through all imaginable means. Sabotage the supply of foodstuffs to Germany.'

On 30 August Christmas Møller calmly described his visit to a fighter station. This was to be his last speech, following the peaceable pattern of the summer.

On 2 September 1942 Sir Archibald Sinclair, secretary of state for Air, broadcast to all the enemy-occupied countries about sabotage, and his speech went out in Danish.

> It is not only from the air that the enemy's transport system is to be attacked. Patriots everywhere from Poland to the Pyrenees, from the North Cape to Athens, are helping to cripple it. It is for this reason that I am speaking to you because you can cooperate with us in cutting off or stopping the pulse of Germany's transport system. The transport system of the Axis is just as fragile as the human body. When one part is damaged, the whole is affected.... This is how we must, with increasing effect, choke and strangle the German transport organization. Get ready to fight, to fight against German transport.[2]

[1] B.B.C. Danish Service, 8 August 1942 (B.B.C. Archives and Danish Archives).

[2] The Danish text is quoted in Jørgensen, *London Kalder*, p. 105.

Christmas Møller followed this with his well-known speech of 6 September 1942.

He began by reminding Danish listeners of Sir Archibald Sinclair's speech the previous week. He then compared it with a speech of Vilhelm Buhl's. 'It was like fire and water, night and day.' He reminded Denmark that this war was a fight between good and evil, and that there was no such word as neutrality.

> Action is required of us all, of each one of us. Not Denmark but the Danish people as such are Allies and have the minds of Allies... The outcome of this gigantic struggle concerns us all.... It is our duty to have only one thing in view, that which hurts Germany most, and that which benefits the cause of our Allies. Whatever the British or the Allied direction of the war thinks is beneficial must be carried out, whatever is harmful must be avoided. Therefore I know well what I am doing when I tell you at home how really deadly serious the situation is for us all. Denmark and you at home must take your share of the burden.
>
> Now it is transport that matters.

Christmas Møller then reminded listeners again of Sinclair's encouragement to sabotage. He went on:

> The destruction of a train in France causes complications on the Russian front. The sinking of a ship or a ferry immobilizes trains which wait to be loaded or unloaded at the harbours, and forces Hitler to move his heavy traffic from the sea to the overloaded railways. Damage and delays, bombing and Resistance action—these are the means by which, with increasing effect, we will suffocate and strangle the German transport organization.
>
> Do your duty—do your work.[1]

[1] B.B.C. Archives. In drafting his speech of 6 September 1942 Christmas Møller originally wrote: 'Now transport is the important thing. All that we can do to destroy it, so that it cannot work for the Germans, that we will do. May it be heard far and wide over the world that the Danish people are in this, in mind and in act. Go into this work, the work of sabotage and destruction, not without having thought it out in advance, but knowing well its risks and its dangers.'

This was somewhat stronger wording than what he in fact said. For the piece quoted above in the draft, Møller substituted in the final manuscript a quotation from Sinclair's speech plus the lines 'the destruction of a train in France... we will suffocate and strangle the German transport organization' (quoted above in the text).

This indicates that the words Møller originally wrote for his speech were considered too strong, perhaps by Møller himself, but more probably by P.W.E. who

At last Christmas Møller had his wish. He was now able to urge active resistance and sabotage over the B.B.C.[1]

Military strategy and the course of the war now made sabotage a necessity. The autumn of 1942 saw the assertion of the allied military initiative on the North African front. Yugoslavia and Greece were in September 1942 strategically important for the allied attack in North Africa.

> With the planning of the final Anglo-American assault on the German positions in Africa, the question of guerilla sabotage and activity on the key German rail communications through Yugoslavia and Greece became of immediate military importance to the Anglo-Americans. In September General Alexander called for widespread attacks on these communications as a prelude to the North African landings and the desert offensive against Rommel.[2]

Military necessity meant that the B.B.C. had now to call openly for sabotage in the enemy-occupied countries, whatever the state of internal politics. It will be noted that General Alexander's call for sabotage in Yugoslavia and Greece came at the same time as Sinclair's speech, and Christmas Møller's open call for sabotage in Denmark over the B.B.C.

On 28 September Ronald Turnbull wrote a letter to the League in which he said that the British General Staff now expected sabotage in Europe against German communications. 'It is for this reason that the various British ministers and also Christian (Christmas Møller) have all begun to advocate

would have been naturally apprehensive had too violent and strong an appeal for sabotage been put out.

It is perhaps debatable whether the final version was in fact more moderate than the draft version. The difference seems to be that there was a stronger and more direct appeal to Danes to take up sabotage in the draft version, whereas in the final version the appeal was more general and was more obliquely expressed.

[1] The general directives of the B.B.C.'s director of European Broadcasts, N. F. Newsome, show that in September increased emphasis was put on Danish Resistance stories in all B.B.C. broadcasts. For example: 'Other news of Resistance should include a note about Denmark. Danish Resistance is not only of vital importance; it is also a most valuable indication of the temper of the Continent as a whole. It is not surprising to find resistance where oppression is great. It is obviously much more indicative of feeling when the oppression is not great' (general directive, 14 September 1942, B.B.C. Archives). The general directives for 9 and 12 September also made specific reference to Danish Resistance.

[2] F. W. Deakin, *Britain and Yugoslavia*, Oxford Conference, December 1962.

sabotage of German communications in a general way... You will see that Christian is not to blame for this, but has actually been acting at the suggestion of the General Staff.'[1]

This letter was the first of many from Turnbull to the League, stating that the British government now expected more action in Denmark. The waiting period of the summer was now over and sabotage action in Europe was to be encouraged, as a preparation for the awaited allied offensive. Further, it was now expected that Denmark should prove herself.

> It would be tragic if the Germans were to take over this year without any sabotage or anything else having been done to harm them in Denmark...I fear that London are absolutely determined to have some activity in Denmark in the nearest future since Denmark is the only country at present in which no organized sabotage has been carried out...I must say that for Denmark's future reputation it would be a very wise thing to make her contribution soon when it will really affect the result of the war, and not later, when the war is already practically won.[2]

The British authorities clearly wanted the League to organize active resistance in Denmark, but in this they were disappointed. During the winter and spring of 1942–3, it became clear in London that the League would not become the leaders of active resistance in Denmark. The League clearly wanted to remain hidden but prepared, until a final struggle with the Germans was imminent. They saw themselves more in the nature of a police force ready to take control of the country after the withdrawal of the Germans. Fear of a Communist take-over was clearly present in their minds.

In contrast S.O.E. now needed months of regular sabotage to undermine the German position in Denmark.

[1] Quoted in *Table Top*, p. 407. [2] Quoted *ibid.*

CHAPTER 7

THE B.B.C. AND THE DANISH CRISIS OF OCTOBER 1942

> If the crisis in Denmark subsides, it will only be because the Government will have sold out completely to the Germans. It must not subside.
>
> General directive from N. F. Newsome, director of the B.B.C.'s European Broadcasts, 7 October 1942

From September 1942, the Danish section of the B.B.C. reflected, as was natural, the ideas that were circulating in official circles in Britain. During the summer of 1942, all editors of the European Service had received a reprimand from N. F. Newsome, director of European Broadcasts.

> We are wandering off the target, not just sometimes but nearly always [he wrote]... Not only do some editors follow their own line without reference to any instructions, but they actually adopt a line directly contrary to that which has been laid down. Now that clearly cannot go on. The principle has been accepted in the highest quarters that the European Service shall act as an entity, as an army attacking certain clearly defined objects, and using a strategy laid down broadly by the Commanding Officer, and not as a series of guerilla bands or groups of partisans, with no cohesion and entirely self-ordained plans and aims.

He added that he did not run a totalitarian régime, and that editors could object to the general line laid down, either in his office to him personally, or at the daily conferences. 'What cannot be tolerated', he concluded, 'is that editors, having received written directions, should ignore them or run counter to them without raising the matter, or that, having received verbal suggestions and even instructions, should neglect or go against them without voicing any contrary opinion.'[1]

[1] N. F. Newsome, director of European Broadcasts, to all editors of the B.B.C. European Service, 18 June 1942 (Danish Archives).

This protest illustrated how difficult it was at times for the editors of the various sections to keep their broadcasts in line with the policy laid down by the Director of European Broadcasts. Some B.B.C. editors followed their own policies as much as possible, and one or two sections of the European Service were reputed to be freer from central control than others. The Danish section was not one of these. At times the editor found himself in difficulties with opposing directives from his director and from P.W.E. If he followed the directive of one, then he received a reprimand from the other whose directive he did not follow. On the whole co-ordination was good, and P.W.E. and the Director of European Broadcasts did not issue opposing directives.

There were exceptions. Four months after Newsome's letter to all the editors of the European Service, Robert Jørgensen was criticized by P.W.E. for mismanaging the broadcasts to Denmark during the Danish crisis of October 1942. This affair showed how confusing it was for an editor when his advisers disagreed, and how warily he had to tread when opinions differed.

The crisis in Denmark was caused by the king's curt acknowledgement of Hitler's telegram of congratulations on the king's 72nd birthday. This precipitated Hitler's demand for 30,000 Danish volunteers, for a change in the government, and the consequent emergence of the foreign minister Erik Scavenius as prime minister in November.

The crisis made the front-page headlines of the *Daily Telegraph* on 6 October.

HITLER READY TO TAKE OVER DENMARK

GESTAPO RULE THREAT TO KING CHRISTIAN

Diplomatic relations between Germany and Denmark have been to all intents and purposes ruptured by the sudden return to Berlin of the Nazi Minister in Copenhagen, Freiherr von Renthe-Fink. This was followed by King Christian's recall of his Minister in the German capital, Herr Mohr, 'for consultations'.

These steps mark one of the worst crises between the two countries since April 1940, when the Germans overran Denmark. Renthe-Fink's journey is explained in German circles as having been caused by King Christian's 'insulting behaviour' in replying to Hitler's fulsome telegram of congratulations on his 72nd birthday with a curt 'Thanks. Christian X.'

The report finished with a warning of what might be expected in the future.

These S.S. men, members of the Frikorps Danmark,[1] are swaggering about in uniform. It is an open secret that they have been brought home from Russia to act against their own countrymen if Hitler's latest scheme is opposed.

The directives from the Director of European Broadcasts between 7 and 13 October encouraged the Danish section to take the strongest line possible. It was hoped that the crisis would not subside. If it did it would only mean that the Danish government had sold out completely to the Germans.[2]

The directive of 9 October stated that the Danish government had already yielded to some of the German demands, and that as a result Hitler was asking for 30,000 volunteers from Denmark. It continued: 'Unless Denmark makes a stand now and chooses the path of honour and ultimate self interest already chosen by Norway and now by France, she will become a Rumania. German, English, Swedish and Norwegian broadcasts, all of which may be heard in Denmark, must take this line.'[3]

On 10 October came a further directive, which the Editor of the Danish section followed. This later caused a complaint from P.W.E. It read: 'We should exert the strongest pressure of which we are capable on the Danish Government to stand up against the Nazi demands. It would be a mistake to suggest that they are resisting. If anything, we should err on the side of suggesting that they are capitulating. Should this crisis blow over we can assume that they have yielded.'[4]

[1] The *Frikorps Danmark* had been formed in Denmark by the Germans for service on the Eastern front.

[2] General directive, 7 October 1942 (B.B.C. Archives).

[3] B.B.C. Archives.

[4] *Ibid.*

Throughout the crisis Robert Jørgensen, editor of the Danish section, followed the directives of the Director of European Broadcasts. P.W.E. were quick to criticize Jørgensen for ignoring their directives. At the weekly meeting with P.W.E. on 15 October the Danish section was accused by Brinley Thomas, director of the Northern Department of P.W.E., of mismanaging its broadcasts.

Brinley Thomas said that an inquiry would have to be held, because the directive which had been agreed upon by the Foreign Office and P.W.E. had not been strictly followed. Furthermore, reports had been received from Stockholm suggesting that the reputation of the B.B.C. in Denmark had suffered because of this. The main complaint was that, at the height of the crisis, the B.B.C. had indicated that the Danish government had made concessions to the Germans and thereby provided the Danish government with an excuse for ceasing to resist further German demands. This apparently had been broadcast in several languages, and Brinley Thomas's argument was that, as it was widely thought in Denmark and in Europe, as the result of B.B.C. broadcasts, that the Danish government had made concessions, then it was most unlikely that a firm stand would in reality be made.

The P.W.E. directive in question had been issued on 10 October. It was entitled 'The Crisis' and read:

> Pending the receipt of more definite information regarding the outcome of the crisis in Copenhagen, continue to report reactions in this country, Sweden and the U.S.A., relate the tension in Denmark to similar ferment in other occupied countries, and make a particular point of the climax which is being reached in France over the labour question.
>
> Emphasize to the Danes that the free world is watching them with interest and sympathy, remind them that the Nazis are meeting a new wave of resistance in occupied territories, point out that the Germans are desperately in need of more labour and food from Denmark. If news is received of the crisis being solved by concessions being given by the Government, attack these concessions vigorously. Avoid commenting on King Christian's attitude while the crisis continues, or if it ends without our being informed on what terms,

emphasize that the free world would find concessions difficult to understand at this stage of the war. There appear now to be only two policies open to Denmark:

1. Successfully to keep the Germans to their undertakings.

2. If the Danes fail in this, to draw the moral, i.e. greatly increase their resistance. Use Buhl's speech at the Rigsdag opening in this connection.[1]

This directive was considerably milder in tone than that issued by the director of the B.B.C.'s European Broadcasts on the same day, 10 October. The P.W.E. directive indicated that confirmation that concessions had in fact been made should be received before the B.B.C. attacked the government.

The B.B.C. directive, on the other hand, required the Danish section to urge the government not to give way, at the same time indicating that so far the government had not stood firm and was in danger of capitulating.

The attitudes were strikingly different. The B.B.C. was too eager to exploit this situation, and obviously hoped that this crisis would be final for the Danish government and that the Germans would be forced to take over in Denmark. For many months the B.B.C. had watched the Danish government concede more and more to the Germans, and had tried to point out to the Danish people that their government could not act in the best interests of Denmark and was only helping the Germans by remaining in office. The B.B.C. hoped that in October 1942 the government would in fact stand out against the German demands—hence the advice to the editors of the European Service to use their broadcasts for encouraging the government to resist—and that as a result the Germans would be forced to assume control and Denmark would at last be brought into line with the other enemy-occupied countries of Europe. It had been the aim of the Danish section since April 1940 to encourage the Danish Home Front as much as possible, so that it would create a situation where it would be impossible for the government to continue. This was an opportunity to encourage

[1] Danish Archives.

unrest further, and was the logical sequence to the B.B.C. policy of rigorous attack on Danish concessions in November 1941,[1] and of encouraging sabotage after September 1942.[2]

P.W.E. on the other hand held a more moderate view of the crisis and this was expressed in their directive of 10 October. Their policy was to await events, rather than to try and force them. As it happened they were correct, as the final crisis for the Danish government did not come until August 1943.

It is probable that neither the Director of European Broadcasts nor the Editor of the Danish section knew at this point of the consultations going on between S.O.E. and the League.[3] They would not have known that in October 1942 S.O.E. was still hoping for co-operation in sabotage work from the League, and that any attempt on the part of the B.B.C. to create opposition towards the Danish government would, because of the views of the League, have prejudiced the negotiations. P.W.E.'s strong reaction to the Danish broadcasts at this time, and the threat of an inquiry, were probably made because militant broadcasts from the B.B.C. during October were likely to hinder the secret negotiations between S.O.E. and the League, and were therefore not desired by the Foreign Office and other British authorities concerned with policy and operations in Denmark.

As it happened, the plan that the League should lead sabotage in Denmark failed, and so no harm was done. This was a case where secrets were too carefully kept, and where the B.B.C. was not informed of what the Foreign Office and S.O.E. were planning. From existing documents this appears to be the only occasion on which the B.B.C. followed a more extreme policy than that laid down by the Foreign Office. During the crisis foreign broadcasts were not in line with foreign policy because the B.B.C. was not informed of the true position of Britain *vis-à-vis* the League. This also showed how difficult it was for a B.B.C. editor when his policy advisers disagreed, for Robert Jørgensen took the blame for what was broadcast by his section, and received the brunt of the criticism from P.W.E.

[1] See chapter 4. [2] See chapter 6. [3] See chapter 5.

The broadcasts during October make interesting reading. In almost every sentence can be read the heartfelt desire of the Danish Service of the B.B.C. that events would lead to the total collapse of the government. A news talk on 9 October stated that, if the Danish government gave in again, 'concessions of the kind referred to might place Denmark in the same category as Hitler's other vassal states, a state of affairs which would make it difficult for the Danish people in future to assert its indisputable right to fight for its freedom on the side of the United Nations'.[1] The *Daily Express* was quoted in the talk: 'In Parliament and in the press, Prime Minister Buhl pleads for calm, good order, unity—all the things that Dollfuss, Schuschnigg, and Hacha asked for in their turn.'

On the same day Christmas Møller spoke to Denmark:[2] 'One feels that there is no such thing as neutrality. Blazing hatred of everything German is the all-pervading feeling.' Also in the same talk: 'We who are abroad know quite well that those at home have to make the decision, have to say yes or no. With all our heart, we hope that it is to be no. It is no use thinking that we should continue to receive preferential treatment. And one feels it will be too hard to bear if we do not show the same resistance as the others...We do not now want to experience a moral and spiritual 9th April.'

On 10 October, the B.B.C. broadcast a statement from Henrik Kauffmann, the Danish Minister in Washington.

While the French people are without question not considered responsible for the statements of the Laval minority government in Vichy,[3] the Danish Coalition Government, on the other hand, is regarded as speaking for the Danish people. Therefore, some of Denmark's best friends abroad are now afraid that if Denmark again makes concessions, there will be a serious danger of Denmark becoming, in the public opinion of the world, classed with countries such as Hungary and Rumania which, albeit against their will,

[1] Danish archives.

[2] Christmas Møller, B.B.C. Danish Service, 9 October 1942 (B.B.C. Archives).

[3] The Danish government was often unfavourably compared with the Vichy government in France, as Stauning had been with Pétain in 1940.

collaborate with Hitler, and have thus associated their fate and future with that of the German *Reich*.[1]

The feelings of Danes abroad were clearly shown and clearly expressed, but to no avail. Concessions were made, and the government did not fall. The B.B.C. was proved right in its statements that concessions would be made, but was, with the Free Danes abroad, misguided in its hopes that the Danish people would take this opportunity to reject their government's decision, and show their true feelings towards the Germans. Denmark was not prepared to force the issue, and the crisis was averted.

Scavenius emerged in November as prime minister. He continued the former government policy of negotiation with the Germans, but his past record, and the fact that he had been more or less chosen as prime minister by the Germans and thrust upon Denmark, made it apparent that the policy of his government was even less anti-German and more conciliatory than that of the previous one. The Danish section of the B.B.C. proceeded therefore to concentrate its attack largely on the person of Scavenius.

On 5 November came the announcement of Hitler's appointment of Dr Werner Best as political chief in Denmark in succession to von Renthe-Fink. Lindley Fraser, formerly a university lecturer and during the war a regular broadcaster on the B.B.C.'s German Service, wrote a talk in which he gave a warning of what might be expected in Denmark under the new régime. 'Best has been appointed to use all the Nazi methods against the Danish people.'[2] The attacks on Scavenius over the B.B.C. intensified during November and December. Blytgen-Petersen and T. M. Terkelsen continually pointed out that Scavenius, by forming a government, was working against true Danish patriots.

During the last two months of 1942 the point that the Danish section wished to bring home to the Danish people was this: that Scavenius was the puppet of the Germans, and that his

[1] Danish Archives. [2] *Ibid.*

appointment was only the means to an end, so that the Germans would be able to exert pressure on him for more concessions, particularly economic. Scavenius was the tool of the Germans, the 'Quisling Dane as Premier', as the *Daily Telegraph* called him.[1] The Germans would only use him to get manpower and war materials from Denmark. Leif Gundel in a talk on 19 December, entitled 'A Mess of Pottage', said that Denmark was run by a 'Government camouflaging the furtherance of purely German interest with care for the well being of the Danish people'.[2] Christmas Møller on the same day said: 'Scavenius is without root in the Danish population and his point of view is not that of our people. He is without understanding of all values which the Danish people, as well as the free world, hold so dear, and for which they are fighting. Today, with an even greater right than ever before, we can maintain that it is we outside who speak the language of Denmark.'[3]

The Political Intelligence Department of the Foreign Office which, as noted earlier, sent directives to the B.B.C., in addition to those sent regularly by P.W.E., was following events closely in Denmark at this point. In a directive on 17 December, it was suggested that the B.B.C. should state that the British press had been reporting Danish affairs with great interest. The *Evening Standard*, particularly, had drawn attention to the need for anxiety that Hitler's rulers in Denmark—Best and von Hanneken—had gone to Norway to compare notes with Josef Terboven on the finer points of occupation rule. The directive went on,

It is stressed in London that the Prime Minister's speech in the *Folketing* last Tuesday can only be regarded as an attempt, behind a nationalist camouflage, to conceal that the course he follows only serves German interests. There can hardly be any doubt that in view of Scavenius' pro-German past, he will not succeed in misleading the Danish public, and thus obtain support for a policy of appeasement which in practical effect can only be of greater help to the German war effort.[4]

[1] *Daily Telegraph*, 10 November 1942.
[2] B.B.C. Archives.
[3] *Ibid.*
[4] Danish Archives.

As a memorandum of the last two or three months' broadcasting in 1942, a report was sent to the director of European Broadcasts, N. F. Newsome, by Grant Purves, Scandinavian Intelligence officer of the B.B.C.[1] This was produced entirely by the B.B.C. itself and consisted mainly of the comments and ideas of the B.B.C. Intelligence section, which studied all the reports and transcripts of outgoing broadcasts. This report, called 'A Memo and Criticism of Danish Broadcasts', was interesting both for its comments on Danish characteristics and also because it reflected a difference of opinion on what was the right policy for Britain to adopt towards the new Danish government.

It began by complaining of too much innuendo and hidden insult in the recent broadcasts to the Danes.

> Broadcasts seem to nag. Of all people the Danes will be the last to respond to such treatment. They are sensitive and choleric people, with a sharp sense of personal justice, and in their own lives they attach even greater importance than we do, I find, to sincerity in speech.

Innuendo would only create enemies, not friends.

> I know policy to Denmark is a difficult problem for the moment and certainly I don't feel able to offer any solution. But whatever policy is finally adopted will have to be put across by us, and until we know exactly and clearly what we must summon the Danes to do, I think we should have only one thought in our head—to build up as large an audience as we can by providing a reliable, authoritative and objective radio service.

It was further suggested that the B.B.C. should refrain at that time from generalizing its attack on Scavenius into an attack on the Danish government as a whole.[2] The Danish section was

[1] Dated 13 November 1942 (Danish Archives).

[2] The view that the Danish Coalition government as a whole should not be attacked was also shared by those who were responsible for the policy of Radio Denmark. The directive for the setting up of Radio Denmark (quoted chapter 16) was dated June 1942, and here the view was expressed that for the time being the coalition government was preferable to 'some authoritarian system'.

Clearly some of the British propaganda advisers called for caution on the grounds that too sudden a take-over by the Germans in 1942 would do more harm than good

also to be reminded that it should not call Scavenius a 'Laval', or associate him too closely with Best until they had clearer proof.

So far, the Danish Government, unlike Scavenius, has a very good record. It never had any trump cards, and in the face of certain very hard realities, with which we ourselves are not faced, it has so far played a remarkably strong defensive game. If Scavenius sells out to the Germans and the Government with him, then I am in favour of letting them have it full blast, but not until then.

As an example of the wrong kind of approach to Denmark, the report quoted a broadcast on 10 November 1942, in which T. M. Terkelsen had said: 'It is felt as a blow in the face when in the headlines in the evening papers one reads "Pro-Nazi Prime Minister in Denmark" or "Denmark's Laval Forms New Government". It feels as if Denmark is at the point of giving in at the moment when the only thing to do is to hold out.'

This last report has been quoted at length as it gives some indication of the problems about Denmark which faced the B.B.C. in December 1942. Between the lines can be read the more moderate view that Britain should not try to precipitate matters in Denmark; this was what was meant by the suggestion

to Denmark, while others were for hastening the day when the Germans would take complete control.

The B.B.C., as it received propaganda guidance from several different sources, tended to steer a course mid-way between the two different schools of thought. On the one hand the broadcasts in October 1942 during the crisis were more extreme than P.W.E. liked. On the other hand the attacks against the Danish government, mentioned in the B.B.C.'s Intelligence report, were not direct, and hardly constituted generalized attacks. They were directed only against Scavenius, and other figures like Gunnar Larsen whose conduct was open to criticism, and not against the other members of the government.

By the summer of 1943 it is interesting to note that propaganda advisers in Britain were united in the view that events in Denmark showed that the issue was about to be forced, and that therefore the propaganda offensive from Britain could be increased.

The divergences of opinion were therefore basically over the timing of the propaganda attacks from Britain.

It should be remembered also that in November–December 1942 S.O.E. was still negotiating with the League, and that therefore there was some need for the B.B.C. broadcasts to be moderate. By the summer of 1943, when the propaganda advisers were in agreement that the time had come for an all-out propaganda offensive from Britain, these negotiations had broken down, and Denmark itself was showing signs that the crisis was about to be reached.

that the B.B.C. should not generalize its attack on Scavenius into an attack on the Danish government as a whole.

The report also showed the difference of opinion on the situation in Denmark. At the time of the crisis in October and for the months following, there were two schools of thought in Britain about policy to Denmark.

On the one hand stood the Director of European Broadcasts with the more extreme view that Scavenius should be attacked and exposed, and that the Danish broadcasts should pounce upon any hint of appeasement or conciliation in Denmark. In this the B.B.C. was supported by the Political Intelligence Department.

On the other hand stood the Political Warfare Executive with a more moderate view, that the B.B.C. should not precipitate matters in Denmark by aggressive broadcasting, that Britain should wait for signs of action in Denmark before openly encouraging it, and not vice versa. This view was surprisingly supported by the B.B.C. Intelligence section, and it suggests that there were internal conflicts and differences of opinion within the B.B.C. itself.

It was not until the late spring and early summer of 1943, when negotiations between S.O.E. and the League had broken down and when, in the general election in March, the Danish people showed their opinion of Nazism and collaboration in Denmark, that all groups in Britain concerned with policy to Denmark were united. By then it was becoming clear that Denmark itself was getting ready to force the issue, and in their battle the Danish people received wholehearted support from all the British authorities concerned.

CHAPTER 8

JANUARY-APRIL 1943

> It becomes more and more obvious that Scavenius is willing to give important assistance to the German war effort, even though it may be that he has managed to get round certain German demands.
>
> B.B.C. broadcast, 9 January 1943

The year 1943, the critical year in the history of German-occupied Denmark, opened with the familiar pattern of B.B.C. attacks on Scavenius and the Germans. The theme that Scavenius was, in reality, working for German against Danish interests was elaborated further.

On 14 January 1943, Tillge-Rasmussen recounted how Scavenius and Best were not only working together against Danish patriots, but were undermining the authority of the king. 'The Germans deliberately try to undermine the position of the King as a symbol of the unity of the Danish nation, and Prime Minister Scavenius is not the one to hinder them.'[1] This was a clever approach, as since the invasion the king had become more and more a symbol of pride and unity to his people. His daily ride on horseback from the royal palace over which the Danish flag always flew, through the streets of Copenhagen, brought him into contact with his people. He would shake hands with many Danes and yet conveniently forgot to return the salutes of German sentries. These rides were of similar meaning to his people as were Churchill's appearances in his siren suit with cigar to the British: 'He sustains us,' said the bishop of Copenhagen at the time, 'he unites us, he guides us.'[2] King Christian represented, throughout the German occupation, the old order of peaceful and democratic Denmark. As German pressure increased in Denmark, King Christian, as the father of his people, became more important. Any oppressed people need a

[1] B.B.C. Archives.

[2] Quoted in the chapter on Denmark in *The Undaunted* by Ronald Seth.

figurehead, and King Christian was this figurehead. Further, his position had been guaranteed by the Germans. Thus any suggestion that he was being undermined by Scavenius was likely to produce the strongest reaction in Denmark. This was part of the B.B.C.'s policy to stir Danish national consciousness and patriotism.[1] Throughout 1943, King Christian was continually mentioned by the B.B.C. as a matter of policy. His accident, while out riding in May 1943, caused great concern and showed how close he had come to his people. Blytgen-Petersen said of the king: 'When the Danish radio brought the news that the King was so far restored in health that he was able to take over the conduct of the Government, all Danes at home and abroad rejoiced.'[2] He also quoted *Frit Danmark*:[3] 'After the 9th April, the Danish people regarded King Christian not only as the strictly constitutional monarch, but also as the man who had the courage of his own opinions. Three years of occupation has only added to the fineness of this picture.'

On 22 January, a broadcast was devoted to the activities of Scavenius, and of Best and von Hanneken, the two German leaders in Denmark. Best and von Hanneken had not applied to be received by the king. Scavenius was frequently dining with Best. 'All these facts tally with the German intention to isolate the king and eliminate the royal family as a factor in the national life of Denmark.' Yet the conclusion, and the hope of the B.B.C. Danish section, was that, despite this, 'King and people will be bound with still stronger ties, and the combination of King and people, Scavenius will not be able to break'.[4]

Direct propaganda such as this was superimposed on a back-

[1] Robert Jørgensen confirmed in an interview that it was part of the B.B.C.'s policy to mention the king frequently in broadcasts, in the hope that Danish patriotic feeling would be stirred. For example the general directive from the Director of European Broadcasts for 13 October 1942 read: 'Feature Nazi attacks on King Christian.'

[2] B.B.C. talk, 25 May 1943 (B.B.C. Archives).

[3] *The Times* announced on 21 December 1940 that a newspaper for the Free Danes had been started in London. This was *Frit Danmark* and its editor was E. Blytgen-Petersen.

[4] B.B.C. talk by Sven Tillge-Rasmussen, 22 January 1943 (B.B.C. Archives).

ground of more general broadcasts, often on the current state of the war. The purpose was to show that the German grip on Europe was gradually being crushed, and that any adherence to Nazi ideals at this stage of the war would be fatal in Denmark. Tillge-Rasmussen on 13 January described the dismal failure of the German campaign in Russia. 'A whole army, which is slowly perishing with cold more than 150 kilometres apart from its retreating allies, is now in front of Stalingrad learning to appreciate the *Führer's* aversion to listening to competent military advice. Their relations will be telling the truth when they say—"they died for the *Führer's* prestige".'[1]

In addition to this picture of the collapse of German military power, it was pointed out in the same month that it was no longer in the *interest* of official Denmark to co-operate with the Germans, now that the Nazi collapse had begun. 'The entire attitude taken by official Denmark may prove fatal for the future position of Denmark in post-war Europe, if the Danish nation does not in time, in an unequivocal manner, make it clear to the free world that it is wholeheartedly on the side of the United Nations in the struggle for freedom.'[2]

The feeling of impending doom for those in Denmark who were pro-German in their views was encouraged too by mention of 'black lists' being drawn up in Britain, of those Danes who were known either to have collaborated with the Germans or to have allowed their factories to manufacture goods on German demand. These lists were being compiled at this point by the Political Intelligence Department of the Foreign Office. In fact, little became of these black lists after the war, and little, if any, direct action in Denmark was carried out as a result of them.

However, this could not be prophesied in the early months of 1943. The 'black list' had a definite propaganda value. It suggested that the British Foreign Office was informed in such detail of Danish activities that no pro-German action in Denmark would pass unnoticed. This fear of being on a British

[1] B.B.C. Archives. [2] B.B.C. talk, 9 January 1943 (*ibid*).

'black list' was likely to be enough to sway many waverers at a point in the war when German fortunes seemed to be growing blacker. The fear of 'backing the wrong horse' must have been very real in early 1943 for many Danish industrialists.

A few of the most blatant collaborators were mentioned by name over the B.B.C. Frits Clausen, Gunnar Larsen and others were frequently named. Occasionally, new and little expected names were broadcast over the B.B.C. On 26 February, Blytgen-Petersen attacked Dr Christiani, the civil engineer, for falling 'for German overtures'. 'It is at times like these that the best men of the nation should prove their mettle as good, strong, Danish men, and as the wise and intelligent men they were thought to be,'[1] was Blytgen-Petersen's rather pontifical conclusion. This particular broadcast ended with a word of praise for Christiani's two maidservants who had handed in their notice on the day after Christiani had dined with Dr Werner Best, the German plenipotentiary in Denmark.

The report of the B.B.C. Intelligence section in November 1942[2] had advised the Danish section of the B.B.C. against generalizing its attack against Scavenius into an attack against the Danish government as a whole. By April 1943 this advice was openly disregarded by the Danish section, and this coincided with the period in the negotiations between S.O.E. and the League when it was becoming apparent to S.O.E. that there was no hope of building up active resistance in Denmark with the help of the army officers. It now became unnecessary for British foreign policy to respect the League's demand for the preservation of the *status quo* in Denmark. There was no reason now in British eyes why an open attack should not be launched over the B.B.C. against the Danish government, aimed at its downfall. The change to an active anti-Danish government policy from Britain began sometime during the spring of 1943, when the talks between S.O.E. and the League broke down. The Danish section of the B.B.C. reflected this change in its broadcasts during the spring and summer of 1943.

[1] B.B.C. talk, 26 February 1943 (B.B.C. Archives). [2] See chapter 7.

On 4 March T. M. Terkelsen made a general attack on the government, comparing it to the previous governments under Stauning and Buhl.

There is a fundamental difference [he said] between the two periods. Renthe-Fink was able to negotiate with a Government which was, in many ways, weak but which had nevertheless a certain strength from the fact that it was elected by the people so far as it was possible. The present Government is quite a different thing. It is the result of a direct German demand. The Scavenius Government can never expect the same degree of loyalty, and developments have shown that the way the Government was created has weakened its authority. In this then lies the great difference between conditions today and four months ago. Germany's political attitude has not changed, but the increasing resistance has shown that a great part of the Danish people feel themselves free from obligation to a Government which they have not themselves elected.[1]

On the following day the *Daily Herald* printed a long article on Denmark. Its conclusion was: 'A new phase is opening up in the history of Denmark under German occupation. The Germans expect and prepare against open resistance to Scavenius' policy of collaboration.'[2]

Blytgen-Petersen had also during the previous month expressed the contempt of the free world for the Danish government.

There is surprise [he said] in the free world every time the Danish Government gives in to Germany again, and the unfortunate thing has happened that as the Germans are fairing worse and worse, the more easily their requests are complied with. That is the impression one is inclined to get, on learning that blankets and arms, and now also ships, are being handed over to the Germans. The more the Germans ask for, the more they get.[3]

As the *Daily Herald* prophesied, the result of the weakness of the Danish government was that there were more frequent outbreaks of sabotage and active resistance. Yet the Danish section of the B.B.C. still had to refrain from making general calls for sabotage during the first three months of 1943.

[1] B.B.C. Archives. [2] *Daily Herald*, 5 March 1943.
[3] B.B.C. talk, 19 February 1943 (B.B.C Archives).

Events between February and April 1943, before the negotiations with the League had finally broken down, were carefully watched by British government departments. A new and lengthy report reached the Danish section from the B.B.C. Intelligence section during February[1] and this brought the most up-to-date criticism of the Danish Service.

A Mrs Coffey, daughter of the late Dr Graham, moderator of the Church of Scotland, had been caught in Copenhagen at the time of the German occupation. She was only able to escape from Copenhagen in January 1943. When she arrived in Britain, she brought a mass of information, which she gave to the B.B.C. Intelligence section.

She reported that the reception of the B.B.C. was, at the time of her departure, poor in Copenhagen, because of jamming. In the provinces it was better. The popularity of the broadcasts was obvious, but 'it was also a fact that the number of listeners was decreasing rather than increasing'. There were many reasons for this, but Mrs Coffey thought that the chief reason was that the Danes 'expected B.B.C. to comment favourably upon their behaviour under German occupation and could not help resenting criticism of which they considered the B.B.C. is allotting them more than a fair share'. Of the speakers, she said that Tillge-Rasmussen was thought to talk down to his audience too much. Terkelsen and Blytgen-Petersen were more popular. Most popular with the Danish people, she considered, was Rodney Gallop. 'They [the Danes] were very flattered when English broadcasters addressed them, and even if their Danish was rather faltering, this seemed to be only a further attraction.'

Apparently, a large percentage of the audience consisted of farmers and intellectuals. A general complaint was that the B.B.C. Danish announcers did not speak the King's Danish, their voices did not sound cultured and some of them apparently spoke with an English accent. This was considered by the B.B.C. Intelligence section to be rather an important point 'as the

[1] Dated 9 February 1943 (Danish Archives).

Danes had rather a cultivated taste and tended to be more interested in the presentation of the news than in the news itself.' Bad Danish would be sufficient to spoil the whole effect of a broadcast.

There was also an interesting return to the main theme of the November Intelligence report. This was that Denmark now needed encouragement, as a spiritual rebirth had begun. 'Instead of nagging and criticism which leads nowhere when dealing with the Danes, the primary object of the B.B.C. should be to restore their confidence in themselves.' Mrs Coffey also confirmed that many Danish people listened to Home and Empire B.B.C. broadcasts, as they were considered more authoritative.

In the same month, the Political Intelligence Department sent in a report on the general attitude in Denmark. This stated openly that German psychology in Denmark had been excellent. Good material conditions had been allowed, so that even now there was a certain section of the population who, because they were afraid of getting 'Norwegian conditions',[1] were prepared to annoy the Germans, but not to wage open war. 'On the other hand there are a good deal of 100 % people who are prepared to do anything.' The Political Intelligence Department report concluded: 'However, Danish girls are often seen with German soldiers. It is said that monuments to the unknown soldier will be erected in front of many maternity homes.'[2]

Several points stand out from these reports. First, much emphasis was placed on the technical details of broadcasting and reception, presentation, voice, and accent. Secondly, two parts of this report indicate that Denmark itself could not, or did not wish to, feel the urgency which the B.B.C. was trying to express. It was not encouraging for the Danish section to read that many Danes were more interested in the presentation of the news than in the news itself, or that the Danish audience

[1] The words 'Norwegian conditions' were used in Denmark to describe what might happen if the Danish government ceased to function, and the Germans began a reign of terror as they had done in Norway.

[2] Political Intelligence Department report, February 1943 (Danish Archives).

thought that the B.B.C. was being too hard on them. P.I.D.'s summary was probably the correct one—that the population was divided between those who were anti-German, who would annoy the Germans but would do nothing to precipitate 'Norwegian conditions', and those who were '100%'. Clearly by the beginning of March 1943, despite the B.B.C. having taken as forceful a line as possible, much ground was yet to be covered before the Danish population would openly show its true feelings and demonstrate against the policy of the government. The complaint was still that the B.B.C. was nagging and criticizing.

To create the desired effect, the B.B.C. had to encourage the Danish population to stand up openly for what it considered to be right. The people were clearly swinging into a more aggressive frame of mind, and this had been encouraged by the B.B.C.'s broadcasts since early 1941. The problem now was how to get the population to show, and not only to think, its protests. This policy the Danish section followed during April 1943.

Several factors were important to the success of the B.B.C.'s objectives. The general situation of the war had now changed for the better. Britain was psychologically and materially in a far better position to support active resistance in German-occupied countries. Material help was an important consideration, which Charles Hambro of S.O.E. had raised in 1940.[1] The principle that there was to be no sustained propaganda offensive over the radio to encourage unrest in Denmark, until Britain was able to give material support in the form of arms and explosives, had been followed. By the spring of 1943 Britain was able to give that support.

Further, two important events contributed greatly to the British decision to encourage action openly in Denmark from April onwards and during the rest of the summer of 1943.

The first was the general election held in Denmark in March. The second was the final breakdown of S.O.E.'s negotiations with the League.

[1] See chapter 4.

CHAPTER 9

THE ELECTION OF MARCH 1943

Vote Danish... Choose a Rigsdag of men who will say no to any further concessions to the Germans.

B.B.C. broadcast, March 1943

It is difficult to be certain why the Germans allowed an ordinary general election to be held in March 1943, or what they hoped to gain by letting the Danish people go to the polls. There are several interpretations. Dr Werner Best, the German plenipotentiary in Denmark, almost certainly pressed Berlin to allow the elections to be held. His decision must have been made on the basis of evidence that there was a certain Danish-German *détente* in the early months of 1943. The political crisis of the autumn of 1942 had been followed by the emergence of Scavenius and a government re-shuffle. Best arrived in Denmark in November, as Hitler's political representative. Throughout the winter of 1942–3, Britain was not urging active resistance over the radio because the League of Danish army officers was opposed to it. Perhaps the relative peace on the Home Front, and lack of encouragement to sabotage from Britain, led Best to believe that the situation in Denmark was more secure than it was. Certainly it was in his own interest, as Hilter's representative in the 'Model Protectorate', to present as peaceful a picture of Denmark as possible to Berlin. To the Danish public he reiterated his understanding of the position of Denmark, and to Berlin he pointed out the very great military and political difficulties the Germans would have if the existing policy of negotiation with the Danish government broke down completely.

By holding the elections Best probably hoped also to demonstrate to Berlin the complete hopelessness of the possibility of Danish Nazis forming a government. His policy was to work together with those Danes in the government who were able to count on some support within Denmark, and to avoid pressure from Berlin which might require him to depend on the Nazi party in Denmark. In this aim at least, Best was successful, because the elections proved that the Danish Nazi party had no popular support, and that any German proposal which required Best to follow a policy of negotiation with a Nazi government in Denmark would end in complete failure, because the population would not have accepted such a government. Whatever his prime motive may have been, he succeeded in presenting his view successfully in Berlin, and obtained the decision that the election was to be held.

The propaganda value of the election to the Germans was obvious. The whole world, not least Berlin, was to see that if Denmark was to be allowed to hold a general election, then it was not in reality writhing under the yoke of the German occupation. The Danish section of the B.B.C. was quick to point this out. T. M. Terkelsen in a broadcast on 11 March warned listeners of the meaning of these elections. 'The Germans have already advertised the elections as a proof of the incredible freedom to move, which Denmark enjoys inside the walls of the prison. Scavenius hopes to be able to exploit the elections as a confirmation of the correctness of his policy.'[1]

Terkelsen might also have added here that Scavenius was only camouflage in the whole operation, that it was in reality Best who sought confirmation of his policy with regard to Berlin.

In this broadcast, the Danes were also encouraged to show by their voting what they really felt. 'The only thing to do is to see that the best Danish men are elected. For the first time since the occupation, the common Dane has a chance to use his influence on the Government of the country—why not take the chance? It is no longer the question of parties—the party system after all is really void under a coalition government. The thing is to choose men who have convictions and the moral courage to fight for them.'

[1] B.B.C. Archives.

The result of these elections was clearly very important for British policy. The Danish section of the B.B.C., from the beginning of the war until April 1943, had had the difficult task of avoiding two extremes. On the one hand, the section was unable, and in fact unwilling, to broadcast openly for sabotage, and the destruction of the coalition government. This would have had the effect, either of turning the Danish population against the B.B.C. or, if the broadcasts had been effective, of causing unnecessary bloodshed, during the long period when Britain was unable to send men or materials to Denmark.

The other extreme which had to be avoided was that of giving the impression that everyone in Britain was satisfied with Denmark, that there was a general realization in Britain that Denmark could not help the events of 9 April 1940,[1] and that it was expected that Denmark would be quiescent under German occupation. This had to be avoided at all costs.

During the long period when Britain was unable to give material support to the Danish Resistance, the Danish section of the B.B.C. steered, as it had to, a middle course veering towards an active line at particular times. The whole of broadcasting from 1940 until 1943 was intended to bring home firmly to Danish listeners that the government of Denmark was not in Danish hands, but in German. The B.B.C. attempted to destroy the myth that the coalition government helped the Danish cause, by saying that this was not possible when every final decision was not made by the Danish prime minister but by a German. This is why at times the Danish broadcasts were a catalogue of the promises which the Germans had broken since 9 April 1940, and why every time pressure was applied to the government and concessions were made, so much was made of it from London. The aim of the Danish section of the B.B.C. had always been that Denmark should enter the fight on the side of the Allies, but that the Danish people would have to show their willingness to do this by spontaneous action in Denmark, whether by riots, strikes, marches or sabotage. The

[1] See chapter 1.

important point—and this clearly was important to the Foreign Office too—was that the Danes themselves should show themselves ready to rise and fight, before the real attack began from London. So every attempt from Britain until March 1943 was directed at making Denmark herself react positively against the Germans. Once the Home Front had shown itself spontaneously, then London needed no longer to exercise restraint. Clearly, isolated outbreaks of sabotage were not enough, although figures for sabotage rapidly mounted. In January there were fourteen successful sabotage actions, in February twenty-nine, and in March sixty.[1] A general and widespread indication of the feelings of Denmark had to make itself evident, before the final attack, aimed at the removal of the Danish government from office, began from Britain.

So the elections were very important both to the Danish section of the B.B.C. and to S.O.E. and the Foreign Office. Best's decision to hold these elections was a massive propaganda gamble, which failed. For just as Best wished to show Berlin the success of his moderate policy in the 'Model Protectorate', Britain hoped that at long last Denmark would 'show' itself, by the safe yet effective method of voting anti-Scavenius and anti-Nazi.

The B.B.C. did not neglect to tell Denmark that the way the voting went in the election might have vital consequences for Denmark after the war. Blytgen-Petersen on 19 March drew attention to discussions in Washington, attended by Anthony Eden, on the future of German-occupied countries after their final liberation by the Allies. Clearly the decision of the Allies would be that free elections would have to be held as soon as possible. 'Such elections will be free elections then, and different from the present occupation elections. But before those first peace elections can take place, Denmark—like all the other liberated countries—must have a German-free Government to administer the country in the interval.' This was one of the many political problems with which the Allies would be faced after the liberation. Blytgen-Petersen continued: 'From this you

[1] Figures quoted in *Panorama Denmark* by Jørgen Hæstrup.

will understand that the elections next Tuesday have a certain significance. You will see that it is particularly important for the time immediately after the war that the Danes even now, during the occupation, utilize this chance to confirm their belief in Danish Government by the people in a free Denmark.'[1] His final exhortation was that the Danish voter should vote *Danish.*

In the week before the election, a great deal of propaganda was broadcast from Britain. Gundel broadcast especially to Danish youth. On 19 March in a talk entitled 'The Young Electorate' he told Denmark that this election was of the utmost importance to the future of the youth of Denmark.

> There are two tasks to perform on Tuesday [he said]. First, to make the elections a great national demonstration, a mighty show of the will of the people to regain its freedom and independence. Secondly, to choose a *Rigsdag* of men who can and will say 'no' to any further concessions to the Germans, to any new humiliation of our traditions as a free and democratic nation—the 'no' which will lead Denmark into the battle for freedom and right on an equal footing with the Allied countries.[2]

Gabriele Rohde made a special appeal to Danish women voters to come out in force and vote for a strong *Rigsdag*, that would not agree to concessions.[3] Sven Tillge-Rasmussen, on 20 March, summed up the pre-election feeling in Britain. 'There will, for us Danes in the both enviable and difficult position abroad, be much to explain and defend when the results of this election are known.'[4]

When the results of the election became known, they were open to several interpretations. They could be seen as a victory for Scavenius and the policy of negotiation with the Germans. The B.B.C. preferred to interpret the vote as a victory for the principle of democracy in an enemy-occupied country.[5]

[1] B.B.C. talk, 19 March 1943 (B.B.C. Archives).

[2] B.B.C talk, 19 March 1943 (*ibid.*).

[3] B.B.C. talk, 21 March 1943 (*ibid.*). [4] B.B.C. talk, 20 March 1943 (*ibid.*).

[5] The general directive from the director of the B.B.C.'s European Broadcasts read, on 24 March 1943: 'In this connection, too, the Danish Election results, a defeat for the Nazis and the Scavenius collaborationist party, are of great interest—one small state votes against the Statute of Europe.'

The only real alternative for the voter had been to vote for the Danish Nazi party, and this the Danish population did not do. The elections proved once and for all, and probably to the satisfaction of Dr Best among others, that any attempt at setting up a Danish Nazi government in Denmark would end in complete failure. The response to the election was certainly not half-hearted and its great importance 'was the tremendous poll which had the practical effect of crushing a couple of small pro-Nazi factions, and so helping to eliminate any possibility that the Germans would find support should the occasion arise in Danish adherents. To that extent the population was unshakably united.'[1]

The B.B.C., interpreting the result as a 'victory for democracy', could breathe again. On 23 March, Terkelsen broadcast:

> The elections to the *Folketing*[2] have for a short spell again brought the name of Denmark into the limelight in the free world. In the midst of great war events arrives the announcement that the Danish people after three years of German occupation have spoken a thundering 'yes' to democracy. For that is how the results of the election are interpreted out here. It has been brought home to the world that out of 148 elected members of the *Folketing*, 143 confess to Democracy, 3 to the Nazi *Weltanschauung* and 2—the peasants' party—adhere to those who pay the highest price for their butter.[3]

On 29 March, he was able to sum up with the words: 'Denmark today presents to the foreign observer the picture of a country where everybody swears to democracy and more and more people take part in the active fight for freedom.'[4]

Paul Palmér, in a talk entitled 'Election Aftermath' on 19 April, drew attention to the split that the results of the election had caused in the pro-Nazi factions in Denmark. He told listeners that even *Fædrelandet*, the official pro-Nazi newspaper, had admitted on 6 April 'that the parties working

[1] Jørgen Hæstrup in *Panorama Denmark*.
[2] *Folketing*—the Danish Parliament.
[3] B.B.C. talk, 23 March 1943 (B.B.C. Archives).
[4] B.B.C. talk, 29 March 1943 (*ibid.*).

together won a decisive victory, owing to the fact they more or less set themselves in opposition to the Government. A good deal of the *Rigsdag* are either partly or entirely in opposition to the Government and only pretend to approve of the foreign policy of the Government.'

Palmér continued with a scathing picture of Frits Clausen, the Danish Nazi leader:

Only three days after *Fædrelandet's* honest confession, Frits Clausen stood up in the *Folketing*—on the 9th April itself—and disowned his own paper and the writer of its leading article, in order to obey his orders from Berlin and to trumpet forth German propaganda in the Danish *Rigsdag*, by saying: 'The elections have shown that Danish democracy unanimously supports that foreign policy which is being carried out by the Foreign Minister, with the exception of the Danish Unity Party, and the whole Danish people, therefore, supports a foreign policy, which according to statements made by the Government itself—aims at effective collaboration with Germany.'[1]

[1] B.B.C. talk, 19 April 1943 (*ibid.*).

CHAPTER 10

THE B.B.C. ENCOURAGES ACTION IN DENMARK

> Sabotage will be one of the most effective weapons against Hitler in 1943.
>
> Emil Blytgen-Petersen in a B.B.C. broadcast on 4 January 1943

London certainly differed in its interpretation of the election results from Frits Clausen. This was marked by the considerably firmer attitude shown in the B.B.C. broadcasts from the beginning of April 1943.

Two factors had influenced the Foreign Office and P.W.E. in the decision to encourage the B.B.C. to strengthen its attack on the policy of the Danish government. The first was the result of the March election. This showed that there was almost no pro-Nazi feeling in Denmark, and it led Britain to believe that the Danish people would now become more and more restless with the Scavenius government because of its weakness in the face of German pressure.

The second was the collapse of S.O.E.'s negotiations with the League. On 26 April 1943, Ronald Turnbull wrote to the League. In this letter it became absolutely clear that London was determined to press ahead with S.O.E. operations and that it had finally been decided not to depend on the League for active resistance, but upon the civil resistance groups which were already undertaking extensive sabotage operations.

> However we [S.O.E. in London] must emphasize again that although we understand the League's attitude, we think that it does not necessarily coincide with the United Nations' strategy, which is that the Germans must be harmed *now*. Nor incidentally do we think that the League's attitude is based on a very clear grasp of the situation. Clearly the Germans are not going to leave a potentially revolt-

ing army in their midst. The first sign of the outbreak of a second front in Europe will bring the Germans down on the League forces.[1]

By April, S.O.E. realized that it would be foolish to expect the League to encourage sabotage, when they would be the first suspects. Further the League was not prepared to carry out enough sabotage actions, as far as S.O.E. was concerned. 'We want action now because we need it now, and because we think it most unlikely that the conditions for realizing the *P*-plan will ever exist...We hope very much that the League will continue to furnish us with Intelligence, but we are equally determined to go ahead with Table plans [S.O.E. operations].'[2]

Now began in earnest the attempt from Britain to support active resistance in Denmark. In March a new S.O.E. leader, Flemming B. Muus,[3] and three others[4] were sent in with instructions to contact as many leaders of civil resistance groups as possible. Muus took over command of all S.O.E. agents then in Denmark, and the supplies of arms and equipment from Britain were increased.

Sabotage now became prominent. Figures have been quoted to show that sabotage actions rose rapidly in the first three months of 1943. They continued to rise. In the month of April, their number was 70. This meant that in four months sabotage had increased fivefold. By the early summer, several Danish Resistance groups were issuing instructions, arranging the reception of weapons parachuted in by canister, and distributing them. The first delivery of arms from Britain by parachute came during March. This was followed by a number of deliveries mainly of sabotage material, but also of supplies of small arms. In July, there were 84 acts of sabotage and during August 198.[5]

[1] Quoted in Hæstrup, *Table Top*. [2] Quoted in *Table Top*.

[3] Flemming Muus had been in Liberia on 9 April 1940 when Denmark had been invaded. From a B.B.C. broadcast he heard that Danes were being recruited into the Buffs Regiment in London for active service. Soon after he arrived in England, he was asked to join S.O.E. and he began special training. He was then parachuted into Denmark in March 1943, where he took over the leadership of S.O.E. For a fuller account of his work for the Danish Resistance see his book *The Spark and the Flame*; also Hæstrup in *Kontakt med England*, ch. 14.

[4] These three were Einar Balling, Paul Jensen, and Verner Johansen.

[5] Figures quoted in Hæstrup, *Panorama Denmark*, p. 27

The decision to try and precipitate action in Denmark had been taken. Britain now actively and publicly supported Danish sabotage and resistance and, as if to support the decision of their government, British newspapers began reporting Danish sabotage actions in detail. The *Daily Telegraph*, in an article headed 'Danes blow up German Barracks', on 31 March, stated: 'Sabotage in Denmark is growing to such an extent that the Nazis are threatening to eliminate Danish control of civil administration.'

During April the *Manchester Guardian* remarked on 'the sudden publicity given to acts of sabotage in Denmark'.[1] The B.B.C. also began again to broadcast about sabotage.

The year had begun with the R.A.F. attack on the workshops of Burmeister and Wain in Copenhagen. On 26 January a member of Parliament had suggested in the House of Commons that as Burmeister and Wain were manufacturing diesel engines for German U-boats, their factory should be bombed. The parliamentary secretary to the minister of Economic Warfare replied that the matter was being considered very carefully.

The day after the question was raised in the House of Commons, the R.A.F. attacked the Burmeister and Wain factory.[2] This was taken to mean that the British meant business in Denmark. It seems likely that there were discussions held at this time between S.O.E. and the Danish Home Front about the method of attacking industrial targets in Denmark. Was it to be by bombing from Britain or by sabotage?

This R.A.F. attack had, despite Danish casualties, been generally welcomed. It was taken as a warning of the choice which lay between bombing and sabotage. There can be little doubt that the increasing sabotage in the first half of 1943 satisfied the British government. The attack on Burmeister and Wain was the first and last attack on an industrial target in Denmark by British bombers. The Danes were quick to realize the necessity of destroying factories which were manufacturing arms and equipment for the Germans. Because of this, there was

[1] *Manchester Guardian*, 1 April 1943.

[2] The R.A.F. attack on Burmeister and Wain was on 27 January 1943.

no comparable damage to the civilian population as there was in Norway when, in November 1943, 158 Flying Fortresses from the U.S. 8th Air Force attacked the 'heavy water' plants at Rjukan and Vemork. The Norwegian historian Professor M. Skodvin wrote of this attack that

> the loss in civilian property and human life was entirely out of proportion to the damage to war production. The bombing seemed all the more unnecessary since nine Norwegian saboteurs had been able ten months before to penetrate into the heavy water production unit itself, and blow it up with no losses. To prove the superiority of sabotage over bombing, they now repeated their feat by sinking the heavily guarded ferry on Lake Tinnsjö with a cargo of 15,000 litres of heavy water (diluted).[1]

It was not until this last attack that there was a notable shift away from bombing to sabotage in Norway.

In Denmark, however, the principle seems to have been accepted well before November 1943, probably by mid 1943. By this time, Danish sabotage had become so effective that there was little need for bombing attacks. However, it is only fair to Norwegian saboteurs to state that there was no industrial target in Denmark of such vital importance as the 'heavy water' plants in Norway. Had there been so, it is possible that the Allies would have preferred to bomb the targets themselves. Only by bombing could they be absolutely certain of what was destroyed and what was not. For vital targets, official policy was to bomb rather than trust saboteurs of a national resistance movement, on the grounds that the success or failure of an allied bombing mission could be checked at first hand, without depending on resistance intelligence links.

The B.B.C. began to report sabotage activities in great detail to draw the attention of Danish listeners. The formation of a corps of Danish sabotage guards for duty in factories was attacked by the Danish section of the B.B.C. Commenting on the setting up of a body of guards of 15,000 men under the

[1] In an essay entitled *Norway and Britain* by Professor M. Skodvin written for the Oxford Conference, December 1962.

Anti-Sabotage Bill, Blytgen-Petersen ended with the words: 'This is because the Danes employ this weapon of sabotage with dexterity and common sense, as also all the other countries do in their fight for liberation. Sabotage will be one of the most effective weapons against Hitler in 1943.'[1]

Scavenius received the brunt of the B.B.C. attack, and was blamed for forming the anti-sabotage corps, so that Danes should do the dirty work of the Germans. 'It becomes more and more obvious', said Gundel, 'that Scavenius is willing to give important assistance to the German war effort.' The forming of the anti-sabotage group was seen as 'a clear admission of the fact that the activities carried on by the Danish patriots under the slogan "sabotage secures victory" have by now grown to such dimensions that they have become a serious threat towards the occupation forces'.[2] Gundel concluded by stating bluntly that Scavenius was now positively helping the Germans. By allowing the formation of this group, Scavenius was saving a German division from doing guard duty.

During May, Terkelsen elaborated, with more detail, the argument against the sabotage guards. He pointed out that, in effect, Dane was now forced to kill Dane: 'Things have arrived at such a pass that it has become a question of who is to shoot first, the saboteurs or the guards. In practice, this means that Danish workers and patriots shoot at one another. From a safe distance, the Germans can stand and laugh, and smile broadly, because they have succeeded in making the wise Danish Government place Danish men in the most exposed posts.'[3] By June 1943, there were real grounds for propaganda attack on the sabotage guards. Terkelsen recounted how the Danish newspapers were forbidden now to call 'sabotage guards' by their proper name. They were now to be called 'factory guards'.[4] Whatever their name was officially, sabotage guards were clearly becoming more and more difficult to get. During June,

[1] B.B.C. talk by E. Blytgen-Petersen, 4 January 1943 (B.B.C. Archives).
[2] B.B.C. talk by Leif Gundel, 9 January 1943 (*ibid.*).
[3] B.B.C. talk by T. M. Terkelsen, 31 May 1943 (*ibid.*).
[4] B.B.C. talk by T. M. Terkelsen, 14 June 1943 (*ibid.*).

the Danish section of the B.B.C. could report with some satisfaction that more and more Danish workers were refusing to serve as factory guards and that the Copenhagen courts were imposing heavier fines on those who refused.[1] This was just the situation which the B.B.C. had hoped to create. By continually exposing the precise nature of the work that a sabotage guard was expected to do, the B.B.C. had affected the attitude of that part of the population from which these guards were drawn. Fewer men were prepared to do the job, and opposition to it grew, as the broadcasts made it plain that the job of a sabotage guard was actively against Danish interests.

The general attitude amongst the working population in Denmark was by June becoming increasingly anti-German. It was in just such a situation that propaganda, repeatedly on the same subject, became so effective. British propaganda can fairly claim a share of the credit for the failure of Scavenius' sabotage guard policy.

Terkelsen had the last word on this subject, brutally exposing the confusion of ideas involved.

> If you put a Dane into a German uniform and send him to the Eastern front to shoot the Russians, then the majority agree to call him a *traitor*. But if you give a Dane a German revolver and give him orders to shoot his own countrymen, then he is called a *factory guard*. There is only one group of men who can prevent the plan from succeeding—that is the Danish workers who have been chosen as sabotage guards.[2]

It was in fact, as Terkelsen hoped, the Danish workers' reluctance that caused the failure of this scheme.

The propaganda attack from Britain on sabotage guards was one of many weak spots probed by the Danish section of the B.B.C. throughout the spring and summer of 1943. The aim of the B.B.C. broadcasts was to foster the growing spirit of unrest in the hope that open resistance would spontaneously break out. The B.B.C.'s methods of fostering Danish unrest were both direct and indirect.

[1] *Ibid.* [2] *Ibid.*

The attack on sabotage guards could be classed as part of the indirect attack. The aim was here to prevent the formation of an effective anti-sabotage corps, by exposing the real purpose behind the German demand. The result was difficulty in recruitment, and consequently easier conditions for industrial saboteurs.

Similarly, the argument that sabotage was in the interest of Denmark's economic future after the war was another propaganda attack which could be classed as indirect. Terkelsen on 31 May 1943 pointed out that the argument used by pro-Nazi Danes, that Danish industry would be useless after the war if it was sabotaged, held no water.

It is no use whatever for Denmark to own the finest production apparatus in the world when the war is over, if the country has by its attitude under the occupation betrayed itself and its past, and therefore finds itself in the wrong camp. Sabotage cannot be seen out of its right context. It has great importance not only for Denmark of today and tomorrow, but far out in the future for Denmark after the war.[1]

In a talk entitled 'Active Resistance in Denmark', Terkelsen warned that the Germans were trying to prevent sabotage 'by endeavouring to work up feeling among the people against the Patriots by describing the acts of sabotage—not as they really are, blows dealt to the German war machine—but as crimes against Danish industry'.[2]

Rodney Gallop joined this propaganda attack aimed at appealing to Denmark's economic self-interest. His talk to Denmark on 9 May 1943 came straight to the point. He asked Denmark to take up sabotage now to ensure her post-war economic future.

Many of you realize how important it is for you that before peace comes, you should pass from *passive* to *active* resistance...A country needs more than territorial integrity and independence. It needs markets and commodities, and a respected position among its neighbours.

[1] B.B.C. talk by T. M. Terkelsen, 31 May 1943 (B.B.C. Archives).
[2] B.B.C. talk by T. M. Terkelsen, 6 April 1943 (*ibid.*).

It may be true that if, by the end of the war Denmark had not helped actively in the common victory, we would not deliberately make her suffer. But I don't see how she could in practice avoid suffering from a depreciation and a neglect which would have serious consequences.

He said that raw materials were likely to be short after the war, and that nations would receive material help, and indeed protection, according to whether they had earned it or not. 'So you will see, apart from anything else, how strong a material interest Denmark has that, by the end of the war, it is clear where Denmark stands.'[1] This, although it was effective propaganda, was a form of economic blackmail.

Another indirect but effective form of attack from Britain was to describe what had happened to the legal system in Denmark since the German occupation.

Each time a new law had been passed which effectively gave more control over the civilian population to the Germans, the B.B.C. was not slow to point this out. This was the case when, in early 1941, a supplement to the Criminal Law was passed. This made criminal law retrospective. A man could, by this law, be imprisoned for acts which, when they were committed, were not even crimes. In May 1943, Terkelsen was quick to point out how impotent the Danish government was, if it allowed German military tribunals to pass the death sentence on Danish citizens. On 8 May, a 35-year-old Dane had been sentenced to death for sabotaging a firm which repaired German military vehicles. From this it was evident that the administration of justice and of the police in Denmark was no longer in Danish hands: 'An end must be put to the fiction that Danish justice is in Danish hands.'[2]

Terkelsen further pointed out that nobody should believe the minister of Justice who, as an excuse for his actions, said: 'We must at all costs keep the administration of justice in Danish hands.' This was a complete fiction. Terkelsen concluded

[1] B.B.C. talk by Rodney Gallop, 9 May 1943 (*ibid.*).
[2] B.B.C. talk by T. M. Terkelsen, 12 May 1943 (*ibid.*).

with the warning that, 'during the coming months, hundreds of Danish patriots, who have shown themselves ready to make the greatest contribution of all, will be put in German prison-houses or concentration camps, just because the Danish prime minister under duress retreated from a bulwark, which at all price should have been held'.[1]

The propaganda attack from Britain during the first part of 1943 was highly effective. Its aim was to show Denmark that it could no longer trust its own government because Scavenius and his ministers were firmly under German control.[2] The lack of justice in German-occupied Denmark, the future economic position of Denmark after the war, the formation of the sabotage guards—these were all used by the B.B.C. in its attempt to show the Danish population that the government was powerless to do anything for Denmark, and that now was the time to take up active resistance despite all. Further, the broadcasts from Britain, by giving full publicity to all acts of sabotage being carried out, gave the impression that sections of the Danish population had already taken up the battle in earnest. There is a great stimulus in being noticed, and the B.B.C. made Denmark as a nation, and the world at large, sit up and take notice. Something real was at last happening in Denmark. The result was that, as the Danish people saw that their efforts did not pass unnoticed, they contributed still more.

Typical of this giving of publicity to Danish acts of sabotage was a broadcast in April 1943, which quoted liberally from the

[1] B.B.C. talk by T. M. Terkelsen, 12 May 1943 (B.B.C Archives).

[2] This is confirmed by the general directive from the B.B.C.'s director of European Broadcasts for 8 April 1943. This read as follows:

'We should draw attention to the fact that the Germans and their agents are giving publicity to sabotage, depicting the saboteurs as dangerous anti-social criminals in the hope of securing Danish public support, and the adoption by the Scavenius Government of drastic measures, including the imposition of the death penalty.

The Germans do not wish to increase their liabilities by taking over the policing of Denmark and they wish Scavenius to do their dirty work for them. We should expose this fact, and we should make it quite clear that the saboteurs in Denmark are causing their country's name to be honoured among the free peoples. They should always be represented as a great national asset to the Danes.'

Swedish newspaper *Världpressen*. This newspaper had brought out a long article in appreciation of Danish sabotage. 'Practically not one day goes by without a fire or a dynamite attempt against Danish firms which work for the Germans. Although the sabotage is not always successful, taken as a whole, it is nearly always both to the point and effective.' *Världpressen* thought that the R.A.F. bombing attack against Burmeister and Wain was partly responsible for the considerable change in attitude towards sabotage during 1943.

The war is still so far away from Denmark that 'official' Denmark still does not tolerate sabotage acts, but the British bombing attack on Burmeister and Wain on January 27th has brought about a considerable revision of the official frame of mind. This invitation to co-operation—the bombing probably was meant as such—has been willingly accepted, and an organization to put the resistance into action is clearly being formed.[1]

This same broadcast explored the complete German confusion over the whole question of sabotage attacks.

The German news agencies announce there is no truth in the assertions about disturbances in Denmark. Yet General von Hanneken called the Danish editors to a meeting in order to make a statement on sabotage. On this occasion he uttered the most violent threats against Denmark unless the sabotage was stopped. He reproached the editors in strong words that none of them had written leading articles on the problem of sabotage, and after having bawled out yet another couple of threats against the editors, he turned on his heel and disappeared through the door rattling his sword.

The broadcast finished by posing a question to Danish listeners. Was it not possible that there was a great deal of confusion in German circles over sabotage? Von Hanneken clearly did not know that all mention of sabotage in Danish newspapers had been expressly forbidden by the German press attaché Meisner, and by the press bureau of the Foreign Ministry.

Exposure of the confusion of the Germans in their attempts to stop sabotage was frequently heard over the B.B.C. at this time.

[1] B.B.C. talk by T. M. Terkelsen, 5 April 1943 (B.B.C. Archives). The article in *Världpressen* referred to in the broadcast was in the April edition of the paper.

This came in the form of warnings to Danish patriots not to take any notice of German propaganda being circulated on the subject of sabotage. Following the policy of 'forewarned is forearmed' the Danish section broadcast German propaganda from London so that Danish listeners would know it for what it was when they were actually subjected to it. Some examples of German-instigated propaganda which were given over the B.B.C. were:

(1) Sabotage is anti-patriotic, dangerous to the people and to the nation, and a crime against Danish industry.

(2) All saboteurs are Bolsheviks, British or Jewish agents, because it is not possible for them to be members of Hitler's 'Model Protectorate'.

(3) Thune Jacobsen [minister of Justice] and his police are doing an excellent job in preventing sabotage. [The B.B.C. here stated that the position of the police was unhappy and unfortunate. The Germans made the police do their dirty work.]

(4) There are vast money rewards for information leading to the capture of saboteurs. [The B.B.C. pointed out that although this may well have been true, it was strange that these rewards were very rarely claimed.[1]]

Rodney Gallop devoted a broadcast to exposing Best's cunning psychology of the Danish people. Best hoped by guile to prevent the Danish people from seeing the need for resistance. 'I don't suggest that you should plunge yourselves into a premature outbreak,' said Gallop. 'I know also that many Danes are of my way of thinking. It is not to them that I speak. I only want to warn all those more cautious and timid souls to whom Best's cunning attitude is so dangerous, to make up their minds now to make all necessary sacrifices at the right moment.'[2] He also reminded listeners of the 'black list' of collaborators and traitors. 'England will not forget the names of Danes on those lists.'[3] He went on to mention certain Danes who

[1] Terkelsen devoted part of his talk on 6 April 1943 to exposing German propaganda methods.

[2] B.B.C. talk by Rodney Gallop, 20 June 1943 (B.B.C. Archives).

[3] B.B.C. talk by Rodney Gallop, 22 July 1943 (*ibid.*).

would be remembered after the war. 'There are quite enough good Danes for the bad ones not to be missed.' By mentioning names of Danes on the 'black list', he reminded Denmark that Britain was so well informed now that, if no resistance took place, there would be many who would suffer after the war. The inference was obvious.

By August, spirits were high in Britain in the hope that Denmark would at last show its hand openly. Gallop explained over the B.B.C. that Britain had of necessity to restrain sabotage in some countries, but that this did not apply to Denmark. He had heard that this had caused some confusion. Appeals to Denmark for increasingly active resistance had coincided with appeals to other German-occupied countries to go slow with forms of resistance which would bring down heavy reprisals on them. Norway was cited as an example where hasty individual actions, which only involved human sacrifices, had to be stopped, but the difference between Denmark and Norway was that between Hitler's 'Model Protectorate' and 'Norwegian Conditions'. 'It is', Gallop said, 'impossible to deny that Danish Resistance still has far to go.'

The concluding words of his broadcast were as follows:

So you will understand that we sometimes find it necessary as part of our wider strategy to encourage some of the occupied countries which have gone to the limit of resistance to put on the brake a little, while we urge you to increase your resistance and above all to reduce the help which the Germans are extracting from you. This should cause no misunderstanding, and you should not assume that those recommendations apply to you, which you hear us make to other countries. This does not mean that we want you to take undue risks, but that we think you can now do more without taking undue risks.[1]

Perhaps the explanation was needed, perhaps not. Denmark did in fact do more. On 13 August, Gundel positively rejoiced into the microphone in his talk '*V* for Sabotage', when the news of increased Danish sabotage activity was received.

[1] B.B.C. talk by Rodney Gallop, 5 August 1943 (*ibid.*).

The great event, for which all Danes out in the free world and the great majority at home have waited and hoped through three long years, has at last taken place. Best has, for the moment, had to draw a blank against the Danish saboteurs...Dr Best, for the first time, has felt himself up against a firmly-constructed Danish common front.[1]

During August the wave of unrest that was passing through Denmark could be seen primarily by the number of sabotage actions, amounting to six or seven daily.[2] This unrest passed through the population, and particularly from the factories into the open streets. The German reaction was the increased use of soldiers both in the streets and sometimes on guard duty outside factories to prevent sabotage, the imposition of a curfew, the threat of taking hostages, in fact the beginnings of a general reign of terror.[3]

Strikes first broke out in the provincial towns, Esbjerg, Odense, and Aalborg in particular, and were the culmination of weeks and months of dissatisfaction, humiliation, and unrest amongst the Danish workers. They began in the provinces, perhaps because friction between the people and German garrisons flared up more easily in the smaller communities rather than in the capital. Unrest was started and kept alive by the frequent outbreaks of sabotage.

By the time Copenhagen was affected and demonstrations

[1] B.B.C. talk by Leif Gundel, 13 August 1943 (B.B.C. Archives).

[2] The general directive from the B.B.C.'s director of European Broadcasts for 20 August 1943 read as follows:

The Danish story is really big. The last train carrying German war material to Norway through Sweden has left and at this moment, when communications through Denmark have become absolutely vital, the Danish Underground Front swings into action with attacks on railways and factories.

The Germans must stop this but they can't afford to tie up the forces necessary to take over Denmark completely. They *must* force the Scavenius Government to do the job for them but the Government refuses so far. If it eventually agrees it will forfeit all Danish support and will have to rule with German bayonets. So, whether Scavenius toes the line, a completely Quisling Government is installed, or the Germans take over, the result will be more strain on German manpower and increased underground resistance and attacks on communications, doubly vital owing to the end of Swedish transit traffic.'

[3] For an account of the events in Denmark during August 1943 see Hæstrup, *Panorama Denmark*, pp. 28–30, and *Kontakt med England*, particularly ch. 21.

took place in the streets, several of Denmark's provincial cities, particularly Odense, were in almost open revolt, with strikes, sabotage, rioting and open clashes in the streets taking place between German soldiers and civilians.

All attempts at conciliation were bound to fail, as the unrest was too widespread. Dr Best was recalled to Berlin to face a rough reception from Hitler.[1] Sabotage increased still more. On 25–26 August the Jutland railway system was sabotaged extensively by Jutland Resistance groups.[2] On 28 August, the Germans placed an ultimatum before the Danish government. This demanded the introduction of the death penalty for saboteurs, and the introduction of martial law throughout the whole country, a complete ban on strikes, meetings and demonstrations, a curfew, strict censorship—in fact all the necessary trappings of a military dictatorship.

To have accepted these terms would have been too invidious even for Scavenius. The government rejected the ultimatum, and this decision was supported by all the democratic political parties, and by the king.[3] The government ceased to function, and control of the country passed from Scavenius' hands to those of the German *Wehrmacht* under General von Hanneken.

The transition of power did not pass without the Danish Home Front making its mark. On Admiral Vedel's instructions, the entire Danish fleet was either scuttled or sent to Sweden

[1] Dr Werner Best was called to Berlin on 24 August.

[2] The general directive to all editors of the B.B.C. European Services from the Director of European Broadcasts for 26 August 1943 read as follows:

'Feature the Danish situation as one of our big stories on accepted lines showing acute German nervousness and the almost insoluble character of their dilemma.

Emphasize that whatever the Danish Government and political parties may be doing now the Danish people have decided that the moment has come to do all they can to embarrass the Germans. Report that Danish patriots have been raiding German arms depots and that in some cases German soldiers have bartered their arms for food parcels for their families. Report sinking German morale in Denmark as in Norway.'

[3] After von Hanneken took over control of the country, the government agreed with the king to offer its resignation, which the king never officially acknowledged. According to the Danish constitution no king can be without a government, and strictly speaking this government held office until after the liberation when a new government was formed. In fact it never resigned, but just 'ceased to function'.

during the night of 28–29 August. Fighting broke out between the German *Wehrmacht* and Danish sailors in the harbour area. During the early hours of Sunday 29 August the Germans made widespread arrests, and took hostages in Copenhagen. The king was at Sorgenfri Castle, a few miles north of Copenhagen, where he was put under armed guard by the Germans.

On 29 August listeners to the B.B.C. Home Service heard the following detailed report:

After three years of Hitler's New Order, the whole of Denmark has today had to be put under a form of martial law by the Germans. Just after four o'clock this morning, the Commander-in-Chief of German troops in Denmark issued the necessary decree; and it was broadcast about three hours later. In other words, it was an accomplished fact by the time the ordinary man's day began. It leads off by saying that events had shown that the Danish Government was no longer able to keep order; and by trying to place the blame on enemy agents for disturbances directed against the German army. The decree then orders Danish officials to go on with their duties, but in accordance with German regulations which are to be laid down. It bans all public and private gatherings—even meetings of more than five people. It forbids the use of postal, telegraph and telephone services. Strikes are prohibited; and people who try to engineer them, to the danger of Germans, are told that the usual punishment is death—a penalty unknown to Denmark for many years. German military courts are to enforce the decree—wherever necessary by the use of ruthless armed force. The decree ends by making out that all this is based on International Law; and by saying that anybody in Denmark who obeys the rules will be safe.

Not long after this first news of a state of siege had been given, the Danish Home Service radio, under German control, began to rub in the explanation that the Danish people, in general, were not to blame, but the systematic underground work of foreign elements and so-called patriots. Month by month, night after night, the foreign agents had carried out dark sabotage work, doing damage which could not be measured in money alone. But, worse than that, the Germans said, was the work of the patriots; it was this which hampered and finally destroyed the relations which for three years—three difficult years, they were called—had existed between Denmark and Germany.

The broadcast then went on to say that yesterday the German Government had asked the Danish Government to declare a state of emergency; but that the Danish Government couldn't or wouldn't. The result was that the request showed itself to be an ultimatum, for the Germans had had to declare martial law. The statement ended with more threats of ruthlessness against anybody not obeying instructions.

Since then, an overseas broadcast from Germany has mentioned another reason why martial law has been imposed—the safeguarding of the European coast. It'll be remembered that the Swedish Government recently cancelled their traffic agreement with the Germans, forcing them to switch their transport of troops (to and from Norway) from the Swedish to the Danish transport systems.

The Nazis are now going out of their way to give the impression that there's a 'business as usual' atmosphere in Denmark today—quiet and restraint everywhere. But reports from Sweden don't bear that out at all. Stockholm correspondents of the three news agencies—Reuter, Associated Press and British United Press—have cabled that at about six o'clock this morning, part of Denmark's small navy is said to have been scuttled in Copenhagen harbour; and that several other Danish warships carrying a large number of civilians had escaped to two Swedish ports. There are also reports from Stockholm that heavy fighting broke out during the night in Copenhagen, where Danish seamen are said to have blown up ammunition dumps and port installations. The correspondents say that speculation about the whereabouts of the Danish Government ranges from stories that some members of it have escaped, to reports that the Government have been interned; and that King Christian is being kept by the Germans in a castle some ten miles outside Copenhagen. Clearly none of these reports can yet be confirmed.

The Swedish Radio says that telegraph and telephone communication with Denmark (which was first reported to have stopped at five o'clock yesterday afternoon) was still cut off today; and it announces that the train ferries between Sweden and Denmark have stopped as from today.

The leader of the Free Danes in this country, Mr Christmas Møller (who escaped from Denmark last year), has issued a statement saying that the people of his country had felt just the same as all other enslaved nations for the past three years—years of occupation, exploitation and injustice, which had finally led to revolt against the Germans.

This bulletin was substantially correct.[1] The king was a prisoner, the government had dissolved, and the control of Denmark was firmly in German hands. The members of the Danish section of the B.B.C. could look with satisfaction over their past three years' work. By continual broadcasting, they had helped the Danish population to see that the government stood for nothing. By their emphasis on sabotage and unrest in 1943, they had encouraged the Danish population to force the issue. The result was the collapse of the Danish government, which was what the section had always hoped for. The broadcasts from London did not, by themselves, force the German ultimatum and the resulting collapse of the government. They had helped to bring the Danish population to such a pitch that the failure of the government and of its policy was the logical conclusion to Danish unrest.

[1] This B.B.C. news bulletin showed how quickly and, on the whole, how accurately Danish news was sent over from Stockholm to London.

It was correctly reported that the king was under armed guard. The government was not interned. It just ceased to have any executive authority in Denmark.

The reports from the news agencies in Stockholm were mainly correct. The navy was scuttled or escaped to Sweden. Probably the explosions reported in the harbour area were in fact the ships being scuttled, and not sailors blowing up ammunition dumps and port installations. Thirty-one ships of the navy were scuttled or blown up, and thirteen escaped to Sweden.

CHAPTER 11

THE EYES OF THE WORLD ARE ON DENMARK

It is said in the free world that it is the whole of the Danish people that, with sabotage and the strike weapon, say no to the Germans and their demands. It is the people who show what decision Denmark takes.

Emil Blytgen-Petersen in a B.B.C. broadcast, 27 August 1943

From 29 August onwards the Danish section of the B.B.C. was able to carry the war openly into the enemy's camp.[1] It no longer faced the extreme political difficulties caused by the existence of a Danish government. How much credit, however, could the Danish section of the B.B.C. take for the events of 29 August 1943?

Radio can be, and was, used for political purposes. Most propaganda whether spoken, written or broadcast is political, but one type of propaganda has more political effect than another. The division between the two main types lies in the extent to which propaganda from an outside source affects the internal political balance of a country. Broadcasts of news bulletins, talks and commentaries, designed to influence the ideas of a group of listeners but leaving the final decision whether or not any action is taken with the listeners themselves, is of the first, comparatively mild, type of propaganda. The second kind is where propaganda is directly aimed at upsetting the political balance within a country, usually by exaggeration, repetition of a particular theme and, if needed, lies and rumours. In this sense the decision whether to act or not is not really the listener's. He has few true facts on which to base a decision

[1] The general directive from the director of the B.B.C.'s European Broadcasts for 17 September 1943 showed that the B.B.C.'s task was easier now that there was no Danish government.

and will usually find himself carried by a wave of frenzy, created by others like himself, who are starved of true facts, but whose emotions cannot resist the continual bombardment. Hitler's propaganda speeches were of this type, and the loudspeakers in offices and in factories in Nazi Germany were intended to reduce the listener to a state in which he did what he was told irrespective of reason.[1] He became almost like one of Pavlov's[2] dogs. This type of propaganda can be used for dangerous political purposes, to upset the internal state of a country. Hitler created the Jewish problem by such methods throughout Nazi-occupied Europe.

The division between these two types of propaganda is ill defined. However, it can be seen partly in the extent to which a propaganda adviser is or is not prepared to go, in the pursuit of his task. It is, too, the extent to which morality becomes nothing in the attempt to achieve a particular end or aim.

The B.B.C. in its wartime broadcasts definitely put out the less extreme kind of propaganda. This was broadly aimed at influencing the listener as much as possible, within the limits of truth and objectivity. The B.B.C. left the listener the power to decide whether to accept or to reject its views because its broadcasts gave facts upon which he could base a decision. If the listener believed, then action might take place as a result.

At times, the B.B.C. was accused of indulging in the second category of propaganda. Certain Yugoslav historians[3] claim that the image of Mihailović as the first great resistance leader of Europe, presented by the B.B.C., was not just an attempt to create a figurehead who would lead Yugoslavia against the Germans. On the contrary the support given to Mihailović has

[1] Lindley Fraser's book *Propaganda* has an interesting chapter on propaganda inside Germany itself.

[2] Ivan Pavlov, Russian physiologist, experimented with dogs in working on his theory of 'conditioned' or 'acquired' reflexes.

For example, Hitler's propaganda, by the constant repetition of the word 'Jew', caused a conditional reflex, that of hatred, in certain sections of the German population.

[3] Notably Professor J. Marjanović of Belgrade in his essay *Yugoslavia and Britain* written for the Oxford Conference, December 1962.

been seen by these historians as an attempt to create an anti-Tito, anti-Communist leader in Yugoslavia, to prevent a Communist bid for power after the war. The decision to support Mihailović was, it is implied, strongly influenced by King Peter and the Yugoslav government in exile in London. It must have been embarrassing for the B.B.C., and for its advisers, that it was not Mihailović's Četniks but Tito's Partisans who later led effective resistance against the Germans.

The Danish situation until August 1943 could have caused an equally difficult situation. Had there been too strong an attack on the Danish government from the start in April 1940, there might even have been voices raised in indignation that the B.B.C. had no respect for reality, and that it supported a left-wing movement which wished to destroy 'official' Denmark once and for all. Had there been the Communist take-over in Denmark feared by some sections of the Danish population during the latter part of the war, the position of the B.B.C., if it had adopted a continuous anti-Danish government policy from the start, would have been difficult. However much the B.B.C. might have protested that a strong anti-Danish government policy was directed at helping to create an effective resistance movement against the *Germans*, there would have been some who would have doubted the motives of the B.B.C.

However, the B.B.C., despite this fear of delving too deeply into the internal Danish political situation, had to support S.O.E. in its work of encouraging resistance against the Germans. Above all, the tendency to be complacent about the situation in Denmark had to be avoided.

The result was that the broadcasts to Denmark were of the first type of political propaganda—an attempt at influencing ideas in Denmark by the presentation of news and commentaries, by stimulating Danes to thought, and by exposing the falsity of German propaganda. By this method it was hoped that the Danish population would see the situation as it really was. When this happened, the Danish section of the B.B.C. hoped the people would act upon its new realization. This was precisely what the B.B.C. succeeded in doing during the first three years of the war, and particularly in 1943.

In *Voices in the Darkness* E. Tangye Lean wrote: 'About half of propaganda must be plucked from the body of the society to which it is addressed. If the wounds are not already there, they cannot be deepened or widened.'

Throughout the period 1940–3, the B.B.C. followed events in Denmark as closely as was possible, probing the weak spots. That was why there could be no definite policy until the Danish population as a whole was prepared to show its feelings. There was pressure from various British departments that a firmer line should be taken. The Political Intelligence Department tended to advocate a stronger line than it was always possible to take. In contrast the B.B.C. Intelligence reports frequently accused the Danish section of being too aggressive and too persistent in suggesting that the Danish people were content to accept domination by the Germans.[1]

It had therefore to be a middle course that Robert Jørgensen and his section followed, veering towards an active policy whenever events in Denmark made this possible. The situation in Denmark provided normal guidance for the section except when allied military or political needs were of overriding importance. During 1943, the election and the breakdown of negotiations with the League gave the Danish section the opportunity of aggravating the 'wounds' in Denmark. The Foreign Office and S.O.E. were now convinced that Britain should encourage Denmark to take action, because events on the Danish Home Front showed that the population was becoming increasingly restless.

During 1943 the Danish section of the B.B.C. probed as many Danish 'wounds' as it could. It encouraged sabotage by giving full publicity to sabotage acts being carried out. It gave direct encouragement to saboteurs. It also exploited the abuses of the legal system, and the dangers for Denmark's economic future if no resistance took place. The formation of the factory

[1] See chapter 7 and notes.

guards was attacked, and Danish listeners were warned about the German lies and rumours that were circulating.

All this undoubtedly helped to stir unrest, and to keep it alive. In this sense, the B.B.C. furthered the collapse of the Danish government, by probing already angry sores. It is impossible to be more precise than this. The only accurate measure of the effectiveness of propaganda to Denmark would be to have proof that certain specific broadcasts from London caused Danish listeners to commit certain specific actions which directly or indirectly caused the collapse of the Danish government. Such an analysis is virtually impossible. It is only possible to say that if propaganda aims are realized by later events, then it is likely that the effect of the propaganda will have contributed something to the final result.

There are, however, two indications that the Danish section of the B.B.C. can take some credit for the success of Danish Resistance in 1943. The first is the series of broadcasts by H. Hørsholt Hansen[1] to the Danish workers. The second is what the Nazis in Denmark had to say about the broadcasts from London.

From the existing copies of Hørsholt Hansen's broadcasts, it appears that he began his broadcasts to Denmark on 9 July 1943.[2] He then broadcast regularly from London until 29 August at least once a week. His talks were all specifically directed at the Danish working population.

It was no coincidence that special talks should be directed at the Danish worker at this point in 1943. London expected that the revolt, when it came, would come first from the working population. Both in peace and in war, the working population was likely to be the first to protest. Strikes and sabotage increased throughout the summer of 1943. Hørsholt Hansen's task was to show the Danish worker how important he was, that he could be the leader of any demonstrations against the

[1] H. Hørsholt Hansen, a Danish journalist in London, contributed regular talks to the B.B.C.'s Danish Service during 1943.

[2] This first talk was on the subject of the post-war plans of trade unionists (B.B.C. Archives).

government, and that by striking he could make the most effective protest possible.

Hørsholt Hansen's broadcasts began quietly enough with a talk on post-war trade unionism.[1] He gave examples of the better conditions for which the American trade unions were then bargaining—a 30-hour week for all, major monopoly industries to be taken over by the government, social security modelled on the Beveridge Plan, and guaranteed full employment. Hørsholt Hansen equated this with Denmark, and said that the Danish working class would have to make up its mind. 'Do you wish the dissolution of the Trade Unions, permanent banning of strikes, lower wages and working conditions, which are not very different from those of ancient slavery, or do you want a free life secure both economically and socially?' He encouraged the rest of the working population to press their demands and fight for their rights like Burmeister and Wain's clerical staff who demanded that they should be allowed to leave their offices when the air-raid warnings went. The result of this demand was that they were told that they could resign if they did not like their conditions of work. If they left the building, part of their salary would be deducted, and their bonus would be reduced. Terms such as these were not to be tolerated.

This was a suggestion that Danish workers should fight for their rights. Another broadcast scorned those Danish workers who worked for the Nazis.[2] '10,000 Danish workers help the Germans in Norway, 25,000 Danish workers are building German fortifications in Jutland, 40,000 Danish workers are working for the German armament industry in Germany. These numbers are not exaggerated. On the contrary, in all 75,000 Danish workers, or more than 10 % of all Danish workers, let themselves be used by Nazi Germany.'[3]

Hørsholt Hansen had two emphatic points to make on this. First, that while the Germans apparently had no difficulty in

[1] B.B.C. talk, 9 July 1943 (B.B.C. Archives).
[2] B.B.C. talk by Hørsholt Hansen, 24 July 1943 (*ibid.*).
[3] These figures were in fact exaggerated.

getting Danish workers, Danish agriculture and particularly the peat industry was suffering from shortage of labour. This work was important, because on it depended 'the provision of fuel for the stoves of all Danish homes next winter, and bread for Danish meals. The Germans do not supply sufficient coal and coke for Denmark, and they deprive Denmark of various kinds of food.'

Secondly, came the warning that the British 'black list' extended to the workers too: 'B.B.C.'s listeners will have heard that a "black list" of the firms working for Germany is being broadcast, and naturally every single worker who for the same motive—profit—volunteers for this work, is no better than the firms.'

Both Terkelsen and Hørsholt Hansen broadcast on the dangers of working for the Germans.[1] These talks were designed to prevent further Danish workers going into German work, and to starve German production, by encouraging a large scale walk-out of German factories. On 2 August Terkelsen described the terrible number of deaths among Danish workers in Hamburg, as a result of British air-raids: 'Thousands of Danish workers are streaming across the border at Padborg and Krusaa. They are the returning survivors from the air-bombardments on Hamburg...How many of them have been killed during the raids nobody knows...of all of them it can be said that they were warned...It soon ought to sink in that German work is dangerous work.' Terkelsen ended with a warning that any factory producing goods for the Germans 'has an irresistible attraction for British bombs'.

Four days later Hørsholt Hansen reported that an estimated 122 Danish workers had been killed by a series of explosions while working on the German fortifications in West Jutland, because the Germans had not bothered to protect their workers from their own minefields.[2]

[1] T. M. Terkelsen broadcast a talk entitled 'Dangerous Work' on 2 August 1943 (B.B.C. Archives). Hørsholt Hansen broadcast his talk called the 'Dangers of Working for the Germans' on 6 August 1943 (*ibid.*).

[2] Hørsholt Hansen, *ibid.*

From 12 August onwards the B.B.C. gave direct encouragement to the Danish workers to strike, cause stoppages, demonstrate or walk out: 'Delay or stoppage of work for the Germans hastens the final result of the war.'[1] Hørsholt Hansen said that the Germans were now finding it very difficult to obtain labour for the fortifications in Jutland. He suggested that this was the result of various B.B.C. broadcasts on the dangers of working for the Germans, although the official reason given for the difficulty was that Danish workers working for the Germans were not entitled to receive higher wages than Danes working for Danish enterprises.

On 16 August,[2] Hørsholt Hansen told Denmark that the British trade union movement was expecting the Danish trade unions to join the fight against the German Nazis now. British trade unionists had received with satisfaction news of resistance in Denmark: 'There has been news of sabotage, demonstrations, and of strikes.'

He then read a message specially written by Patrick Gordon Walker to the Danish workers.[3]

We in the British Labour movement have been extremely encouraged by the news of demands and strikes by the Danish workers. From the reports we have received, we gather that these are organized actions. The free workers of the world welcome every act that slows up this war machine—*every* act that advances the day of Hitler's defeat is a service to free Labour—whether or not it would, in normal times, be justified. We in the British Labour movement cannot believe that the Danish workers' sole aim is to improve the conditions under which they must work for Hitler. There can be no question of satisfactory conditions, of an end to industrial struggle, until the day that sees the final defeat of Hitler and his whole system.

On 21 August[4] the B.B.C. announced that strikes had broken out in several Danish towns.

[1] B.B.C. talk by Hørsholt Hansen, 12 August 1943 (B.B.C. Archives).

[2] B.B.C. talk, 16 August 1943 (*ibid.*).

[3] Patrick Gordon Walker worked for the European Service of the B.B.C. during the war.

[4] B.B.C. talk by Hørsholt Hansen, 21 August 1943 (B.B.C. Archives).

A wave of strikes is sweeping Denmark. It began with small isolated strikes in several provincial towns but soon spread to other small towns. In the cement factories in Aalborg work stopped; the shipbuilding workers in Odense, through their strike, obtained their demands that German sabotage guards should be taken away from the yards, and the general strike at Esbjerg constituted a full and decisive proof that it is not without use to resist the Germans.

This same broadcast paid tribute to the Danish working class, and praised its solidarity with other working classes abroad who were now fighting tooth and nail against the Nazis.

In Yugoslavia there is open rebellion. In Russia partisans destroy the German lines of communication. In Holland and Italy and other places, the workers strike in order to have their political demands carried through. In Norway the workers have to be carried forcibly to the places where they work for the Germans, where the work is sabotaged in countless ways.

And in Denmark it has now, in a most convincing way, been expressed that the Danish workers realize that they carry the responsibility for one section of the long Home Front, which paralyses Germany's ability to fight. The Danish workers hold their section as well as the workers in other countries hold theirs.

On 27 August:[1]

The Danish population has gone over to active resistance. Acts of sabotage are daily carried out by Danish patriots. Recently, there have been open conflicts in the streets between the Danes and German soldiers, and the Danish workers have not hesitated to use general strikes as a political weapon.

On 28 August,[2] Christmas Møller made his last request before the collapse of Scavenius' government: 'Whatever happens in Denmark and whatever order Best brings back from Berlin, there is no doubt that the people will *act*.'

The people *did* act, and it was the working population that precipitated the crisis which eventually brought down the government. Hørsholt Hansen's broadcasts had considerable

[1] B.B.C. talk by Hørsholt Hansen, 27 August 1943 (*ibid.*).

[2] Christmas Møller's talk entitled 'The Unknown Danish Soldier' was broadcast on 28 August 1943 (B.B.C. Archives and Danish Archives).

effect in making the Danish worker realize what power he held, because both Scavenius and the Germans were so dependent on his co-operation for affairs running smoothly in Denmark. The working population was the most closely knit and the largest section of the Danish population. The term 'working population' included the agricultural and the industrial workers. On the fringe of this section were the office workers and the shopkeepers, who were likely to be influenced by any industrial demonstration. It was this section of the Danish population which began by striking in Odense and other provincial towns.

It is probable that without these popular demonstrations the Danish government would not have collapsed as quickly as it did. These strikes and demonstrations led to the German demand for a military dictatorship, a concession to which even Scavenius could not agree. The B.B.C., as far as it is possible to judge, can claim some credit for making the Danish worker realize during July and August 1943 what a powerful part of Denmark he was.

Evidence of the effect of British radio on events in Denmark can be found in the pages of *Fædrelandet*, the Danish Nazi newspaper, during 1943. *Fædrelandet* declared that London was greatly responsible for much of the sabotage carried out in Denmark. Harald Bergstedt, writing in *Fædrelandet* on 7 April 1943, commented on the sabotage action against Aarhus Stadium. He wrote that those who had carried out the sabotage would be severely punished, but that there was little use in this, as they would only smile and consider themselves as heroes: 'The true originator (of sabotage) is the London Radio over which Christmas Møller and other escaped Danes daily say that it is a *Holger Danske*[1] deed to sabotage the Germans to the utmost.'

In the same month the editorial in *Fædrelandet* was entitled 'Sabotage and Incitement'.[2] It blamed the Danes who spoke

[1] It was said that Holger the Dane would always rise from the past to help Denmark in its hour of need.

One well-known resistance group took its name from *Holger Danske.*

[2] The editorial was dated 3 April 1943.

over the B.B.C. as the real instigators of sabotage: 'They have a larger audience than the ordinary Danish radio news broadcasts, and many simple-hearted people, who are behind the times, consider this radio a kind of official institution. At a certain hour the London broadcasts boom through the quiet streets and spread poison and incitement in thousands of Danish homes.'

The British press too made frequent references to *Fædrelandet* in support of the view that British propaganda helped to stir up unrest during 1943. The *Newcastle Journal*, on 10 April, quoted *Fædrelandet* on 'Danes who speak over the London Radio to stir up anti-Nazi resistance in Denmark':[1] 'These Danes have a larger audience than the ordinary Danish radio news broadcasts, and many people consider it [B.B.C.] as a kind of official institution.' Two days later, the *Evening News*[2] printed a Reuter report which quoted the same article in *Fædrelandet.*

British propaganda had also been a considerable factor in the discussions between Nazi-Danes and Germans on whether or not to hold the elections in March. Hartel[3] had spoken in the *Rigsdag* and said that elections during an occupation were a bad thing—'among other things, because the British wireless might easily choose to take the opportunity to create unrest'.[4]

During August *Fædrelandet* used much space on discussions about propaganda from London. It suggested that there was going to be a change of propaganda policy:

It may possibly be quite a new one or possibly a further concentration of the present policy. Of this, it may be said that it has served its purpose, and there is no reason to refute the fact. Radio has proved a dangerous weapon, and has done far more than ever Lord Northcliffe could achieve with his papers in the last war.

This is a matter about which we are competent to speak because

[1] This article in the *Newcastle Journal* clearly referred to the editorial in *Fædrelandet* dated 3 April 1943.

[2] *Evening News*, 12 April 1943. This referred to the same editorial in *Fædrelandet.*

[3] A Danish member of Parliament.

[4] Quoted in a B.B.C. talk by T. M. Terkelsen, 29 January 1943.

we have noticed the effect of its propaganda here in this country. It has brought about a hitherto unknown uniformity of reasoning. It is possible that fanatics will call it 'unity of purpose among the people' but individuals with common sense will take the view that it is simply an instance of the public being misled, on a hitherto unknown scale. When the tradesman and his errand boy have the same view on matters of foreign policy, something is wrong, and when exactly the same arguments are put forward by different people to excess, it becomes obvious they have been through a machine which has made their brains identical.

This propaganda against government and king's wishes will no doubt result in the entire population, excluding only the most sensible, being seized by a mass hysteria which can well lead us into bitter misery.

What matters is that we should control ourselves and not let ourselves be swept away by these new methods of influencing public mentality. We, after all, are in a position in which we cannot afford to play a part in the war.[1]

During November 1943, the British newspaper *Reynolds News* brought out a leader which was entitled 'Smuggled Voice Roused Denmark'. The article stated:

The day on which the people of Denmark revolted against their Nazi overlords, August 29th last, was the day—it can now be revealed—on which the B.B.C. broadcast a stirring appeal by a prominent leader of the Danish Resistance movement, recorded on a disc, and smuggled past the Gestapo. The voice on the disc was that of Dr Mogens Fog, a brilliant young professor of Psychiatry in Copenhagen University.[2]

He recorded an appeal to the Danish people on a disc, which was smuggled out of Denmark and brought to London. On August 29th it was broadcast by the European Service of the B.B.C.

It was heard in Denmark—and recognized—and on that day the Danish people took action and rose against the Nazis.

[1] *Fædrelandet*, 23 August 1943. It is interesting that *Fædrelandet* now brought the question of sabotage into the open. When sabotage became widespread *Fædrelandet* could not ignore it, and it seems to have been the policy of the Germans and the Danish Nazi party to blame all sabotage on the B.B.C., and in particular on Christmas Møller, or on British agents, or Communists.

To this extent *Fædrelandet's* evidence of the effect of the B.B.C. is probably exaggerated.

[2] Mogens Fog was in fact professor of Neurology, not of Psychiatry, as stated by *Reynolds News*, 28 November 1943.

It was a coincidence that Professor Fog's message was broadcast to Denmark on the day the government ceased to function, but the fact remains that the British press was aware that events in Denmark during 1943 were being affected by the London broadcasts—not perhaps to a great extent but enough to be noticed. The Danish Nazi newspaper *Fædrelandet* was clearly forced to bring the subject of British propaganda to its readers' notice, because the B.B.C. broadcasts provided an excuse, or at least an unhappy reason, for the behaviour of the Danish people during 1943. 'Radio has proved a dangerous weapon,' wrote *Fædrelandet*.[1] This was the clearest evidence of the success of the B.B.C.'s policy since April 1940. It had become an enemy to be reckoned with.

[1] *Fædrelandet*, 23 August 1943.

CHAPTER 12

THE FREEDOM COUNCIL AND THE QUESTION OF ALLIED RECOGNITION

> The valuable contribution which is being made to the defeat of Germany by the work of the Danish Council of Freedom...is warmly acknowledged by His Majesty's Government.
>
> Anthony Eden in the House of Commons, July 1944

From October 1940 until August 1943, the Danish section of S.O.E., under Commander Hollingworth, had worked to increase and support Danish Resistance. The B.B.C. had given open support to this policy whenever possible. S.O.E., as it was a subversive organization, could afford a far more extremist policy than it was possible for the Danish section of the B.B.C. to follow in its broadcasts. It was S.O.E.'s intention from the start, and the policy of the Ministry of Economic Warfare, to disrupt Danish-German co-operation as much as possible. It was the B.B.C.'s policy to help achieve this object by probing every sensitive spot, in the hope that the Danish people would rebel against their government's policy of negotiation with the Germans and thereby force its collapse.

The events of 29 August 1943 produced this, but they also produced a political vacuum in Denmark. Who was in control of the country now that the government had ceased to function?

The government fell because of the extreme demands of the occupying power. The Germans claimed that they had the right to force the government out of office because of articles 42–56 of the Hague Convention.[1] These articles, however,

[1] See Hæstrup, *Panorama Denmark*, p. 30. The Hague Conference of 1907 had laid down 'Regulations Respecting the Laws and Customs of War on Land'. Articles 42–56 dealt with 'Military Authority over the Territory of the Hostile

presupposed a state of war between occupier and occupied, but no declaration of war had been made between Denmark and Germany.

The situation was confused in the extreme. In effect the government had disclaimed responsibility and had refused to function. This had been accepted by the king. The Germans continued in their efforts to produce a puppet government.

> All efforts to this end [wrote Dr Hæstrup] were met by point-blank Danish refusal and the final, practical outcome was that the heads of the ministerial departments carried on the administration, each being responsible to his own department. Political responsibility ceased to rest on Danish shoulders, but through skilful administrative work, there still remained scope for defensive action and passive resistance to the reign of violence which now set in.[1]

Dr Werner Best, the German plenipotentiary, now became in reality the ruler of Denmark. This again posed certain problems during the weeks after 29 August for S.O.E., for the Foreign Office, and for the Danish section of the B.B.C. The situation had simplified somewhat since the fall of the government. There was now no Danish intermediary between the Germans and the Danish people to be considered when planning Danish operations, but the lack of any kind of leadership clearly worried those concerned with policy towards Denmark.

One obvious solution would have been to increase S.O.E.'s position in Denmark to such an extent that it would have become the undisputed leader of Danish Resistance. With many more agents to organize resistance groups, to arrange for the

State', and laid down the principles and conditions which an occupying power should observe.

The Germans were probably (if they needed a legal reason) acting on article 43 which read: 'The authority of the power of the State having passed *de facto* into the hands of the occupant, the latter shall do all in his power to restore, and ensure as far as possible, public order and safety, respecting at the same time, unless absolutely prevented, the laws in force in the country.' Although the Germans might claim that they had the right to take over control of the country because public order and safety were (as far as they saw it) not being maintained by the Danish government, their recourse to the Hague Conference was invalid, because these articles presupposed a state of war; a state of war had never existed between Denmark and Germany in 1940.

[1] See *Panorama Denmark*, p. 31.

reception of British arms and explosives, and to carry out large-scale actions, this might well have been possible. Under Flemming Muus, S.O.E. in Denmark was strengthening rapidly and making wide contacts amongst all groups resisting the Germans.

This, however, was the kind of position in which S.O.E. could not place itself. S.O.E. was primarily a military organization, aimed at dealing effective blows at the German economy. It was a weapon of economic warfare, not of politics. Had S.O.E. tried to build up the leadership of the Danish Resistance round itself, it would have been open to all the criticisms of meddling in internal politics which it has received since from, for example, Yugoslavia.[1]

There would have been serious opposition too from the Danish Home Front if S.O.E. had attempted to follow this policy. The leading Danish Resistance groups, at this time finding political expression in many different illegal newspapers, would have been unlikely to accept an essentially foreign leadership.[2] Flemming Muus, too, was Britain's leading agent in the field and chief representative of S.O.E. in Denmark. Despite his undoubted courage and brilliance, he did not inspire confidence in many of the leaders of the Danish Home Front.[3]

The answer to the problem of who should lead the Danish Resistance was found in the Freedom Council.[4] The Freedom Council consisted of a group of seven resistance leaders who met

[1] See notes to chapter 11.

[2] Danish Communist groups would never have accepted a British-led resistance movement in Denmark, nor probably even a Russian-led resistance. It is a very doubtful point whether any national resistance movement would ever have accepted the *leadership* of a foreign power. Support and material aid was different, and Tito for example was prepared to accept this, but not instructions and orders from Britain.

[3] Flemming Muus, although undoubtedly a very brave man and one who contributed greatly to the growth of Danish Resistance was, however, convicted after the war of embezzling resistance funds in 1943 and 1944. He was sentenced to two years' imprisonment but was later pardoned.

[4] See Hæstrup, *Kontakt med England*, ch. 22. The Freedom Council—*Danmarks Frihedsraad*—consisted at the beginning of seven resistance leaders, later changed and increased, who gathered in Copenhagen to co-ordinate the resistance activities carried out by various groups. It had no constitutional basis, but its influence grew rapidly. As an organizing committee for resistance it was of vital importance to Denmark. It was recognized publicly by the British government in July 1944.

in Copenhagen with the purpose of co-ordinating the various resistance groups. Now that the government had fallen, leaving a political vacuum, there was a definite need for a strong central leadership of the Resistance. At the inaugural meeting of the Freedom Council on 16 September 1943 were Mogens Fog, Erling Foss, Børge Houmann, Frode Jakobsen, Aage Schoch, Jørgen Staffeldt and Flemming Muus.

It is significant that Muus was at this meeting not as a representative of S.O.E. but as a representative of the Free Danes abroad. On 7 October he left for Sweden to go to Britain, and he remained in London until the middle of December.

This period was for him one of intensive activity. Extracts from his book *The Spark and the Flame* show that the subject of many of his discussions with British officials was the Freedom Council.[1]

Busy weeks followed. There were negotiations with the Air Ministry, meetings at the Ministry of Economic Warfare, and in the Foreign Office. In the latter I attempted to explain how important it was that the Freedom Council should be supported. It was a great help to be able to point out that although neither Vilhelm Buhl nor Hedtoft-Hansen were members of the Council, they were nevertheless in contact with it. I made a great deal of this point, although the contact existed through me, and had in fact been made against the wishes of other members who did not wish to cooperate with the old politicians.

The Freedom Council did not receive the support of the B.B.C. until 31 October. For this delay in giving important publicity over the radio to the Freedom Council, the Danish section of the B.B.C. cannot be blamed. The decision to support the Freedom Council over the B.B.C. was one of policy, which could not be made by the B.B.C. alone. It was a matter for P.W.E. and for the Foreign Office.

Erling Foss, a Danish Resistance leader and a member of the Freedom Council, had written to Ebbe Munck in Stockholm on 25 September 1943, raising the question of getting publicity for

[1] See ch. 16, *The Spark and the Flame.*

the Freedom Council.[1] Foss asked Munck to try and get the 'greatest possible publicity' for it, and said that they were drawing up an appeal to the B.B.C.

The first letter from the Freedom Council to the B.B.C. was dated 1 October, but for some unknown reason, probably the uncertainties and delays in the post at this time, it never reached London.[2] At the beginning of November the B.B.C. received a much longer letter from the Freedom Council, dated 14 October, asking for the support of the B.B.C. in a propaganda attack which the Danish underground press was making on certain sections of the Danish population.[3] This letter asked the B.B.C. to direct its broadcasts particularly at civil servants, the police, farmers, business men, and industrial workers. This propaganda drive was aimed at stopping any form of co-operation between these sections of the community and the Germans. Requests for the exact type of propaganda to be directed at each section were extremely detailed. The letter finished by stating that it would be of great assistance to the Freedom Council's work if the B.B.C. would agree to broadcast this kind of propaganda. It also asked the B.B.C. for support in general terms:

> The Freedom Council's formation, so far as we have been able to find out, has still not been announced on the London radio, whereas it has been discussed in a Swedish broadcast. We hope soon to get the support for our work and for our influence, which a talk and a commentary on the London radio would mean. Where our proclamation has so far been received in Denmark, the formation of Denmark's Freedom Council has met with satisfaction and support.

It is known that this letter was passed on by Robert Jørgensen to the director of the B.B.C.'s European Broadcasts on 5 November.[4] Jørgensen wrote a further minute to Newsome on the subject of supporting the Freedom Council on 17 November.[5]

[1] Letter from Erling Foss to Ebbe Munck, 25 September 1943 (Danish Archives).

[2] See Hæstrup, *Hemmelig Alliance*, vol. 1, ch. 2, and Leif Gundel, *Her er London*, p. 131.

[3] Letter from the Freedom Council to the B.B.C., 14 October 1943 (Danish Archives), quoted in *Hemmelig Alliance*, vol. 1, ch. 2, p. 56.

[4] *Ibid.*

[5] Letter from Robert Jørgensen to N. F. Newsome, director of the B.B.C.'s European Broadcasts, 17 November 1943 (Danish Archives).

On 31 October Christmas Møller was allowed to welcome the setting up of the Freedom Council over the B.B.C.[1] This was some six weeks after its formation. The non-arrival of the Freedom Council's letter of 1 October, and the fact that the second letter from the Freedom Council to the B.B.C. dated 14 October did not arrive until the beginning of November, may partly explain the delay. It cannot, however, explain why there was no mention of the Freedom Council over the B.B.C. during the first six weeks when the Council was trying to establish itself in Denmark. S.O.E. must have known definitely of the formation of the Freedom Council as Flemming Muus, S.O.E.'s leader in the field, was present at the inaugural meeting of 16 September. Permission to publicize the Freedom Council over the B.B.C. cannot have depended on the letter to the B.B.C. from the Freedom Council dated 14 October. Had it done so, the Freedom Council would not have been mentioned on the B.B.C. until mid November when the letter was with the Director of European Broadcasts. Christmas Møller in fact began publicizing the Freedom Council over the B.B.C. at the end of October, before the B.B.C. had even received the letter of 14 October. Although he had received a letter from Mogens Fog and others in Denmark by mid October announcing the formation of the Council,[2] it is unlikely that he would have been permitted to introduce the Freedom Council into the B.B.C. broadcasts without official permission. It seems that either the Foreign Office or P.W.E. took six weeks before deciding to allow the B.B.C. to give the Freedom Council the support it asked for, and that permission to publicize the Council was only received by the B.B.C. at the end of October.

From this time onwards the support of the B.B.C. was never withheld and became a very valuable contribution to the effective control of Danish Resistance by the Freedom Council.

[1] B.B.C. talk by Christmas Møller, 31 October 1943 (B.B.C. Archives and Danish Archives).

[2] Letters from Frode Jakobsen and Erling Foss to Christmas Møller, 30 September and 1 October 1943. Letter from Christmas Moller to Mogens Fog, 14 October 1943. (Danish Archives). See *Hemmelig Alliance*, vol. 1, ch. 2, p. 56.

The proclamations of the Council were spread in Denmark mainly by the underground press, but this was often a lengthy process. It was much quicker and more effective for the proclamations to be read over the B.B.C. to the whole Danish population. A proclamation would be agreed by the Council, sent to Stockholm, relayed to London, from where, within 24 or 48 hours, it became public knowledge in Denmark.

Such proclamations, relayed over the B.B.C., were particularly valuable when the Freedom Council was trying to exert its control to prevent an uprising of the population, because of German provocation, which would only have led to bloodshed. This was the case in October 1944 when T. M. Terkelsen emphasized in a B.B.C. talk the importance of obeying the Freedom Council's order.[1]

> Denmark's Council of Freedom have issued a new proclamation warning the Danish people against allowing themselves to be provoked by the Germans. The Council says that Pancke[2] and the Gestapo will try to create a new situation of conflict, in order to tempt active resisters into the open at a too early stage. It would suit German plans beautifully to have an occasion to crush the Home Front before it gets the chance to be properly effective. The Freedom Council requests the population and the Resistance groups to keep cool and avoid precipitate action. On this point there is complete unanimity between the Freedom Council and the Allied Supreme Command, who have themselves intermittently warned the organized resistance movements in the occupied countries against hasty actions.

Again on 9 October 1944 Terkelsen reiterated the same warning of the Freedom Council.

> What is required now is not minor isolated actions but close collaboration between all the forces within the active Resistance movement so that the blow, when it is struck, is completely effective.

[1] B.B.C. talk by T. M. Terkelsen, 2 October 1944 (B.B.C. Archives).

[2] Günther Pancke was leader of the S.S. and the German police in Denmark. After the crisis of August 1943, the powers of the Reich plenipotentiary Dr Best were modified considerably, and the German police began to arrive in Denmark in force. They were under the orders, not of Best, but of Pancke, who was personally responsible to Himmler. By August 1944, when he had taken over judicial power in Denmark from the German courts martial, Pancke was the most dominant and the most feared German in Denmark.

In the B.B.C. the Freedom Council had the best means of publicizing its proclamations to the greatest extent possible.

Why did it take several weeks for the British authorities to accept that the Freedom Council filled the political vacuum left by the collapse of the government, and that it deserved British support? Clearly, any new development in Denmark required a certain amount of time for consideration by the Foreign Office. In this case, it was clearly the Foreign Office, by its control of policy matters through P.W.E., which restrained the B.B.C. from giving its immediate support to the Freedom Council. There were, during this period, positive moves to find out what was happening in Denmark. Probably, the main reason for bringing Flemming Muus out of Denmark in October was to get first-hand information on the state of affairs in Denmark. This is suggested by one brief passage in Muus's book *The Spark and the Flame*, where he writes of his visit to the Foreign Office: 'I attempted to explain how important it was that the Freedom Council should be supported. It was a great help to be able to point out that although neither Vilhelm Buhl nor Hedtoft-Hansen were members of the Council, they were nevertheless in contact with it.'

Much of Muus's activity during the summer of 1943 had been an attempt at forming close links with political circles in Denmark. Whether it was he or Herman Dedichen[1] who considered this necessary, it was probable that it was also desired by the British for the following reason.

It was natural for the Foreign Office to want to know what the Freedom Council stood for, and of whom it was composed, before it approved British support over the B.B.C. When the names of its members became known to the Foreign Office, there would have been relief at finding amongst them conservatives such as Erling Foss and Aage Schoch, counterbalancing

[1] Herman Dedichen worked in close co-operation with S.O.E. in Denmark. He also had valuable connections with both the Danish political leaders and the resistance groups. During the winter of 1944–5 he acted as the leader of the S.O.E. parachutists in Denmark.

Communists such as Børge Houmann.[1] There was, however, a conspicuous absence of the orthodox, respected and established political leaders, such as Vilhelm Buhl and Hedtoft-Hansen, who had not joined the Council. This was probably the reason for Muus's attempting to reassure the Foreign Office in October that the Freedom Council was in contact with Buhl and Hedtoft-Hansen. It perhaps also explains why he and Dedichen were so active in political circles throughout the summer. Reginald Spink of S.O.E.'s London headquarters also felt that the Social Democrats should be represented on the Freedom Council.[2]

The Foreign Office had to think, too, of long-term policy. The Freedom Council had no constitutional right to exercise authority in Denmark. It had no mandate, no authority from the king, and the Foreign Office was in the habit of conducting its relations with governments and not with self-appointed councils. Further, until 29 August 1943, the Foreign Office and other British departments were receiving regular intelligence material via Stockholm from the League. It may well have been that certain elements in the army, who were known to be hostile to the civil resistance groups and particularly to the Communists, were warning the British authorities to be cautious in supporting any new developments in Denmark.

S.O.E. as part of the Ministry of Economic Warfare held the attitude from the beginning that the Freedom Council should be supported. S.O.E.'s job was economic warfare—the disruption of the enemy's production and communications, and the strengthening and encouragement of all forms of resistance against the Germans. S.O.E. was unwilling to involve itself deliberately in internal politics, but the political consequences of its actions were only secondary in importance to the destruction of the enemy. Support for the Freedom Council, which was to unite and lead Danish Resistance, was natural for S.O.E.

[1] Foss, Schoch and Houmann were all at the inaugural meeting of the Freedom Council on 16 September 1943.

[2] Reginald Spink had been in Denmark before the war and had established relations with Danish Social Democrats.

The Freedom Council provided the leadership of the Home Front with which S.O.E. itself did not wish to be directly involved. Hugh Dalton, in his memoirs, illustrated frequently the tensions that existed between his Ministry of Economic Warfare, and the Foreign Office.[1] The Ministry of Economic Warfare was interested in quick results wherever possible, while the Foreign Office had more often to think in terms of future policy. If Foreign Office hesitation was caused partly by intelligence reports from the League sent before the fall of the Danish government in August, then British reluctance to support the Freedom Council, with its extremists and its absence of known and respected politicians, was understandable. The history of resistance in other countries showed that extensive British support of resistance groups during wartime might later in peacetime have the most unfortunate political consequences.

There is evidence to show that the position of Denmark was being reviewed by the Foreign Office after the formation of the Freedom Council, and particularly during November and December 1943. There were strong Foreign Office reactions to a B.B.C. Danish broadcast on 7 December 1943. The broadcast, entitled 'North Sea Powers', began with the following words:

> Denmark was today recognized as an Ally in speeches by British ministers of the Crown, and representatives of Norway, Holland and Belgium, at a function given in London by 'the Knights of the Round Table of King Arthur', given in honour of King Haakon of Norway, and honoured guests from the North Sea powers, Great Britain, Norway, Denmark, Holland and Belgium.[2]

This statement was inaccurate. Denmark had not been officially recognized as an ally. As a result of this broadcast, the

[1] Dalton's autobiography contains several references to the difficulties and tensions that existed between the Foreign Office and S.O.E.

For example: 'There was indeed a suspicion that even now, through S.O.E., I was trying to "control foreign policy", or run a foreign policy of my own' (ch. 26 of *The Fateful Years*).

[2] B.B.C. talk dated 7 December 1943 (Danish Archives).

Controller of the B.B.C. European Services received a complaint from the Foreign Office.

> The point of complaint is that it [the broadcast] speaks of Denmark having been recognized as an Ally, whereas the speakers, so the F.O. say, were carefully briefed beforehand so that they were careful in their references to Denmark, *not* to describe her as an Ally.[1]

Despite this reprimand from the Foreign Office, and the British attitude towards Denmark which it implied, there was at this time some new consideration of policy towards Denmark. Perhaps the events of August 1943, the emergence of the Freedom Council, and the number of Danes fighting in the allied ranks had convinced the Foreign Office that Denmark should be accepted as a fighting ally. In early 1944 S.O.E. worked out the provisional text for a declaration on Denmark's position by the three powers, Britain, U.S.A., and Russia. The text read:

> For over four years Denmark has been subjected to the Nazi yoke. Her King is virtually a prisoner, her Government has ceased to operate and her people are unable to express their feelings openly. But the whole Danish people were united behind the King in determination to refuse the new and humiliating German demands provoked in August last by their stubbornly growing resistance. Inspired by the same beliefs as Danes abroad, who sail and fly and fight in the ranks of the United Nations, the Danes at home, with their comrades in other occupied lands, contribute by active and passive opposition to weaken the Nazi hold. There is no Danish Government which can give expression to the feelings of Denmark by adhering to the United Nations Declaration. The Governments of Great Britain, the United States of America and the U.S.S.R. recognize, however, that the Danish Nation has placed itself side by side with the United Nations and, like them, is determined to contribute to the common struggle for Victory over Hitlerism and for the attainment of the aims of the Atlantic Charter.[2]

Although the declaration avoided using the terms 'associated' or 'allied' about Denmark, it was nevertheless an acceptance by the Allies of the fact that Denmark fought with them against

[1] A minute from the Assistant Controller European Services to Robert Jørgensen, dated 17 December 1943 (Danish Archives).

[2] Text quoted in *Hemmelig Alliance*, vol. 1, ch. 9.

the Germans. Britain and the U.S.A. agreed on the text initially, and after it had been sent to Denmark during May 1944 for the approval of the king, it only remained for the third party, Russia, to give its agreement.

At this point, through Russian disapproval, the whole scheme fell through. Until June expectations were still high, and Ebbe Munck wrote of the expected declaration by the three Foreign ministers, Eden, Hull and Molotov.[1] About 1 July the Russian answer was received, and it was negative. The Russians were not prepared to grant any recognition to Denmark, because it was considered that Danish-Russian relations had been broken off completely in December 1941, shortly after Denmark signed the Anti-Comintern Pact. The fact that Russia had recognized 'Fighting Denmark' and had received its representative, Thomas Døssing, in Moscow did not mean that the Danish policy of 1941 was forgotten. This answer was final. During August Christopher Warner of the Northern Department of the Foreign Office told Ebbe Munck that there was little possibility of Britain and the U.S.A. persuading the Russians to change their opinion. Warner thought that Eden and Hull had done all they could.[2]

There the matter had to rest. Both the foreign secretaries of Britain and the U.S.A. made separate declarations on 12 July. Cordell Hull's declaration followed very closely the wording of the original text. Eden in an answer to a question from Ivor Thomas, M.P., stated the British view on Denmark in the House of Commons.

It is the policy of His Majesty's Government in the United Kingdom to support all those who help in the fight against the enemy. Denmark is an enemy-occupied country. Her King regards himself as a prisoner of the Germans and her Government ceased to operate last August. It is not therefore possible at present for Denmark to become formally belligerent and join the United Nations. But it is clear that the people of Denmark as a whole are inspired by the ideals of the

[1] Ebbe Munck's diary, 15 June 1944 (Danish Archives). Quoted *Hemmelig Alliance*, vol. 1, ch. 9.

[2] The meeting between Warner and Munck was on 11 August 1944.

United Nations, many Danes are actively engaged in the ranks of the United Nations for the liberation of their country, and inside Denmark ever increasing active resistance is contributing to the common struggle against the Axis.

Last Autumn, representatives of various resistance bodies in Denmark formed a committee with the name of Council of Freedom, which, pending the restoration of liberty and constitutional government to Denmark, plays a conspicuous part in the life of occupied Denmark as a focus of resistance to the Germans. The valuable contribution which is being made to the defeat of Germany by the work of the Danish Council of Freedom and by all who contribute to resistance in Denmark is, like that of the Free Danes abroad, warmly acknowledged by His Majesty's Government.[1]

The position as stated by Eden in the Commons was somewhere between the position adopted by the Americans and that adopted by the Russians. After stressing that Denmark was enemy-occupied, the king a prisoner and the government not functioning, and that therefore Denmark could not formally become a member of the United Nations, Eden then emphasized the contribution of fighting Denmark, and of the Danes serving in the allied ranks. There was clearly in his mind, as in the Russians', a sharp division between 'official' Denmark and 'fighting' Denmark.

This remained the British attitude throughout the war, and it seems that the Russian refusal to agree to the terms of the original common declaration influenced British policy. Britain was even less prepared than the U.S.A. to give any formal recognition to Denmark.

Eden's statement on Denmark in the House of Commons showed, however, that Britain gave its official support to the Freedom Council. The words 'pending the restoration of liberty and constitutional government' show the terms of the support which the British government was prepared to give to the Freedom Council. Clearly, it was only temporary support.

In the circumstances limited recognition, as a contributor to the fight but not as a formal ally, was all that Denmark could

[1] Anthony Eden in the House of Commons, 12 July 1944. Quoted in *The Times*, 13 July 1944.

expect. For both legal and diplomatic reasons the British government could not recognize the Freedom Council as acting as an allied government. This would have led to many post-war problems. The Norwegian foreign minister in London, Trygve Lie, was also reputed to be firmly opposed to Britain granting allied status to Denmark. His attitude was that as Denmark had not fought from the beginning as his own country had done, then Denmark, despite the undoubted courage of its resistance, should not be granted formal recognition as an ally.

Formal recognition as an ally had to wait until Denmark was invited to take part in the San Francisco Conference in 1945.[1]

The Freedom Council, however, received British support. The decision whether or not to recognize the Council involved the Foreign Office in some thought, because of its relatively sudden appearance and its self-appointed membership. There was, however, one factor which contributed little to the easy finding of a solution by the Foreign Office at this time. This was that the Intelligence service from Denmark via Stockholm to London was disrupted on 29 August 1943. For some time after 29 August little or no intelligence, or news of Danish affairs, arrived in Britain. This was confirmed in a letter from Dr J. W. Varley, deputy director to Brinley Thomas in the Northern Department of P.W.E., to Ronald Turnbull of the British Legation in Stockholm. Varley, at this time answering criticism of the B.B.C., wrote: 'None of us have forgotten that dreadful time after 29th August 1943 when we were virtually starved of news from Denmark.'[2] It was during this time that the British authorities were forced to make up their minds on the Freedom Council.

[1] The U.S. government sent out invitations on 1 March 1945 to a 'founding conference of the United Nations' to be held at San Francisco on 25 April. Denmark was invited to participate.

[2] Letter from Dr J. W. Varley of P.W.E. to Ronald Turnbull of the British Legation in Stockholm dated 19 May 1944 (Danish Archives).

CHAPTER 13

INTELLIGENCE AND NEWS MATERIAL

It is legitimate to point to good intelligence as the foundation of good propaganda.

Ivor Thomas in *Warfare by Words*

April 1940–August 1943

Information on events in Denmark was the fundamental need of the Danish section of the B.B.C. For without knowledge of what was happening in German-occupied Denmark, the Danish section was unable to probe any weak spots, to influence the population, or indeed to show any knowledge of what conditions were really like. Intelligence was vital for good propaganda. Those who were responsible for broadcasting to Denmark had to know what the Danish population was thinking and doing, what effect their propaganda had, how many listened to broadcasts from London, how much fuel, how much food they had, what restrictions were imposed, and whether there was sabotage and rioting. Before the propagandists knew this, they could not direct propaganda on to the sensitive issues where it would have effect.

The broadcasts of the Danish section of the B.B.C. depended on two main sources of information.

The first was secret intelligence passed out from Denmark to Stockholm, and thence to London, upon which the propaganda directives from P.W.E. and P.I.D. were based. This intelligence material was mainly military and naval, but there were also political reports. These were of the utmost importance for propaganda policy-makers in Britain. It was this Intelligence service to which Field Marshal Montgomery gave the highest praise after the war.[1]

[1] Field Marshal Montgomery had written to General Gørtz of the Royal Danish army on 12 May 1945 stating that the Danish Intelligence was the best of all the Intelligence services which operated in the occupied countries (see Hæstrup, *Hemmelig Alliance*, vol. 1, ch. 5).

Preparations began in April 1940 when Ebbe Munck, a Danish journalist working in Finland for the paper *Berlingske Tidende*, heard of the German occupation of his country, and decided that he and other Danes, for the sake of Denmark's reputation, had to contribute to the allied battle.[1]

Munck returned to Denmark, and secretly contacted the officers of the army Intelligence Corps (later given the code name of 'the Princes' or 'the League'), who agreed to work with him.[2] He then arranged that he should be appointed as his newspaper's correspondent in Stockholm. The plan was that the army Intelligence officers, who were not disbanded after the German occupation, should send all information to Munck in Stockholm, where he would transmit it to the British. The officers were in an excellent position to obtain this information. They were strategically well placed behind the German lines, they were trained in intelligence work and therefore knew what kind of information would interest the Allies, and they had the machinery and the contacts necessary for the collection and the disposal of this information.

The first intelligence reports from this source reached England during the autumn of 1940. During November Charles Hambro of S.O.E. was in Stockholm, where he held discussions with Ebbe Munck. It was agreed then that an S.O.E. representative should be sent to the British Legation in Stockholm, primarily to maintain close links with the Danish Resistance. In February 1941, Ronald Turnbull arrived in Stockholm, having travelled via South Africa, Egypt, Turkey and Moscow. His roundabout route was necessary because of difficulties in making normal travel arrangements, but it also made any guessing of his eventual destination more difficult.[3] The Danish section of S.O.E. had been set up in October 1940, and with Turnbull's arrival in February 1941, the arrangements for the transmission of intelligence material were complete. This flow of intelligence

[1] For the background to this see Hæstrup, *Kontakt med England*, ch. 3.

[2] See chapters 5 and 6.

[3] For a description of the discussions between Hambro and Munck, and of Ronald Turnbull's journey, see *Kontakt med England*, ch. 3.

was maintained throughout the course of the war, with one short interruption.

This interruption was in August 1943 when the officers of the army Intelligence Corps were forced either to flee to Sweden, or to go underground. The Intelligence service was temporarily broken off, between about 29 August and the middle of October. It was this period that Varley mentioned in his letter to Turnbull, 'when we were virtually starved of news from Denmark'.[1]

During the autumn of 1943 Danish Intelligence was entirely reorganized under the leadership of Svend Truelsen.[2] The net was spread wider and even extended into northern Germany. The three main headquarters of the intelligence network were in Jutland, Copenhagen and Stockholm. It has been estimated that, from the time of this reorganization until May 1945, 15,000 pages of intelligence material, in addition to urgent information which was telegraphed direct, reached London. Most of the material consisted of very detailed reports of German military installations, troop movements, and naval intelligence.[3]

Most of the material was routine information which was of general use in assessing German military strength. The most valuable information sent out of Denmark was considered to be the very early warning of German naval movements in the Baltic and North Sea, reports on the V-bomb, and correspondence between allied scientists and Professor Niels Bohr, the Danish nuclear physicist, who in 1943 was able to escape with the help of the Resistance to the United States, by way of Stockholm and London.

When the British Admiralty records are made public it will be interesting to see how valuable the naval information sent out by the Danish Intelligence service was. Quite clearly this intelligence was an important factor in the negotiations between

[1] See notes to chapter 12.

[2] See *Hemmelig Alliance*, vol. 1, ch. 5. Truelsen left Denmark in June 1944 and joined the S.O.E. headquarters staff in Baker Street, London.

[3] Hæstrup, *Panorama Denmark*, p. 36.

the officers of the League and S.O.E. during the winter and spring of 1942–1943.

For the first three years of the war, the Danish section of the B.B.C. depended almost entirely for its propaganda material on the intelligence material sent from Denmark via Stockholm to London. A great deal of this material was purely military, and this of course could not be broadcast back again to Denmark, nor would it have served any particular purpose to do so. Erling Foss, in his description of the setting up of the Intelligence service, wrote that not only was it the best way of getting military information to London, but that 'it also gave an exceptional opportunity to help the Danish radio in London influence public opinion in Denmark in the right way against the Germans'.[1]

Robert Jørgensen confirmed that the problem of information on Danish affairs was a very real one in the early months of the war.[2] Intelligence from Denmark reached S.O.E. and anything which provided the basis of propaganda was passed on to either, or both, the Political Intelligence Department and the Department of Propaganda to Enemy and Enemy-Occupied Countries. The Danish section of the B.B.C. received very little material on events in Denmark from these departments during 1940.[3] Only reports on the general situation could be used for broadcasting back to Denmark. The wide publicity given over the B.B.C. to the Danish Council's formation was partly due to lack of any other information on Danish affairs. This is why for the first six months the Danish broadcasts consisted almost entirely of news bulletins, summaries and encouraging talks by Danish correspondents in London. There was very little opportunity of introducing matters of specific Danish interest, other than news of the Danish Council, simply because there was a lack of suitable news material.

[1] Erling Foss in his book *Fra Passiv til Aktiv Modstand*, pp. 62–3.

[2] Interview.

[3] That there was practically no information coming out of Denmark during 1940–1 is shown by Sten Gudme's account deposited in the Danish Archives. The report that he wrote for the Foreign Office and the Ministry of Information soon after his arrival in Britain in May 1941 was the first detailed information on the situation in Denmark which the British had received.

As the links with Denmark through Ebbe Munck grew stronger, more information which could be used by the B.B.C. was sent to Britain. The growth of the Danish underground press helped the circulation of news within Denmark. Couriers from Denmark to Sweden gradually increased in number as the Resistance movement grew. Sources of propaganda material are extremely difficult to trace, and it can only be assumed that, as more couriers crossed the sound between Denmark and Sweden during 1941, so the material available for Danish broadcasts from all sources increased too.[1]

The confusion amongst the propaganda departments in Britain during 1940 and 1941 cannot have ensured the best distribution of the material available. When P.W.E. was formed in August 1941, all material from the British Legation in Stockholm which could be used for propaganda purposes reached its Northern Department, and was transmitted to the Danish section of the B.B.C. in the form of weekly directives. To summarize:

From 1941 the main sources of secret intelligence used by the B.B.C.'s propaganda advisers were twofold:

(1) Material from the Danish Army Intelligence Corps, sent via Stockholm to S.O.E. This material reached the B.B.C. via P.W.E. and on occasions via the Political Intellience Department of the Foreign Office. P.I.D. probably had sources of information in Stockholm, separate from the Munck–Turnbull channel.

(2) Information not publicly available in Britain which was taken from the European press and from monitoring reports. Soon after the outbreak of war, the Royal Institute of International Affairs undertook to survey the foreign press for the Foreign Office. They worked as a group, eventually at Balliol College, Oxford, where they produced 'Foreign Research and

[1] Refugees from Denmark also began to become a useful source of information. Robert Jørgensen was able to interview several refugees and used any useful information he gleaned from them in the Danish broadcasts. Information from censored correspondence also gradually became available to the Editor of the Danish section.

Press Service' reports at regular intervals.[1] Their main task was to produce an accurate summary of conditions in enemy-occupied countries. This was done, in the case of Denmark, by regular and close examination of Danish, German and Swedish national and provincial newspapers which were smuggled out to Britain. Newspapers formed the basis of regular reports on conditions in the German-occupied countries and frequently the Danish provincial newspapers revealed much more useful material than the national, as they were less rigidly censored. The reports of the 'Foreign Research and Press Service' were distributed amongst British government departments.[2]

The monitoring of German, Swedish and Danish radio was also used as a source of information. The monitoring service transcribed every important detail and fact broadcast by foreign radio stations. It is not surprising to find that many of the early B.B.C. broadcasts to Denmark were based on Danish newspapers and Kalundborg Radio. It was not difficult for skilled propagandists to read between the lines.

There are few specific instances where it can be proved that Danish intelligence material formed the basis of propaganda to Denmark. That it did so is almost certain, but sources of intelligence material still tend to be shrouded in mystery. It can only be assumed that after Turnbull reached Stockholm in February 1941, the volume of intelligence material which was of value to the B.B.C. increased.

Probably as a result of the improvement in intelligence links, the B.B.C. broadcasts became much better informed. The B.B.C. Intelligence report of, for example, August 1941 was able to quote Danish reactions to B.B.C. broadcasts.[3] The statement that listeners in Denmark had heard too much about the Danish Council and, under 'General Policy', that more resistance was now to be encouraged, must have been based on reports coming through Turnbull in Stockholm. Not all the

[1] These reports are filed in the Foreign Office Library in London.

[2] Information about the reading of foreign newspapers was given to me by a member of the staff of the Royal Institute of International Affairs who worked at Balliol College, Oxford, during the war.

[3] Danish Archives.

information transmitted to London from Turnbull came through Munck from the Danish Intelligence officers. Albert Christensen, an S.O.E. agent acting as British consul in Gothenburg, was able to supply information from refugees crossing the Øresund. Stockholm was an international espionage centre, and the British Legation was able to receive information wherever it came from.

There were other intelligence links between Britain and Denmark where the Legation was also involved in transmitting information back to Britain. Herman Dedichen regularly sent back reports on the situation in Denmark to both S.O.E. and the British Intelligence service.[1] One of Flemming Muus's main tasks during the spring and summer of 1943 was to gather intelligence and send it back to S.O.E. In March 1944, Muus was sent two men specially trained in intelligence work and in the distribution of propaganda. Their duties were to 'organize the reception and distribution of propaganda material and to collect and forward to S.O.E. material suitable for the B.B.C.'.[2]

Precisely what use was made of Danish material will not be known for many years. Ivor Thomas, a member of Parliament, wrote in 1942:

> An outsider cannot know, and an official may not say, with what success this task [the best possible use of intelligence material] is being accomplished; but it is legitimate to point to good intelligence as the foundation of good propaganda, and to ask whether the propaganda services are fully supplied with all the available material. It cannot be too strongly emphasized that intelligence material is for use, not contemplation. The Official Secrets Acts can be drilled so hard into the heads of officials that they become terrified of passing on information to the only people who can make use of it.[3]

It was the breakdown of this valuable intelligence service in the autumn of 1943 which was partly responsible for the Foreign Office's, P.W.E.'s and the B.B.C.'s delay in giving support to the Freedom Council.

[1] See notes to chapter 12.

[2] These two men were Herschend and Hecht Johansen (see *Hemmelig Alliance*, vol. 1, ch. 10).

[3] In *Warfare by Words* by Ivor Thomas.

The second source of material upon which the Danish broadcasts depended was distinct from the secret intelligence network just described. This was news material which was obtained mainly from press circles in Stockholm, and provided the basis of most of the regular news bulletins and news talks.

News of Danish affairs was quickly gathered in Stockholm and telegraphed back to London. The B.B.C. kept in constant touch with the four main press agencies which distributed foreign news in London—Reuter, Associated Press, Exchange Telegraph and British United Press—and had its own correspondent in Stockholm who had direct radio contact with London.[1] This meant that the B.B.C. received regular news material in London very shortly after it was known amongst journalists in Sweden. The B.B.C. European Services also received other material from the British press, the European underground press, and from the monitoring service.

It was important that all the incoming news material should be accurate and that the outgoing broadcasts should be coordinated. In the central newsroom news material from all sources was tested for accuracy by a 'copy taster'. Where necessary he chose some reports which seemed to be more accurate than others. He was able to decide how accurate a news telegram was by comparing it with other reports.

The 'copy taster' had in front of him a timetable of all the broadcasting times of every European section. If urgent news was received by telegram, he could have it sent to the relevant regional editor in a matter of minutes for immediate broadcast, by reading the message into a microphone at his side. This loudspeaker system was in touch with all the various section editors. After the 'flash' was given over the loudspeaker, it was translated and broadcast as soon as possible.[2]

In addition, the European Service of the B.B.C. had its own naval, military and air correspondents, who analysed and

[1] See the B.B.C. publication *De Hører B.B.C.*

[2] *De Hører B.B.C.*, and E. Tangye Lean, *Voices in the Darkness*; both have descriptions of how news was circulated within the B.B.C.

commented daily on the news as it came in from all sources. For example, Brian Tunstall, the B.B.C.'s naval correspondent, gave a special talk to Denmark on 29 October 1943 on the importance of the Baltic to German control of North Europe.[1]

The director of European Broadcasts, N. F. Newsome, was responsible for the co-ordination of all the various regional sections. Twice daily, morning and evening, the section editors were summoned to a conference in his office to discuss the day's news from all points of view. Military and other experts gave their view on the news at these conferences. These meetings ensured a certain degree of co-ordination amongst the regional broadcasts. The editors also discussed their news individually with the director.[2] It was these meetings, and the material which was discussed, which formed the basis of the straightforward news service which the B.B.C. provided for Denmark.

The division between intelligence and news material was not always distinct. Many of the sources of information overlapped. The absence of any material on Danish affairs immediately after the events of 29 August 1943 meant that the service of both the League, which was supplying Munck and Turnbull with intelligence, and of the underground press in Denmark, which supplied Stockholm journalists, was temporarily interrupted.

September 1943–May 1945

After the collapse of the Danish government, it became easier to trace the flow of both intelligence material and news material from Denmark to Britain. For, at this time, the Danish Press Service—*Dansk Presse Tjeneste* (D.P.T.)—was set up in a room in the Grand Hotel, Stockholm.[3] This Press Service continued until the liberation, and through it the free world received the great majority of its Danish news.[4]

[1] B.B.C. Archives.
[2] *De Hører B.B.C.*

[3] The Grand Hotel, Stockholm, was the headquarters of foreign news correspondents and it was therefore a suitable place for D.P.T. to begin work (Report by Erik Seidenfaden on how D.P.T. news reached the free world—Danish Archives).

[4] The description of D.P.T. is based on a confidential report on the activities of D.P.T., written in about November 1944, and now deposited amongst the papers of Ebbe Munck in the Danish Archives.

After 29 August, Stockholm became of even greater importance than before. Both for Norway and for Denmark, it was the one contact with the free world. Stockholm was therefore the obvious choice for the Danish Press Service, which began work during August 1943. The task of transmitting news and information to the free world through the Danish Press Service was begun on the initiative of Danish journalists in Stockholm, who saw the paramount importance of setting up the machinery by which the world could hear and read of events in Denmark.

As the Press Service grew, the number of those who received its bulletins of Danish news, two or three times daily, increased. By August 1944, D.P.T. sent regular news bulletins, usually in telegraphic form, to thirty Swedish newspapers, the Swedish radio, the B.B.C., the American Broadcasting Station in Europe (A.B.S.I.E.), Reuter, United Press, Associated Press, and all the correspondents of the free world's newspapers in Stockholm. By this date, D.P.T. employed twenty journalists, two secret correspondents in Copenhagen, two in Malmö and one in Hälsingborg.[1] Its net was spread widely in Denmark itself. As soon as regular reports started to come in to London from D.P.T., the B.B.C. began to use them for its broadcasts to Denmark.

The B.B.C. Danish section did not have direct contact with D.P.T. until 1 February 1944.[2] Until that date most of the B.B.C.'s general news of events in Denmark came through the B.B.C.'s Stockholm correspondent. He naturally drew very heavily for Danish news on D.P.T., although in the B.B.C.'s broadcasts the source quoted was 'the B.B.C.'s Stockholm correspondent' rather than the Danish Press Service.

After 1 February 1944, the B.B.C. received telegrams direct from D.P.T. This established a firm and regular connection between the B.B.C. and D.P.T.—the organization which, as

[1] The agencies to which D.P.T. sent news telegrams, and the number of journalists employed by D.P.T., were given in a letter dated 15 August 1944 from Erik Seidenfaden to Brewster Morris of the U.S. Legation in Stockholm (Danish Archives).

[2] The date by which D.P.T. had begun to send telegrams direct to the B.B.C. was given in an undated letter from Erik Seidenfaden to the Freedom Council (Danish Archives).

Erik Seidenfaden, one of the founder journalists, said, 'aimed at and largely got a monopoly of all Danish news'.[1]

From then onwards the Danish section of the B.B.C. had first-class news material at hand for broadcasts to Denmark.

The most important factor in the organization of D.P.T. was its sources of information in Denmark. Immediately after 29 August 1943 when information on Danish affairs was very scant, D.P.T. reports consisted almost entirely of interviews with Danish refugees who arrived in Stockholm, and of any documentary material which they or others who crossed to Sweden were able to smuggle with them. It was difficult to obtain information in this way, and even more difficult to check it, as the British authorities found until about the middle of October 1943. By then, however, contacts and intelligence links between Denmark and Sweden were being reopened and the volume of information was increasing.

The bulk of D.P.T.'s news was based on the Danish underground press. The B.B.C. therefore owed a great deal to the illegal Danish newspapers, for most of the Danish news which was broadcast to Denmark by the B.B.C. came originally from the Danish underground press. An examination of D.P.T.'s sources of information shows that it was news gathered by the illegal Danish press which provided the basis of the telegrams from D.P.T. to the B.B.C. This was the first of D.P.T.'s two main sources of information.

The second was the organization which kept open the illegal routes within Denmark itself and between Denmark and Sweden. Ebbe Munck's papers referring to D.P.T. show that 99 per cent of the news sent out by D.P.T. came from documents composed in Denmark. 'There exists at home (in Denmark) a news organization, or one can more properly say, a system of news services, which are in fact more comprehensive than the best we have had in peace time,' he wrote in 1944.[2] The news

[1] Interview.

[2] Report on D.P.T. in Ebbe Munck's papers, about November 1944 (Danish Archives).

organization was based on a network of correspondents spread over all parts of Denmark. These correspondents, despite the German control of the postal services and telephones, managed to send or take their news to a central collecting point. The result was that D.P.T. knew of every event of any importance in Denmark, even though it might not have found its way into the Danish newspapers, within 24 hours of its happening. 'Behind the news which the free world gets, lies in almost every case, not the telephone call of the journalist, but the work of a fighting resistance. They take part in a dangerous fight for free information.'[1]

A more specific examination of this underground news service shows that the main supplier of news to D.P.T. was the illegal newspaper *Information.*[2] *Information* was received by D.P.T. regularly and provided the basis of news on Danish affairs. It was, however, supplemented by bulletins from other underground news services of lesser size.[3] The underground press had its own sources, and there is no doubt that much of the information received by D.P.T. via the Danish underground press came from the police and from the various ministries.[4] D.P.T.'s secret correspondents in Denmark sent their news through to Stockholm, as also did the correspondents in Malmö, Hälsingborg and Göteborg. The D.P.T. correspondents on the west coast of Sweden facing Denmark had instructions to telephone urgent news direct to Stockholm. Normally it was sent by post.[5] After the underground connections between Denmark and Sweden had been rebuilt, not a great deal of information was collected from interviews with refugees. This

[1] Report on D.P.T. about November 1944 in Ebbe Munck's papers (Danish Archives).

[2] *Ibid.* Confirmed by Erik Seidenfaden in an interview.

[3] Report on D.P.T., about November 1944, in Ebbe Munck's papers (Danish Archives).

[4] Interview. Erik Seidenfaden said that much of D.P.T.'s secret information came from the police and the ministries. In his three books, Hæstrup lists several instances of co-operation between police and Resistance, e.g. *Hemmelig Alliance*, vol. 1, ch. 5.

[5] Report on D.P.T., about November 1944, in Ebbe Munck's papers (Danish Archives).

happened only for the weeks immediately after 29 August 1943.

A great part of the news from Denmark became available in Stockholm soon after it reached D.P.T. It was handed out in bulletins, which usually varied in size between two and four sides.[1] It was given to those Swedish newspapers, both national and provincial, who subscribed to D.P.T. It also went in English to the international press agencies.[2]

Munck himself laid great emphasis on the importance of the telegram service from D.P.T. to the Danish section of the B.B.C. Telegrams were sent day and night to the B.B.C., containing the great part of all the information received by D.P.T.

> The Danish broadcasts from London must really be considered as Denmark's most important newspaper and so they [B.B.C.] receive also Danish local news of less importance, which would not interest Swedish and other foreign presses, but which is of interest in Denmark. In the last five or six months [May–November 1944], Danish news in these B.B.C. broadcasts has occupied more space than corresponding local material in some of the other foreign broadcasts from London.[3]

During September 1944 D.P.T. decided to discontinue its telegram service to A.B.S.I.E., the American Broadcasting Station in Europe, on the grounds that it could easily obtain the material from the B.B.C.[4] D.P.T. also supplied a weekly résumé of events in Denmark,[5] and a service of press photographs taken secretly by D.P.T. cameramen in Denmark.[6]

A memorandum written in January 1944 on the subject of Danish news in Stockholm showed how Danish news was sent out of Sweden, and that restrictions on the release of news were sometimes necessary for security reasons.[7] This memorandum

[1] Report on D.P.T., about November 1944, in Ebbe Munck's papers (Danish Archives). [2] *Ibid.* [3] *Ibid.* [4] *Ibid.* [5] *Ibid.*

[6] D.P.T. provided many photographs taken in German-occupied Denmark by D.P.T. cameramen. A letter from John Ray of the British Legation in Stockholm to Erik Seidenfaden dated 24 July 1944 stated that the Foreign Office requested copies of photographs of as many sabotage operations as possible (Danish Archives).

[7] 'Memorandum concerning Danish news from Stockholm', January 1944 (D.P.T. papers, Danish Archives).

listed three main sources of information on Denmark which were available to the British in Stockholm:

(1) Secret reports, such as *Ugen* (the Week), from both Danish and British (S.O.E.) sources within Denmark;

(2) the Danish Press Service (D.P.T.);

(3) Danish and Swedish newspapers.

As far as time restrictions were concerned (2) and (3) were not usually affected. Most of D.P.T.'s information went out very soon after it was received, although it was frequently held for a few hours so that better news value could be made of it. Danish and Swedish newspapers (3) were sent to London regularly from Stockholm, and it was from this source that the group working at Balliol College, Oxford, and producing the 'Foreign Research and Press Service' reports, received their newspapers.

Some information from D.P.T. had to be considered secret, and sometimes delayed or even suppressed because, had it been known publicly, it would have compromised people in Denmark. Practically all news was sent out by telegram. The newspapers were quoted in telegrams and then sent complete by air. All the top secret reports from (1) went by diplomatic bag.

The same memorandum stated that both the British authorities and the Danish Council were interested in the information coming from Stockholm. The British authorities were interested in the material primarily for the B.B.C. and 'special purposes'. 'Special purposes' referred to S.O.E. and the propaganda departments. The Danish Council used Stockholm material for publication through the British press and agencies, and for the Free Danish newspaper, *Frit Danmark*.

It was suggested, at the end of this memorandum, that there should be more co-operation between Danish and British circles in Stockholm as well as in London, and that a trusted Danish journalist should be given an office near the British Legation in Stockholm. His job was to be responsible for selecting and transmitting suitable information to London for use by the British authorities and the Danish Council.

It seems probable that this suggestion was acted upon.

Dr. J. W. Varley of P.W.E. wrote to Turnbull at the British Legation in Stockholm on 11 May 1944.[1] The subject was financial support for D.P.T. from Britain. Varley wrote that he had obtained approval for an increase in Britain's subscription to D.P.T. of 800 Swedish kroner per month. This now made the total 1,800 Swedish kroner per month.

This increase was approved on condition that D.P.T. put at British disposal Gunnar Næsselund Hansen, a Danish journalist in Stockholm and one of the founder members of D.P.T. The letter made it clear that the British had no objection to his taking over the job of leader of D.P.T. as long as it was understood that he was to be at British disposal. He was to 'handle without reference to D.P.T. such material as may be placed at his disposal by the British Legation for transmission to London'.[2] It is probable that this referred to secret material received from S.O.E. men in Denmark.

Næsselund Hansen's job was to sort out useful propaganda material for the British from the information coming from Denmark, and then to transmit it to London.

D.P.T. itself saw the importance of controlling its output of news, so that it would receive the widest publicity. This was simply the journalistic technique of timing the release of news so that it made the greatest impact. D.P.T. was acting in Denmark's interests, and wanted Danish news to receive the widest publicity. If an important news item from Denmark was received, it was not handed out by D.P.T. to one particular newspaper. This would have given that newspaper the chance of making an exclusive story of the news. The general impact, however, would have been small, as circulation would have been limited to the small percentage of the population who read that particular newspaper.

D.P.T.'s technique was this. For example, news of a sabotage action in Svendborg was received by D.P.T. at midday.[3] A news

[1] Letter from Varley to Turnbull, 11 May 1944. (D.P.T. papers, Danish Archives). [2] *Ibid.*

[3] This example is given in the report on D.P.T., in Ebbe Munck's papers (Danish Archives).

telegram announcing this was sent immediately to the Danish section of the B.B.C. in London.

At this point neither the Stockholm newspapers nor the Swedish radio were informed of the news by D.P.T. The Swedish radio put out a news bulletin at 12.30 daily, but D.P.T. made sure that the news did not reach the Swedish radio until 18.30. By this time the B.B.C. had already announced the news in its 18.15 broadcast. By this system D.P.T. ensured that the Danish section of the B.B.C. was not only the first to receive the news, but also the first to broadcast it back to Denmark. The B.B.C. insisted that if D.P.T. news bulletins were to be used, they had to be sent first to the B.B.C., and only released later to the other agencies and to the Swedish radio.

D.P.T. made doubly sure of its contact with the B.B.C. The Svendborg message was originally telegraphed to the Danish section of the B.B.C., but at 17.00 D.P.T. delivered the story in English to the B.B.C.'s special correspondent in Stockholm, who at 17.45 sent his daily report to the B.B.C. News Desk in London. The news, once it was received at the B.B.C., was then distributed from the News Desk to the various regional sections. By this time the original message sent direct to the Danish section of the B.B.C. by D.P.T. had arrived, and had been passed on to the News Desk. As a result the News Desk received Danish news from two sources—from the B.B.C. correspondent in Stockholm, and from D.P.T. via the Danish section.

The same story was delivered to foreign newspaper correspondents and subscribers at 16.00. They received it simultaneously and used it as their own news. This usually appeared in the following morning's newspapers. At about 19.00 the news was given general release to the Stockholm newspapers. It was deliberately kept back until after the evening newspapers had gone to press, as D.P.T. reckoned that the news appearing in the following morning's newspapers was likely to get wider circulation. Swedish provincial newspapers were informed during the course of the evening by telephone.

In this way news of Danish sabotage actions received the widest possible publicity.

From this example it can be seen that D.P.T. kept a very tight control over the release of its news. The usual result was that the news was known in Britain before it was in Sweden, and that the B.B.C. Danish section was able to broadcast important news items direct to Denmark, knowing with complete certainty that it was the first to bring the news. This was of incalculable assistance after 29 August 1943 to the B.B.C. in its role of 'Denmark's most important newspaper'.

This technique of distribution applied to news material—material which eventually found its way into newspapers and news bulletins. D.P.T., however, received a certain amount of secret material which was not for publication, but for the use of various British government departments, particularly P.W.E. This secret material consisted largely of reports from the police and from Danish civil servants who had access to official papers.[1] Also included in this category were the political reports sent out by Herman Dedichen for S.O.E. and the British Intelligence service.

D.P.T. had therefore the dual character of both an intelligence and a news organization, although the great majority of its work was that of a press agency. Because it received some secret material from Denmark, D.P.T. maintained very close relations with the British Legation in Stockholm, and in particular with S.O.E.'s representative there, Ronald Turnbull, and his assistant John Ray.[2]

D.P.T., and in particular its leaders Erik Seidenfaden and Gunnar Næsselund Hansen, were in a good position to give reports on the situation in Denmark to the British Legation, on the basis of the information which they received. Seidenfaden's relations with both Turnbull and Ray were very close

[1] Interview with Seidenfaden.

[2] Seidenfaden laid great emphasis on the close relationship which existed between D.P.T. and the British Legation in Stockholm. This relationship was an essential link in the information and intelligence network between Denmark and London.

throughout, and he provided numerous reports on specific subjects for the British Legation. He sometimes contributed reports without being asked for them.

For example, Seidenfaden received a letter from Turnbull on 23 October 1944, requesting information for the British Foreign Office.

I have received [wrote Turnbull] the following letter from the Foreign Office: 'All reports indicate that the Danes are having nothing to do with Pancke's proposal for the formation of a new Danish police force. This is no doubt due to the leadership of the Freedom Council and the line taken by them in their proclamation of the 22nd September and the 6th October. What we would like to know is whether the political leaders (Buhl and company) approve this line. The protest which they sent in to Best after the dissolution of the police suggests that they do, but we have had no specific information about their attitude since their protest, and should be interested to hear if you are able to find out anything.'[1]

The letter ended with the request that Seidenfaden should provide specific information on the matter if he could.

Again on 7 January 1945 Seidenfaden received an inquiry from Turnbull about one of his articles on Danish-Russian relations in *Fremtiden* (*The Future*).[2] This was a fortnightly paper published by D.P.T. reproducing international information on war and post-war problems.

Apparently Seidenfaden's article had been quoted in a broadcast about Denmark on the Swedish radio, but the quotation was not accurate. A sentence had been inserted: 'As far as the future government of Denmark is concerned Moscow has no desire whatever to influence conditions, it is stressed in authoritative Russian circles.'

Turnbull had been instructed by the British Foreign Office to find out from Seidenfaden if anything concrete had been said about this in Stockholm by an official of the Russian Legation.

Seidenfaden also received at other times requests for

[1] Letter from Turnbull to Seidenfaden, 23 October 1944 (Danish Archives).
[2] Letter from Turnbull to Seidenfaden, 7 January 1945 (*ibid.*).

photographs. He was informed by Ray of the British Legation that the Foreign Office required as many photographs of Danish sabotage operations as possible.[1]

The Danish Press Service had a certain political importance. Its system of distributing news gave a definite propaganda advantage to the Danish section of the B.B.C., primarily because the B.B.C. received the news before any other newspapers or agencies. The B.B.C. was therefore able to broadcast fresh news to Denmark, and was able to put its own point of view across before the news became generally known.

The use made of D.P.T.'s news was very important to the Danish Resistance movement. When news was heard over the B.B.C., it had the intentional effect of encouraging resistance. Swedish radio, in contrast, presented the same news with a neutral flavour. The sources of D.P.T.'s news did not risk their lives gathering information in Denmark, only to have it broadcast over the neutral Swedish radio, which, as far as they were concerned, did not make the best use of their material. The Danish section of the B.B.C. became the mouthpiece for Danish news because it was prepared to give maximum publicity to Danish Resistance activities.

The Germans were aware of this, and made every attempt to get the Swedish authorities to suspend the operations of D.P.T. In official protests they complained that D.P.T.'s news, and particularly the B.B.C. broadcasts in Danish based on D.P.T. news bulletins, contravened Swedish neutrality, and were espionage against Germany's position in Denmark.[2] However, Munck wrote in 1944: 'Right from the start we [D.P.T.] have received the greatest understanding and support from the Swedish authorities.'[3]

In October 1943, the Germans tried to counteract the effect of D.P.T. by giving a correspondent of the Swedish press agency *Tidningarnas Telegram Bureau* (T.T.) permission to work in Copenhagen with more freedom than any other press men had

[1] See p. 166, n. 6.

[2] Report on D.P.T. in Ebbe Munck's papers (Danish Archives). [3] *Ibid.*

previously been given in German-controlled areas. The German plan was clear. They hoped that if they let out a certain amount of news about themselves from Denmark through T.T., then fewer people would go to D.P.T. for Danish news. Swedish T.T. news was most unlikely to be as dangerous for the Germans as D.P.T. news, because it was not intended to support the Danish Resistance movement.[1]

This was a clever German counter-move, which caused a certain amount of alarm amongst Danish Resistance leaders in early 1944. For example, the Swedish radio mentioned Danish sabotage actions in general terms only and never stressed that there was a definite distinction between sabotage actions carried out by Danish patriots and *Schalburgtage*, which was the name given to German-inspired sabotage reprisal actions against innocent parties.

The fact that broadcasts from the B.B.C. had more fighting spirit than the Swedish radio can be illustrated by the different versions of a popular demonstration in Denmark.[2] One Sunday evening, a group of Danes took a gramophone to the top of a high building overlooking Copenhagen's main Town Hall Square, and proceeded to play at full volume 'It's a long way to Tipperary'. The record was accompanied by remarks from the Danes, of a most uncomplimentary nature, about the Germans. This caused a great deal of excitement amongst the Danes who began to gather in the square. It also caused a great deal of embarrassment to the German guards below at Dagmarhus, the Gestapo headquarters in Copenhagen, who began shooting wildly into the air.

Swedish T.T. merely reported that a demonstration, with a certain amount of anti-German feeling, had been held in the Town Hall Square. When D.P.T. received the story, it handed it on with all details, so that the B.B.C. was able to place stronger emphasis on the story in its Danish broadcasts.

The presence of the T.T. correspondent in Copenhagen was a definite threat to D.P.T. as he often managed to get his news to

[1] *Ibid.* [2] *Ibid.*

Sweden before D.P.T. was informed by its own underground sources. He was able to telephone direct to Sweden, and this was a quicker way of transmitting news than by underground methods. The Germans had further made it a condition of allowing the T.T. correspondent to work in Copenhagen that Swedish radio used no bulletins from D.P.T.[1]

For a time therefore there was a dual news service from Denmark.[2] The advantage of the T.T. correspondent, that of being able to telephone news direct to Sweden, broke D.P.T.'s monopoly and skilful timing of the release of Danish news. This was not quite as effective as expected. The press in Stockholm soon realized that although T.T. brought news out quicker, it was not nearly so detailed as D.P.T.'s bulletins. Nothing of real interest or really damaging to the Germans was ever allowed out of Denmark through the T.T. correspondent. For this reason the majority of the European newspapers continued to subscribe to D.P.T. and based most of their Danish news on D.P.T bulletins.

The German scheme began to break down during the first half of 1944. The real weakness of T.T.'s position was shown up by the general strike in Copenhagen in June 1944.[3] The T.T. correspondent sent out a miserably uninformative flow of news, while it was quite obvious that events were taking place in Denmark which were really damaging to the German position. None of this was reflected in the T.T. bulletins, and so almost all newspaper reports about events in Denmark in June 1944, and from then on, were based on D.P.T.'s more informative bulletins.

At this time, during the strike, although Copenhagen was encircled by German troops, *Information* was able to give up-to-date news to D.P.T. several times a day. Never, it appears, was D.P.T. better informed than when the Germans made every

[1] Report on D.P.T. in Ebbe Munck's papers (Danish Archives).

[2] From October 1943 to September 1944.

[3] June 1944 saw the first mass strike in Copenhagen, caused largely by the execution of Danish nationals and the imposition of a curfew. The people of Copenhagen disregarded the curfew, and the crowds filled the streets, erected barricades, waved allied emblems, and sabotaged shops run by collaborators.

attempt to cut its lines of communications with Denmark.[1] The European press in Stockholm realized this, to the disadvantage of the T.T. correspondent.

The German concessions to the Swedish T.T. were withdrawn completely shortly after the German action against the Danish police in September 1944.[2] The T.T. correspondent was placed in exactly the same position as he had been in June. He was unable to report anything which might have damaged the German reputation in Denmark as far as the free world was concerned. He was recalled to Sweden, and after that date D.P.T. remained the one source of Danish news, apart from the little of any interest which the Germans themselves thought fit to release from Denmark.

[1] c.f. *Hemmelig Alliance*, vol. 1, p. 295 ff.

[2] Report on D.P.T. in Ebbe Munck's papers (Danish Archives). On 19 September 1944 the German authorities pounced on the Danish police, and arrested about 2,000 men, most of whom were sent to concentration camps in Germany. About 7,000 escaped arrest and organized an illegal police force which operated under the Freedom Council.

On 20 September 1944 *The Times* stated: 'A broadcast proclamation by the German Police General Pancke accused the Danish Police of actively supporting sabotage and murder and encouraging the "underworld" to organize a general strike.'

CHAPTER 14

CRITICISM OF THE B.B.C.

> The Danish broadcasts from London must really be considered as Denmark's most important newspaper.
>
> Ebbe Munck, November 1944

> The primary purpose of the Danish B.B.C. is to project British views on the war to the Danish people.
>
> Dr J. W. Varley of P.W.E., May 1944

During early 1944 the Danish section of the B.B.C. was severely criticized from Stockholm, particularly by Danish journalists working for D.P.T. Their complaint was basically that the B.B.C. was not making proper use of D.P.T. material. They felt that the Danish section had, perhaps of all the other European sections of the B.B.C., the best and most detailed news service upon which it could base its broadcasts. Yet it did not use enough of the Danish material sent to London, and what was used was sometimes reproduced inaccurately. The main purpose of D.P.T.'s sending out detailed Danish news was that the B.B.C. should broadcast it back to Denmark and thereby give Danish news the widest possible circulation in Denmark itself. This, they complained, the B.B.C. failed to do.

Criticism began to mount in Denmark too. In January 1944 a report entitled 'Comments from Denmark on B.B.C.' reached the Danish section.[1] Karsten Meyer, a leading figure in Danish legal circles, was quoted as saying: 'We only want facts from Danish B.B.C.'

In early 1944 the Danish section created further unrest by reporting a rumour of Gestapo action against the Danish police, several months in fact before any action took place.[2] This was not received well in Denmark and it damaged, to a

[1] 'Comments from Denmark on B.B.C.', 26 January 1944 (Danish Archives).

[2] The action against the police did not in fact take place until September 1944.

certain extent, the reputation for reliability which the B.B.C. had built up. A report from a senior Danish police official which reached the B.B.C. showed that the police were not satisfied with the B.B.C.'s treatment of their position. The police official was quoted as saying:

> The false news from the B.B.C. concerning the arrest of the Danish police did not do much harm. But what annoyed all the senior Danish police officials was the talk [over the B.B.C.] about Leifer describing what he had done. This can only induce the Germans to more severe steps against Danish police officials. Never praise a man, even if he is in safety out of Denmark. The results may be disastrous.[1]

The offending text appears no longer to exist. Clearly what had happened was that Leifer, a senior Danish police official, had escaped to Sweden, where he must have been interviewed. The complaint quoted here suggests that Leifer described his activities supporting Danish Resistance during his time as a police officer. It was a mistake for the B.B.C. to devote a talk to this subject as it might well have led to reprisals against some of his colleagues in Denmark and, consequently, less information and less help for Danish patriots from the Danish police.

Although this kind of mistake was dangerous, it could be forgiven. It was an error of judgement which must to some extent have occurred at various times throughout the war in other European sections of the B.B.C. It was not the occasional inaccuracy like this which caused mounting criticism from both Denmark and Stockholm during early 1944, but the more serious complaint that the B.B.C. was persistently ignoring D.P.T. cables and broadcasting less and less Danish news.

[1] Although the B.B.C. had to be responsible for every word that was broadcast, in this instance the original mistake was D.P.T.'s and not the B.B.C.'s. The news about the Gestapo action against the police was the result of a false D.P.T. message. This damaged the reputation for reliability of D.P.T. for some months, and this was held against D.P.T. by the B.B.C. during the controversy described in this chapter.

The remark in Varley's letter of 19 May 1944, answering criticisms of the B.B.C.—'your memory will not need to be refreshed on instances where our discretion has proved to be wise'—probably refers to this false report.

However, the B.B.C. used the report and therefore were, as far as their listeners were concerned, responsible for it, and this did not improve the B.B.C.'s reputation.

The political implications of the lack of Danish news in the B.B.C. broadcasts to Denmark were stressed in a letter which Erling Foss, a member of Denmark's Freedom Council, wrote on 4 March 1944.[1]

Foss began by stating categorically that the B.B.C. was the most important source of news for the Danes about events in *Denmark itself*. It could therefore help patriot fighters greatly, by encouraging a spirit of resistance. Although in September and October 1943 the Freedom Council had asked the B.B.C. for help in propaganda work and for an increase in news of Danish affairs, this had apparently been without effect.[2] Since then news about events in Denmark had become scarcer and scarcer.

In his letter Foss warned that the B.B.C. now risked losing most of its listeners to the Swedish radio, and he said that Hermansson, the Swedish T.T. correspondent in Copenhagen, sent out much more news of local events in Denmark. His reports went to the Swedish radio. As Danish listeners found out that they could hear more and more of Danish affairs from Sweden, so the B.B.C. was quickly losing its audience.[3] Few people could listen to both the B.B.C. and the Swedish radio, and 'for the sake of the United Nations and fighting Denmark the B.B.C. must improve'.[4]

It was further thought in Denmark that other countries, particularly Norway, France and Germany, were much better

[1] Letter from Erling Foss, 4 March 1944 (Danish Archives). It is not clear whether or not this letter was sent direct to the B.B.C. Probably it was written as a report by Foss, and handed to the British Legation in Stockholm for forwarding to the B.B.C.

[2] See chapter 12.

[3] This probably applied more in Copenhagen than in other parts of Denmark. The feeling that the B.B.C. was rapidly losing listeners in 1944 seems to have centred largely in Copenhagen, where Swedish radio could be heard clearly, and where the B.B.C. suffered more interference from German jamming apparatus. In Jutland for example, the B.B.C. probably lost far fewer listeners than it was thought to have done in Copenhagen. In the country districts the B.B.C. probably remained throughout this period the main source of news.

Erling Foss, although he was at this time in Stockholm, was in fact from Copenhagen, a member of the Freedom Council and therefore in close contact with Copenhagen views. Dissatisfaction with the B.B.C. appears, from the evidence available, to have centred very largely on the capital.

[4] Letter from Erling Foss, 4 March 1944 (Danish Archives).

served by the B.B.C. than Denmark. Many Danes were listening in to the German broadcasts from London rather than the Danish broadcasts, despite their obvious distaste at hearing German spoken.

Foss's letter then had a concrete proposal to make. He asked that Denmark should be warned in advance when the best Danish commentators—he mentioned Christmas Møller and T. M. Terkelsen—were to broadcast. This proposal was followed by personal criticism of the Editor of the Danish section of the B.B.C.

There were four other practical suggestions:

(1) All Danish news received from both D.P.T. and T.T. should be broadcast by the B.B.C., if possible.

(2) More articles from the Danish underground press should be quoted in the B.B.C. broadcasts.

(3) Danish commentaries should follow directives to a much closer degree.

(4) The B.B.C. should not be afraid to repeat news items throughout the day, as people never listened three times a day and seldom twice.

The letter closed with the remark that the Danish section of the B.B.C. was completely missing its target in Denmark and that the Freedom Council definitely needed the help of the B.B.C. in its fight for freedom.

During March Danes in Stockholm carried out a detailed survey of the B.B.C. broadcasts to prove the validity of their arguments.[1] From 1 to 10 March they monitored the 12.15, 18.15 and 21.15 B.B.C. broadcasts in Danish. Their conclusions were these:

Danish news which was desperately important for listeners in Denmark did not interest the Editor of the B.B.C. Danish section. The B.B.C. made little attempt to use D.P.T. telegrams, and to write commentaries round them. The need was for more Danish news, which should be broadcast early in the programme, immediately after news of the war and of political events.

[1] Report on the B.B.C. broadcasts in Danish, March 1944 (*ibid.*).

The short talks, apart from Christmas Møller's and one or two others, were so banal in presentation that they did not receive much attention in Denmark. A frequent mistake was that most of these broadcasts gave the impression that the Danish people might be converted to Nazism at any time. This was indicated by the frequent ideological and theoretical refutations of Nazi doctrines. These broadcasts suggested that the B.B.C. thought that German propaganda was a serious opponent of British propaganda in Denmark.

It was suggested also that the B.B.C. might draw more heavily for subject-matter on the Danish bulletin *Fremtiden*. However, it was conceded that there was a very limited number of Danes in London available to give commentaries, and that this was part of the problem.

The criticism then passed on to the main body of the broadcasts—the war and political material. From the monitoring, it became obvious that one of the B.B.C.'s central news staff worked out a common manuscript for all the different sections.[1] Much of this was considered to be trivial and could, with profit, be cut out of the Danish Service.

The final observation was interesting. The period from 1 to 10 March, when the B.B.C. broadcasts were monitored by Danes in Stockholm, was a time when Finland was making the headlines. They claimed that the B.B.C. had failed to realize that the Danish public, on this subject, should not be treated in the same way as Bulgarian or Arabic listeners.

The general conclusion of this report, which was submitted to the B.B.C.,[2] was that there should be much closer co-operation between Stockholm and London, and that there should be a change in the leadership of the B.B.C. Danish section. As an appendix, various examples of the monitoring transcripts were added. One for 10 March 1944 gave the following information.

B.B.C. broadcasts monitored on that day in Stockholm showed that there was only one item of Danish news announced

[1] Central Desk material was in fact common to all sections.
[2] Again probably through the British Legation in Stockholm.

during the whole day. This was the news that an informer, Fru Delbo, had been killed. On that same day the Danish section of the B.B.C. had before them, from both D.P.T. and Swedish T.T. sources, eight Danish news items. These were reports of:

(1) the attempted assassination of a wounded man in hospital;

(2) a brawl between students and Germans in Tagensvej, Copenhagen;

(3) the arrest by the Gestapo of Erik Eriksen, of the newspaper *Fyns Tidende*;

(4) the complete destruction of a factory in Aalborg as the result of a sabotage attack;

(5) the setting fire to a cinema in Peter Bangsvej, Copenhagen;

(6) the arrest of a police inspector by the Gestapo;

(7) the balance of the National Bank;

(8) the murder of Fru Delbo. This was the one item which was used in the Danish broadcasts on that day.

This was the most serious attack yet made on the Danish section of the B.B.C. Not only had Danes in Stockholm made several complaints, but they also provided evidence from monitoring reports to prove their point. More complaints were to follow before P.W.E. finally took up the challenge on behalf of the Danish section of the B.B.C.

Dr J. W. Varley, deputy director of the Northern Department of P.W.E., wrote to Ronald Turnbull on 19 May 1944 in answer to the criticisms.[1] Turnbull was asked to pass on the contents of this letter to Seidenfaden, Munck and Foss who had led the attack on the B.B.C. from Stockholm.

Varley's letter began in a conciliatory fashion. 'There is', he wrote, 'a willingness to accept genuine criticism, since the aims of the B.B.C. and those in Stockholm are clearly the same, to help fight against the common enemy.' He refused to accept 'that B.B.C.'s credit in Denmark now stands at zero', nor was he prepared to allow Robert Jørgensen and the rest of the Danish

[1] Letter from Varley to Turnbull, 19 May 1944 (Danish Archives).

section to accept the blame for whatever mistakes had been made. He admitted, however, that it was known in London that the B.B.C. had lost some ground in Denmark, particularly with the active Resistance movement, and that as a result the Swedish radio had gained more listeners.

Before answering the specific complaints, Varley said that he thought there were other factors which should be taken into consideration by those in Stockholm. First, that German jamming of the B.B.C. broadcasts in Copenhagen was at that time extremely successful.[1] Secondly, that the Swedish radio had an advantage in having a T.T. correspondent in Copenhagen itself—an advantage which the B.B.C. did not have. Finally, and this he considered most important, Stockholm's dissatisfaction with the B.B.C. sprang primarily from disappointment that large-scale allied operations in Western Europe had not begun.

Probably realizing that these general remarks were not enough to silence the critics of the B.B.C., Varley gave specific answers to the three main points of complaint. These were:

(1) the inadequacy of the time devoted to Danish news;

(2) the inaccuracy or the poor quality of the news given;

(3) inferior presentation.

In answer to the first complaint Varley pointed out that the amount of time that was devoted to Danish news was not entirely for the Editor of the Danish section to decide. 'The primary purpose of the Danish B.B.C. is to project British views on the war to the Danish people, and it is far from easy to hold the balance fairly as between centrally provided material relating to the war at large, and purely domestic Danish issues.'

The second criticism from Stockholm was countered by the remark that 'it was surely aimed at the wrong target for the quality of the news we are able to give is entirely dependent upon the quality of the news we receive'. Then came the statement which has been previously quoted: 'None of us have

[1] This was a doubtful excuse. The Germans continually tried to jam the B.B.C. broadcasts but Danish Resistance actions against German jamming apparatus were also very effective during 1944 (see chapter 1).

forgotten that dreadful period of several months after August 29th last when we were virtually starved of news from Denmark, and it was in that period particularly, that the Swedish radio made headway at our expense.' He continued by saying that London reserved the right to exercise discretion over the news received from D.P.T. 'Your memory will not need to be refreshed on instances where our discretion has proved to be wise.' His argument was that the B.B.C. news service had to be provided with as much news as possible, and it was up to D.P.T. to provide that news. London had to insist on choosing what to include and what to leave out. He then praised the way in which D.P.T. already obtained its news from sources in Denmark.

Foss's and Seidenfaden's suggestion that the B.B.C. should use T.T. bulletins as well as D.P.T.'s was not accepted. The reason for this was that the B.B.C. had no access to Swedish radio except from monitored reports which were not received until the following day: 'It is not our business to advertise the Swedish radio, by continually quoting it as a source of our information.' Further, T.T. news was not regarded in London as completely untainted: 'Presumably the Germans have an interest in what they allow to go out, and the Swedes may likewise have an interest which is not entirely synonymous with our own.' The remedy suggested was that D.P.T. should incorporate in their own bulletins any information from other sources which would be of value to the B.B.C.

Varley admitted that the third criticism of poor presentation was not easy to answer. During this period Robert Jørgensen was away ill, and the translation staff of the section was depleted through illness in March when the B.B.C.'s broadcasts were monitored in Stockholm. No more reasons were given.

The last part of the letter expressed gratitude for what was already being done by D.P.T. in Stockholm. 'In conclusion', wrote Varley to Turnbull, 'I do want them [D.P.T.] to be assured of one thing, that the voice with which we speak to Denmark stands now, as it always has done, firmly behind those who are resisting the Germans on Danish soil and elsewhere.'

The contents of this letter were passed on to D.P.T. by Turnbull. This reply was clearly not satisfactory to D.P.T. and they took the most drastic measures open to them. They cut off the supply of news to London completely.

The following telegram, dated 26 June 1944, was received by Ronald Turnbull and John Ray, both of the British Legation, Stockholm. It was sent by Foss, Munck and Seidenfaden.[1]

Last few days brought momentous events Denmark, and through daring liferisking enterprise exclusive information brought Swedenwards in record time. D.P.T. wired you all details starting Friday and following up. Nevertheless during first 48 hours London Danish transmissions mentioned only Syndicate sabotage,[2] but not martial law, sensational rocket demonstration Dagmarhus, Freedom Council's Day Order, and big terroristic Schalburgtages. This terrible disappointment [for] all of us and more important unencouraging [for] Resistance Movement for whom your approval important. [In] view [of] long history unforthcoming backing ex [from] London broadcasting we [have] decided [to] stop further news Londonwards pending explanation of omission and delays.

The telegram was accompanied by a bitter covering letter to Turnbull asking him to forward the message without delay to London.

As a result of this measure the authorities in London took notice of D.P.T.'s complaints. They had no alternative, for without news from Stockholm, they risked a complete breakdown of the B.B.C. Danish broadcasts.

A reply was not long coming from London. Four days later, on 30 June 1944, Ray wrote to Seidenfaden enclosing the reply from London to the attack from D.P.T. on the 26th.[3] The British Legation had received two telegrams from London.[4]

The first was from the B.B.C. It stated that D.P.T.'s telegram

[1] Telegram, 26 June 1944, to Turnbull and Ray from Foss, Munck and Seidenfaden (Danish Archives).

[2] The 'Syndicate sabotage' referred to the large-scale sabotage attack against *Riffelsyndikatet* carried out on 22 June 1944. For an account of the events in Copenhagen at the end of June, see Hæstrup, *Hemmelig Alliance*, vol 1, ch. 13.

[3] Letter from Ray to Seidenfaden, 30 June 1944 (Danish Archives).

[4] The contents of the telegrams, and also several quotations from them, were conveyed to Seidenfaden in Ray's letter of 30 June 1944.

of 24 June had been delayed in transmission. No further explanation of this was given, but this statement was presumably meant to indicate that because of the delay in transmission, the B.B.C. was unable to use D.P.T.'s news of events in Copenhagen on that day.

The B.B.C. expressed its disapproval of the suspension of the D.P.T. telegram service, 'without warning at this critical time'. 'Nevertheless we admit strong grounds for criticism of the B.B.C. output.' The telegram ended with the promise of immediate reform, and with the request that 'Danpress [D.P.T.] telegrams be resumed immediately'.

The second telegram was a much briefer one from the Foreign Office, and was considerably more direct about the justice of D.P.T.'s actions. It expressed complete agreement with D.P.T.'s views, and stated that the Foreign Office was pressing for 'immediate reform at high level'.

The Foreign Office telegram also requested the British Legation to do all in its power to get D.P.T.'s telegrams to London resumed. 'Rapid news service is vital for operational control which must take precedence over any disagreement in propaganda policy.'

Ray's covering letter remarked that these replies seemed to be satisfactory, especially the one from the Foreign Office which showed how important D.P.T.'s news was for operational purposes.

During July the controversy continued. On 5 July Seidenfaden wrote to the editors of *Information* and 'all those co-operating in the Freedom Movement's News Service', to inform them of the state of affairs regarding the B.B.C.[1]

> The main point is that conditions in London have been marked by a pretty impenetrable bureaucracy. It must be noted in this context that the Danish Council and Christmas Møller have no influence as far as news broadcasts are concerned. It must not be forgotten that B.B.C.'s prime object is to spread British news and propaganda, but

[1] Letter to the editors of *Information* and all those co-operating in the Freedom Movement's News Service, 5 July 1944 (Danish Archives).

interest in stimulating the Home Front and understanding that Danish news creates interest in the broadcasts to Denmark, has been growing.

Quite clearly during the summer of 1944—and lack of more documentary evidence makes a more definite calculation of the time impossible—a great deal of rethinking of Danish broadcasting policy was being done in London. Reports from independent sources reaching the B.B.C. showed that D.P.T.'s criticisms were in fact justified, as far as Danish listeners were concerned. The B.B.C. Intelligence section reported to Robert Jørgensen the results of interviews on 27 July 1944 with six young Danish fishermen.[1] They were quoted as saying:

> If we want a pack of lies we listen to the Danish Radio; if we want to hear the Allies we listen to London, but if we want to hear the truth we listen to Sweden. Of course the English and Americans are interested in putting over their point of view, so that you can't always believe everything they say, but the Swedish are neutral, and therefore are unbiased in their reports, and tell us only the bare truth.

On 16 August from the same source, the Danish section of the B.B.C. was informed that 'the B.B.C. transmissions go through well and the speakers are satisfactory. The main criticism can be summed up as follows: The B.B.C. is out of touch with popular feeling at home. People crave unbiased and reliable news from the outside world and more especially from Denmark itself where all official sources of information are controlled by Germans.'[2] A further intelligence report in the same month, reporting an interview with a Danish fisherman who left Denmark on 4 August, confirmed that there was still a lack of authentic and badly needed Danish news in Denmark. The fisherman had referred to sabotage and had said that 'where he lived in

[1] Extract from the B.B.C. European Intelligence report sent to Robert Jørgensen (undated). The interviews with the fishermen were, however, held on 27 July 1944, so the report was probably compiled at the end of July or beginning of August 1944 (Danish Archives).

[2] Extract from the B.B.C. European Intelligence report dated 16 August 1944 (*ibid.*).

Esbjerg, they never heard any mention of sabotage at all, and when they did, it was via the B.B.C.'.[1]

These intelligence reports confirmed D.P.T.'s criticism. Denmark expected the B.B.C. broadcasts to be an active part of the Danish Resistance movement. Only by broadcasting stories of action in Denmark could the B.B.C. produce the feeling of unity so essential to a national resistance movement forced to work mainly underground. The Esbjerg fisherman's report had shown how vital it was that the whole of Denmark should be told of the actions of its patriots, so that a fighting spirit should be maintained and encouraged throughout the country.

It appeared that during the first half of 1944, the Danish section of the B.B.C. failed to play the part expected of it. To what extent was this true, and why had it happened?

The main criticism from Stockholm was that the B.B.C. did not devote enough time in its broadcasts to Danish news. On certain occasions, notably in June 1944, the lack of information in the broadcasts from London about important events in Denmark was not only discouraging for the Resistance movement, but possibly even harmful. The telegram sent on 26 June by Foss, Munck and Seidenfaden complained that, despite the fact that D.P.T. had sent full reports of events in Denmark to London, the B.B.C. had broadcast only the news of the sabotage attack against the *Riffelsyndikat*. This in fact was only one of the several actions then being undertaken by the Resistance against the Germans. The telegram complained that nothing was broadcast by the B.B.C about German counter-measures, and in particular about *Schalburgtage*. It was understandable from a Danish point of view that there should have been considerable disappointment and anger at what was considered the failure of the B.B.C. at this time. The fight of resistance was in part the battle for the minds of the national population. The greater the success of the Home Front the more likely it was that more Danes would join the active fight. The war in

[1] Extract from the B.B.C. European Intelligence report dated 21 August 1944 (*ibid.*).

Denmark was largely a propaganda war. None were forced to do anything, and many Danes went through the war without taking any positive action against the Germans, although there can be little doubt where their real sympathies lay. So to a great extent the Resistance movement needed a mouthpiece. It was not enough that action should be taken. People had to hear about those actions. Only in this way could the sense of unity and purpose be maintained in the continually difficult conditions. Rightly or wrongly, the Danes in Stockholm felt that it was the duty of the Danish section of the B.B.C. to act as a weapon of resistance, by being its mouthpiece throughout the whole of Denmark. Their fears that Danes would listen to Swedish radio were not unfounded. Danish Resistance leaders did not expect the support from the Swedish radio which they demanded from the B.B.C. If the B.B.C. had lost its audience in Denmark it would have damaged the Resistance movement. The Danish listener to Swedish radio was likely to accept Danish news in the objective and neutral way it was presented. He would not feel himself a part of the events going on around him. If he listened to the B.B.C. it was hoped that he would be stirred, possibly to action.

Foss's letter of complaint of 4 March had stated that it was thought in Stockholm that other European countries were better served than Denmark by the various sections of the B.B.C. European Service. In fact he was correct in this assumption, but he was wrong to blame the Editor of the Danish section for this. There is evidence that Robert Jørgensen was aware very early on in this controversy that the amount of local news used by the Danish Service was restricted. Further he made definite moves to counter this.

In early 1944 Jørgensen sent to his director, N. F. Newsome, a summary of the content of the Danish broadcasts, comparing them with other European broadcasts.[1] An analysis of the broadcasts for the month of December 1943 showed that Danish local news occupied only 11·36 per cent of all broadcasts in the

[1] Minute from Robert Jørgensen to N. F. Newsome, undated (Danish Archives).

Danish Service. Jørgensen further remarked in his report that, as this figure covered Christmas and New Year material, it seemed likely that the normal figure was under 10 per cent. This was borne out by the figures for the first half of the month—9·5 per cent.

He compared this with the percentage of time given by the B.B.C.'s European Service to allied countries for their local news:

the Norwegians received over 20 per cent;
the Dutch received 21 per cent;
the Belgians received 40 per cent.

The Dutch and the Belgians received special time for broadcasting local news.[1] For example *Radio Oranje*, the Free Dutch radio from London, was devoted almost entirely to Dutch internal affairs. In addition to this 'free' broadcasting time, Dutch local news would feature in the regular broadcasts in Dutch from the European Service of the B.B.C. Denmark did not have the privilege of any 'free' time over the B.B.C. The reason for this was that Denmark was not an allied country and could not therefore be on an equal footing with other European countries as far as time for local news was concerned. The Editor of the Danish section had to fight hard for the inclusion of Danish local news in the broadcasts of the Danish section of the B.B.C. For him there was no special time set aside for broadcasting local news as there was for *Radio Oranje* or for *Radiodiffusion Nationale Belge*. There was little doubt that the Central Desk of the B.B.C. was mean in its allocation of only about 10 per cent for local news in the Danish broadcasts, but this was a policy which was in line with that of the Foreign Office.

This analysis showed Foss to be right in one respect, that other European countries were better served than Denmark, but wrong in his conclusions. The Editor of the Danish section definitely could not be blamed for the lack of local news. Varley in his letter of 19 May had written as much in Jørgensen's

[1] The Norwegians did not have any 'free' broadcasting time, but the closest relations were maintained by the B.B.C. Norwegian section with the Norwegians in London, and there was no difficulty in including Norwegian local news in the B.B.C. broadcasts.

defence, when he said that the amount of time that was allotted to Danish news was not entirely for the editor to decide.[1] Clearly the amount of time allocated to various countries for local news differed widely, and the decision appeared to be made at the Central Desk of the B.B.C. During the winter of 1943–4 Denmark was allowed less time for local news than any of the allied European countries, as the figures show. This meant that about 90 per cent of the Danish news broadcasts were based on Central Desk material.

It is possible that this allocation was decided upon in the weeks immediately after 29 August when news of Danish events was very scarce. Varley's letter to Stockholm of 19 May spoke of 'the several months after August 29th last when we were virtually starved of news from Denmark'. The length of time was probably exaggerated as it is now known that the Intelligence service from Stockholm had resumed at least during November.[2] Still it would have been a logical solution for the B.B.C. to maintain a very high percentage of Central Desk material in the Danish broadcasts while there was a scarcity of Danish news. It can only be assumed that if this was the answer, the same allocation continued throughout the first three months of 1944, despite the fact that more and more Danish news was being received in London.

Robert Jørgensen had, however, noted that the Danish broadcasts for December 1943 had contained very little Danish news, and he had informed the Director of European Broadcasts. So this was known at the Central Desk. Perhaps Varley's remark that 'the primary purpose of the Danish B.B.C. is to project British views on the war to the Danish people' signified a definite policy towards Denmark. By saying this Varley denied that the Danish section of the B.B.C. was mainly a weapon of the Resistance movement, because if 90 per cent of the Danish broadcasts were based on Central Desk material, it could hardly be regarded as 'Denmark's most important newspaper'. A national newspaper expects to devote most of its space to

[1] See p. 181, n. 1. [2] See *Hemmelig Alliance*, vol. 1, p. 121.

national affairs. It can only be assumed that Varley realized the implications of what he was writing. In fact he was denying that the prime aim of the Danish Service was to help the Danish Resistance. More important was the projection of the British view of events in Denmark.

It is again an assumption that if Varley meant this, he would not have written it on his own authority, as deputy-director of the Northern Department of P.W.E. If it was a policy decision, it would have been made by P.W.E. in consultation with the Foreign Office, and the policy would have been incorporated in a directive to the B.B.C. Propaganda control over the Danish section of the B.B.C. seems, on the evidence available, to have been fairly strict from the time control first became effective in 1941–2. Jørgensen's reprimand from the Foreign Office for allowing it to be announced that Denmark had become an ally in December 1943 indicates this.[1] It seems probable that the same hesitation which accompanied the slow recognition of the Freedom Council remained in the Foreign Office attitude to Denmark after October 1943. Denmark was still not recognized as an ally. How much Communist influence was there really in the Danish Home Front? Would the Freedom Council make a post-war bid for power? Why had the well-known politicians kept out of the Freedom Council? Were they suspicious, too, of the Council's post-war ambitions? Such might have been the reasoning of the Foreign Office, if it was a definite policy decision which kept the control and content of the Danish Service strictly British. The hesitation of the Foreign Office seems to be reflected here. Throughout the war Denmark was one of the most difficult political problems, because the country was neither at war with Germany nor was it clearly friendly towards the Germans. Here, again, the confused legal and constitutional situation in Denmark had its repercussions. Had there been an allied Danish government in London, propaganda control over the Danish section of the B.B.C. would probably have been less—as it was reputedly over other sections broadcasting to

[1] See chapter 12.

countries with exile governments in London. From the beginning there would also have been 'free' broadcasting time allocated for Danish local news, just as there was for Dutch and Belgian local news.

As far as Robert Jørgensen knew, it was the Central Desk of the B.B.C. which was so spare in its allocation of time for Danish local news. N. F. Newsome, the director of European Broadcasts, was considered partly responsible, at least by Jørgensen and also by Terkelsen.[1]

Later in the year, in October, when the controversy had died down, Terkelsen wrote to Varley who was then in Stockholm. D.P.T. had by then won its battle. More Danish local news was being broadcast over the B.B.C. than ever before. Terkelsen wrote:

> If you listen to the B.B.C. in Danish you will notice that they are now using more Danish material than at almost any time before. The resistance of the Central Desk which was held up as a bogey seems to have been overcome. Whether that is due to the imaginary nature of most bogies, to the fact that Newsome is no longer director of European Broadcasts (therefore can no longer hold his sermons against parochialism), or to the fact that A.B.S.I.E. [American Broadcasting Station in Europe] has become a competitor of growing importance, I cannot say.[2]

Whatever the reason behind it, it was clear that it was Newsome and the Central Desk who were instrumental in cutting down the amount of Danish local news to a minimum, and the Foreign Office which was perhaps ultimately responsible.[3]

[1] Robert Jørgensen expressed this view in an interview.

[2] Letter from Terkelsen to Varley, 5 October 1944 (Danish Archives).

[3] As channels of communication between the Controller of the European Services and the Foreign Office were constantly kept open, frequently by telephone and not by letter, it is difficult to establish exactly what directions the Foreign Office would have given the B.B.C. concerning this matter. Danish local news seems to have become a policy matter, at least from the time the Foreign Office replied to Seidenfaden's, Munck's and Foss's telegram of 26 June, and probably before. It is therefore reasonable to assume that the Foreign Office had some responsibility for the decision to limit, and then to increase, Danish local news in the broadcasts. Although the B.B.C. had complete control of programme content, Danish local news was more a question of policy and therefore it concerned the Foreign Office and the propaganda departments.

The other major criticism from Stockholm was that the news given in B.B.C. broadcasts was often inaccurate, and of poor quality. Again Robert Jørgensen had been largely blamed for this. Varley, in his defence of the B.B.C., countered this with the remark that 'the quality of the news we are able to give is entirely dependent upon the quality of the news we receive'.

Both the B.B.C. and D.P.T. were unable to avoid occasional inaccuracies. D.P.T.'s criticism, however, was that the B.B.C. mishandled certain news material from Stockholm.

This was true of the report concerning the police in early 1944.[1] It was also true of a story the B.B.C. put out in Danish about the supposed flight to Sweden of Helge Bangsted, editor of *Fædrelandet*, the Danish Nazi newspaper. This involved the B.B.C. in a certain amount of ridicule in Denmark.

The story of Bangsted's flight to Sweden was broadcast in the dawn bulletin of 9 October. The part of the broadcast which was later found to be quite untrue was as follows:

> The chief Editor of the paper *Fædrelandet* Helge Bangsted has also gone to Sweden and been placed under arrest by the Swedish police. He crossed the sound in a small boat which ran aground just outside Höganäs. A boat from Höganäs went out to save him. Bangsted's pockets were stuffed with Swedish money and ration cards. Danish circles in Stockholm consider that Bangsted's plan was to sneak into Sweden and work as an informer against the Danes over there. It may also be possible that he had fled because he was afraid of the Danish patriots' revenge.[2]

The German-controlled Danish home service ridiculed the B.B.C. in its 18.35 broadcast on the same day. The following report on this broadcast was sent by the B.B.C. monitoring service to the Danish section.

It was headed '*Fædrelandet* Editor not in Sweden', and read:

> There was an interview with Helge Bangsted editor of *Fædrelandet*. The announcer said that Editor Bangsted was supposed, according to the B.B.C., to be in Sweden. He was however in the studio. Bangsted said that he had spent almost the whole of last night in his editorial

[1] See p. 176, n. 2.

[2] Danish Archives.

office, and had not left the city yesterday. Rumours concerning his departure to Sweden began to reach him this morning, and there had been a steady stream of telephone calls all day long.

Bangsted said that it was strange that the B.B.C. should waste its time on such nonsense. He had no reason to flee, nor did he possess Swedish money and ration cards. He had no creditors whom he wished to avoid. Although he had been on many adventurous journeys in his youth, he hardly thought it was his task today to do anything but stay here in order to carry out his journalistic work. With regard to the task which the Swedish Radio believed he was to carry out in Sweden he thought it was so worthless that he did not wish to make any comment.[1]

The reference to the Swedish radio concerned the problem of the sources of Danish news in London. The report of Bangsted's supposed flight was broadcast by the B.B.C. as a result of a monitored bulletin from the Swedish radio. Leslie Tudor, sub-editor in the Danish section, took full responsibility for broadcasting the Bangsted story. He said that he had made the mistake partly because of his insufficient knowledge of how D.P.T. worked. He thought that as the original news report included the words 'Danish circles in Stockholm', this meant that it had the authority of D.P.T. He felt that D.P.T. had somehow overlooked sending the story in one of its own news bulletins, and he had therefore decided to broadcast it.

D.P.T.'s general policy on news material which was not their own was that the B.B.C. should use it if it was needed, but that it should be carefully checked. Foss in his letter of 4 March stated quite definitely that the B.B.C. should use Swedish T.T. reports in addition to D.P.T. bulletins. Foss's one aim was that the Danish section of the B.B.C. should use as much Danish material as possible, preferably all D.P.T.'s bulletins, and any other reports such as those from T.T. or from the Swedish radio, provided they were used carefully.

Varley had flatly disagreed with this view in his reply on 19 May. He said that the B.B.C. could not use T.T. reports because they had no access to Swedish radio in London except

[1] Danish Archives.

from monitoring reports which were not received until the following day. He felt that the B.B.C. should not advertise the Swedish radio by quoting it as a source of information, and said that T.T. news was regarded in London as not untainted. His view was that D.P.T. should be the one source of information, and that they should make very sure that their service was as comprehensive and accurate as possible.

Robert Jørgensen had definite views himself on the question of whether or not to use material other than D.P.T.'s. It was not known by Foss, who blamed the editor for these troubles, that Jørgensen himself was very much in favour of using other sources of information, in addition to D.P.T. bulletins. Jørgensen complained to Varley about the rule of 'D.P.T. news only' laid down by P.W.E., and he was able to quote an instance when it was very important for the B.B.C. that they were able to draw on reports from Sweden other than those from D.P.T., which could itself make mistakes.

This occurred in October 1944 when Erik Seidenfaden wrote to Varley warning him that the B.B.C. had to be very careful in using material which was not received from D.P.T.[1] Seidenfaden did not say that the B.B.C. should not use other material but warned the Danish section to exercise caution when it did. Seidenfaden quoted a broadcast by the B.B.C. on 6 October 1944 which said that the Swedish T.T. correspondent in Copenhagen, Hermansson, had been expelled from Denmark. This, according to Seidenfaden, was incorrect.

Varley took up the matter with Robert Jørgensen, who denied that the B.B.C. had ever reported the expulsion of Hermansson. In his reply to Varley, Jørgensen quoted the text of the broadcast:[2]

Commenting on what *Västmanlands Läns Tidning* terms the lack of Danish news over the Swedish Radio since the last crisis in Denmark, the paper writes: 'The reason is that some time ago the Germans

[1] Letter from Seidenfaden to Varley, 7 October 1944 (*ibid.*).

[2] A report on Robert Jørgensen's discussions with Varley is in the Danish Archives (October 1944).

informed T.T. that its Copenhagen correspondent Hermansson would be refused a permit if illegal news material was quoted by the Swedish Radio.[1]

Jørgensen pointed out that what the B.B.C. said at the time was subsequently proved to be correct, and was in fact confirmed by D.P.T. some ten days later.

He then went on to disagree strongly with Varley's suggestions that the B.B.C. should only use news sent by D.P.T., and should ignore reports from other sources. He was able to quote an example when additional information from Stockholm led to the B.B.C. broadcasting an accurate bulletin. In this case, had the B.B.C. relied solely upon D.P.T., the result would have been inaccuracy.

His example was the action taken by the departmental chiefs in Copenhagen in protest against the dissolution of the Danish police. In this case Jørgensen used the B.B.C.'s Stockholm correspondent's version and this later proved to be correct.

What happened was this. A telegram from D.P.T. arrived at 20.30 saying that the departmental chiefs had resigned. At 20.45 the Danish section received the B.B.C.'s Stockholm correspondent's report which said that it was the Council of the Departmental Chiefs that had resigned. When these two different stories had been received Jørgensen decided to run his own story in the 21.15 broadcast on the lines that the Council of the Departmental Chiefs had dissolved. Later the Danish section of the B.B.C. received a correction from D.P.T. of their first story to the effect that the departmental chiefs were functioning after all. So at 23.30 the Danish section of the B.B.C. gave confirmation of the correct version, and credited D.P.T. with this.

Jørgensen finished his report to Varley with the words: 'Therefore the very fact that we had news from another source enabled us to give a correct version of the story, thus saving ourselves and D.P.T. from disseminating incorrect news.'[2]

The dissension during 1944 about inaccurate news was not

[1] Danish Archives.

[2] Report on the discussions between Robert Jørgensen and Varley, October 1944 (*ibid.*).

of major importance, because mistakes were not made too frequently. Maximum accuracy was, however, necessary, and it was understandable that the B.B.C., D.P.T., and P.W.E. were all concerned about it. As the B.B.C. had built up its reputation on accurate reporting, it was important that this accuracy should be maintained, particularly during 1944 when the Swedish radio was reputedly making ground in Denmark at the expense of the B.B.C. The examples quoted show that neither the B.B.C. nor D.P.T. deserved to bear the full blame for inaccuracies. The complaints themselves were not always fair, and any mistakes that were made were the occupational hazards of wartime news reporting. Both the B.B.C. and D.P.T. were responsible for mistakes at various times. Despite the fact that T.T. news and other reports from Stockholm were used by the B.B.C., D.P.T. remained the chief source of supply for Danish news. Without this supply from D.P.T. the Danish section of the B.B.C. would not have been able to maintain its broadcasts to Denmark, and Sweden would have captured the ear of Danish listeners. Jørgensen, Varley and the Foreign Office were fully aware of this.

The criticisms of the B.B.C. during 1944 were not without effect. The discussions, raised as a result of complaints from Stockholm, ironed out several problems.

Perhaps the greatest change was in the amount of Danish local news broadcast by the B.B.C. at the end of 1944. Robert Jørgensen submitted a report on 3 November 1944 on the Danish section's average weekly output.[1] This showed that Danish output was as before based mainly on Central Desk news. This is not surprising and would have applied to all the broadcasts to other European countries. The report showed, however, that there had been a significant rise in the output of Danish local news. The figures for the week's output were quoted as:

1. Central Desk material, including news and inscripts	3,354 lines
2. Danish news	990 lines
3. Talks, commentaries	556 lines
4. Code messages	150 lines

[1] Danish Average Weekly Output, report by Robert Jørgensen, 3 November 1944 (*ibid.*).

Danish news during the week consisted of just over 20 per cent of the section's total output (excluding the code messages). The amount of Danish news had doubled since the beginning of 1944, when the corresponding figure given by Jørgensen was approximately 10 per cent.

The effects were soon noticed in Denmark too. The answers to a questionnaire circulated in Denmark in October and November 1944 showed that the B.B.C. had regained some lost ground.[1] The answers showed that it was news in all forms, both of Danish and general affairs, which was demanded most. This demand was apparently satisfied more and more. The B.B.C. was reported as more popular than A.B.S.I.E. because it was considered to be doing a better job in satisfying the desire for news. People who replied to the questionnaire were quoted as saying: 'The B.B.C. is better liked because it seems to have better information on conditions in Denmark and gives clearer and more concise news'; 'I prefer the London broadcasts because they bring the best reviews about the progress of the war and they also bring news of conditions in Denmark'; 'The English broadcasts are better informed about Danish conditions.'

Erik Seidenfaden, one of the B.B.C.'s fiercest critics in mid 1944, showed that he was more satisfied in November when he delivered a lecture in Stockholm on the work of D.P.T.[2] He described the connection between D.P.T. and the B.B.C. and then showed how the problem of proportioning Danish local news in the B.B.C. broadcasts had been solved.

> D.P.T. sends the greater part of the messages it receives to B.B.C.'s Danish section, which also receives Danish local news of less importance. This is not really of interest to Swedish and other correspondents, but is of great interest at home. Through the last five or six months Danish news in these B.B.C. broadcasts has taken up a greater place than corresponding local stuff in the other foreign language broadcasts from London.

[1] Report based on the answers to 32 questionnaires which had been completed by listeners in Denmark in October–November 1944 (Danish Archives).

[2] Lecture by Seidenfaden, 8 November 1944, in Stockholm (*ibid.*).

The end of October 1944 brought the very skilful attack by the R.A.F. against the Gestapo headquarters at Aarhus.[1] The propaganda made over the B.B.C. about this attack showed that co-operation between D.P.T. and the B.B.C. had been completely restored.

The B.B.C. produced two first-class broadcasts about this attack by Ole Kiilerich and T. M. Terkelsen. The first news of the attack was announced by the B.B.C. Danish Service on the same day. Kiilerich then followed this with a talk entitled 'R.A.F. Help Danish Patriots', in which he said:

In Denmark the greatest admiration and enthusiasm is felt about the R.A.F.'s brilliant precision attack on the Gestapo headquarters in Jutland.

It was a tactical operation carried out by Mosquitoes from Great Britain's tactical Air Force. That is to say it was a military operation carried out in intimate connection with the land forces, and the land forces in this case mean the voluntary but nameless soldiers of the Danish Resistance movement.

If England did not value the contribution to the Allied offensive against the German war machine made by the Danish Resistance movement, she would not have risked 62 of her best airmen and 37 planes in one single operation against two German-occupied buildings in Aarhus—so far away from the main front where Montgomery is in the midst of a great offensive, and has plenty of use for tactical air support. The Danish contribution on land was regarded as being worth an expedition to Aarhus.[2]

Four days later Terkelsen followed this up with a talk entitled 'After Aarhus':

The official report heard by B.B.C.'s Danish listeners a few hours after the Gestapo's headquarters in Aarhus had been wiped out by British Mosquitoes stated, among other things, that the attack was made to support the Danish Resistance movement in its admirable struggle. There is reason to believe that the Gestapo's archives were

[1] On 31 October 1944 Mosquitoes of the R.A.F. Second Tactical Air Force attacked the Gestapo headquarters housed in the University of Aarhus, Jutland. The Gestapo chief and an estimated 200 of his agents were killed, and files containing thousands of names of Danes wanted by the Gestapo were destroyed.

[2] Talk by Ole Kiilerich called 'R.A.F. Help Danish Patriots' on 2 November 1944 (B.B.C. Archives).

completely destroyed. It is also regarded as probable that a number of the highest Gestapo officials in Jutland have perished, as the Gestapo concentrated its élite personnel in Aarhus in order to combat the increasing railway sabotage.[1]

Both Kiilerich and Terkelsen stressed the important co-operation between Britain and the Home Front. The B.B.C. played its part in relaying the news back to Denmark as quickly as possible, in a way which could not have earned anything but praise and satisfaction from D.P.T., as it was from them that the news material was so quickly sent to London.

On 7 November Terkelsen wrote to Varley, who was then in Stockholm, referring to the R.A.F. attack on Aarhus.[2]

You will probably have realized that in this case, thanks to the whole-hearted co-operation of all who took an active interest in the bombing of this particular target, we have been able to make what I consider first class political warfare. The Danish Service carried the story on the day of the attack, i.e. 18 hours before it appeared on the Home Service, and at least five minutes before the Germans were able to put out their garbled version on Kalundborg.

This was a very different situation to that of March when Foss had written his original letter of complaint about the B.B.C. The views of Newsome, of P.W.E. and the Foreign Office had altered, and Danish local news was allowed to occupy from November 1944 much the same percentage of time as did local news in the other B.B.C. foreign broadcasts. It is likely that it was only the complete stoppage of D.P.T. telegrams to London in June 1944 which made the Foreign Office and P.W.E. alter their views on the broadcasting of Danish news to Denmark. The original decision to limit Danish local news, and its reversal, cannot have been the B.B.C.'s alone for two main reasons.

First, Foreign Office influence through P.W.E. and P.I.D. over broadcasts to Denmark had been fairly strict from the end of 1941 onwards, as has been shown. It is therefore unlikely that

[1] Talk by T. M. Terkelsen called 'After Aarhus', 6 November 1944 (B.B.C. Archives).

[2] Letter from Terkelsen to Varley, 7 November 1944 (Danish Archives).

a decision about limiting Danish local news, which was a matter of policy, could have been taken without reference to the Foreign Office and P.W.E.

Secondly, it was Varley of P.W.E., and not the B.B.C., who answered the complaints from Stockholm. The criticism in Foss's letter of 4 March was directed at the B.B.C., and not at P.W.E. Had the decision to limit Danish local news been made by the B.B.C. alone, the obvious person to answer the criticism would have been either the Controller of the European Services of the B.B.C. or the Director of European Broadcasts. As it was, the complaint was passed on to P.W.E. for Varley to answer. This indicates that criticism from Stockholm raised a problem of policy which was not handled by the B.B.C. alone but also by its propaganda advisers.

CHAPTER 15

THE B.B.C. AND MILITARY OPERATIONS

Action signals will be given via the B.B.C.
S.H.A.E.F. operational order sent by S.O.E. to Denmark in June 1944

The Foreign Office telegram which was sent to Stockholm at the time of the discontinuance of D.P.T. telegrams to London had stressed the importance of the intelligence and news service for planning operations in Denmark. The Foreign Office had urged D.P.T. to resume its service because it was 'vital for operational control'.[1]

During 1943 and 1944 S.O.E.'s operations in Denmark reached a peak. The bombing of Burmeister and Wain in January 1943[2] had served its purpose, for after this attack there was no need for more bombing of industrial targets. The Danish Home Front and S.O.E. increased the number of their sabotage attacks. The number of actions in the first three years of the war was 151, and from January 1943 until May 1945 the number greatly increased to 2,523 attacks.[3] In addition to these industrial actions, Danish patriots carried out extensive sabotage on railways and communications within Denmark. The number of these attacks for the years 1942–5 was 6, 175, 328 and 1,301 respectively.[4]

The reply to the criticism of the B.B.C. from Stockholm had shown that the British were initially unwilling for the B.B.C. to be used for propaganda purposes by the leaders of the Danish Resistance. P.W.E. had stated that the B.B.C. was primarily to project British views in Denmark, and it followed from this that the B.B.C. was not to be used purely for Danish Resistance pro-

[1] See chapter 14.
[2] 27 January 1943.
[3] Figures given in Hæstrup, *Panorama Denmark*.
[4] *Ibid.*

paganda. This attitude was effectively overcome by the attack from D.P.T., and as a result the B.B.C. began to devote more broadcasting time to Danish affairs.

In military matters there was no similar problem of how the B.B.C. was to be used, as there was no difference in outlook between the leaders of the Resistance and the British authorities. The British had no doubts about using the B.B.C. for military operations, because they were planned and carried out by S.O.E., and were approved by the allied military authorities. Had the Danish Home Front wanted to use the B.B.C. for communicating orders to their own military groups, the same divergence of interests and problems of control as had occurred in propaganda matters would undoubtedly have appeared in the military sphere. The British authorities were naturally cautious about allowing the B.B.C. to be used solely for the benefit of a foreign organization, just as they were about interfering in purely Danish domestic issues. Control had to remain firmly British. Apart from one or two incidents, the interests of the British and the leaders of the Danish Resistance were one and the same.

The B.B.C. was therefore used to its full capacity as a means of communication in military matters between Britain and the Danish Resistance. By 1944 the B.B.C. had become an important tactical arm of both S.O.E. and S.H.A.E.F. The use made of the B.B.C. in the communication of signals, codes and orders was of great importance to the Resistance.

The underground army in Denmark rapidly increased from the autumn of 1943 onwards, and by Christmas 1944 it was estimated at 25,000 men.[1] During the spring of 1944 armed groups were built up all over Denmark. The problem was who was to command this underground army, and this led to many difficulties and suspicions amongst Danish Resistance leaders of different political views, even to the withholding of arms from certain groups which badly needed them.[2] The K-committee

[1] Number given in *Panorama Denmark*.

[2] See Hæstrup, *Hemmelig Alliance*, vol. II, ch. 17.

under the Freedom Council eventually became responsible for these groups, but not until the Freedom Council in its attempt to maintain both military and political control over the Danish Resistance had found once again its lack of a formal position a serious handicap. Britain was vitally interested in the leadership of the Danish underground army. Co-ordination between the leadership of the Danish underground army and S.H.A.E.F. was very necessary before the invasion of the Continent.

Before D-day and even afterwards no one could guess which way the tide would turn in the battle for Europe. It was quite possible that at some stage of the war the battle would turn northwards beyond Hamburg into Denmark and perhaps Norway. Therefore co-ordination between the underground armies and S.H.A.E.F. became an immediate military necessity.

At one stage the Allies thought that they would be able to control the Danish underground army direct through S.O.E.'s chief representative in Denmark, Flemming Muus, who had returned to Denmark in mid December 1943.[1] This short-sighted view neglected two main factors. First, that the Freedom Council was not prepared to allow military control to pass from it at this critical time. Secondly, that Muus's personal position made it unlikely that he would be accepted as general commander of the Danish Home Front. In fact he himself was wise enough to recommend that military orders from S.O.E. should pass through the Freedom Council. This was in fact what happened. Denmark was divided into seven regions for military purposes and in each of these regions armed groups were built up.[2]

Agreement with S.H.A.E.F. came after Hollingworth of S.O.E. visited Stockholm in April 1944 to discuss plans with the Freedom Council.[3] The plans had been discussed in detail in February with Colonels Gyth and Hvalkof, the Danish army

[1] See *Hemmelig Alliance*, vol. 1, ch. 6, pp. 145–6.

[2] There were six regions at first. Then Bornholm was added to make the seventh in autumn 1944.

[3] These discussions and their result are described in *Hemmelig Alliance*, vol. 1, ch. 7.

representatives in London. Finally, after many disagreements, a decision was reached. It was settled that the Freedom Council would retain direct control of the armed groups until such time as they would operate together with an allied invasion force. If the Allies marched into Denmark it was agreed that the command would then pass to S.H.A.E.F.

After a great deal of discussion which had shown chiefly how jealously guarded was the leadership of the Danish Resistance by the Freedom Council, a compromise plan had been accepted. It was clear that some degree of co-ordination was necessary but also that the command of the Danish underground army was to be kept in Danish hands until the last possible moment.

In fact formal control of the Danish Resistance groups never passed to S.H.A.E.F., as the allied armies never undertook any military action in Denmark against the enemy. By the time Field Marshal Montgomery crossed the border into Denmark the Germans had already surrendered at Lüneburg Heath on 4 May.

S.H.A.E.F. had originally hoped to have direct control over the resistance groups, particularly as D-day drew nearer. In S.H.A.E.F.'s plan the B.B.C. had a definite part to play, even though it was never called upon to play quite the role that was intended.

The aim of S.O.E. and S.H.A.E.F. was that each of the seven regions should be independent and that the groups should be organized in such a way that they could go into action independently, on receipt of instructions from the B.B.C.[1] S.H.A.E.F. was insistent that decentralization was vital. A telegram to Muus in May 1944 showed this:[2]

> Experience has shown centralization at action stages is dangerous and has already caused disasters in other countries. Therefore Supreme Allied Commander will not support any movement depending on centralized control in field and insists passing warning and action signals direct to regions concerned. This method gives speed with security.

[1] *Ibid.* p. 165.

[2] *Ibid.* p. 168.

The plan was that all orders from S.H.A.E.F. would be given direct over the B.B.C. to the individual groups, while S.O.E.'s direct radio service with London would be used by S.H.A.E.F. to maintain contact with the Freedom Council.[1]

An operational order sent from S.H.A.E.F. through S.O.E. to Denmark dated 14 June 1944 showed in detail how important a part the B.B.C. played in military strategy.[2] The B.B.C. was the one means of contacting underground fighting groups, not only in Denmark, but in the rest of Europe where these armies existed.

S.H.A.E.F.'s instructions were as follows:

Information

Danish Resistance is now fully co-ordinated. The whole of Denmark is divided into regions with each region possessing its own commander and staff. This co-ordinated Resistance movement will be known as the Chair Organization. The Chair Organization will prepare and plan:

(1) to carry out harassing and delaying tactics against enemy troop movements to and from Denmark.

(2) to assist in any operation carried out by S.H.A.E.F. on Danish soil.

(3) to take action in such diversionary operations as S.H.A.E.F. may consider necessary.

(4) in the event of the enemy withdrawing from Denmark before the arrival of Allied forces the Chair Organization will make every effort to prevent the destruction by the enemy of public utility services and other vital installations.

Method

The Chair groups will only be called into action for military reasons and the signal for such action will be given from London over the B.B.C. as set out in Appendix 3.

Appendix 3

Action signals will be given via the B.B.C. It is also important to inform all group leaders that either code names or code numbers may be used on the B.B.C.

[1] *Hemmelig Alliance*, vol. 1, ch. 7, p. 172.

[2] Operational order from S.H.A.E.F., sent by S.O.E. to Denmark, dated 14 June 1944, and called 'Operation Order No. 1' (Danish Archives).

Code signals transmitted over the B.B.C. will cover the following:

'Stand by'
'Utmost damage'
'Limited damage'
'Protect'

Each action signal, and each type of target to be attacked, will have a code name or a code number. These code names or code numbers and their meaning will be sent direct to the Regional Commanders. They will vary according to regions.

'Stand by' means 'make all preparations but await further signal before taking action'.

'Utmost damage' means 'attack target, if possible in such a manner that the damage will be difficult or impossible to repair'.

'Limited damage' means 'attack target in such a manner that the damage could, if necessary, be repaired within a few days'.

'Protect' means 'take counter sabotage measures'.

Regional leaders were then given general guidance about the type of targets to aim at but were told to plan their own tactical movements and choose their own particular targets. The signal for the actual attacks was still to be given by the B.B.C. Regional commanders had, therefore, independence in the choice of target, but not of timing.

The targets listed by S.H.A.E.F. were:

(1) Railways. Attacks were to be directed not only against railway lines, but also stations and locomotives. The most common operation was to destroy a line in the path of an on-coming train, to cause derailment.

(2) Telecommunications in general, and in particular the Danish and German telegraph systems.

(3) Harbours and port installations.

(4) Electrical supply systems.

The action signals in code were then given. Each region was given different signals.

For Region I they were as follows:

Stand by—lykønsker (congratulate).

Take Action

(*a*) Utmost damage—*sender en hilsen til* (to send greetings to)

(*b*) Limited damage—*har inviteret* (has invited)
(*c*) Protect—*er paa skovtur* (is on a picnic)

Railways—maleren (the painter)

Telegraph and telephone—vognmanden (the lorry driver)

Electric system—bryggeren (the brewer)

Harbours—ministeren (the minister)

German telecommunications—advokaten (the barrister)

The code words used over the B.B.C., *Fotografen sender en hilsen til ministeren* (the photographer greets the minister) meant 'take action (utmost damage) against harbours in Region I'. *Fotografen* was a word taken at random which meant nothing, and only served to complete the sentence. To facilitate this kind of action printed instructions on, for example, 'How to Derail a Locomotive' were infiltrated from Britain to the various groups.

By June 1944 the B.B.C.'s integration into military operations in Denmark was elaborate if theoretical.

Since 1941–2 the B.B.C. had been used by S.O.E. for more simple but no less important operations—the parachuting of arms and men to Danish reception committees. Instructions to the Resistance were issued through the personal messages and special messages, which were usually broadcast at the end of the news in the B.B.C.'s Danish transmissions.

The first personal messages sent by the Danish section of the B.B.C. were transmitted on 22 December 1941.[1] They began with Christmas and New Year greetings from Danish sailors, fishermen and volunteers in the British forces to their homes in Denmark. In 1942 the B.B.C. sent out an increased number of personal messages in Danish throughout the whole year. These were genuine messages.

In early 1942 the French section of S.O.E. hit upon the idea of giving instructions through the B.B.C. French Service to their men in the field, that men or arms were to be dropped, or that

[1] *De Hører B.B.C.*, p. 28.

certain actions were to be undertaken at a prearranged time and place. Colonel Buckmaster, head of the French section of S.O.E., wrote:[1]

> These messages [to the field] were sent as most people know through the *messages personnels* after the news. They were, of course, not code messages in the usual sense, for they conveyed only that a previous instruction was to be acted upon, not the text of the orders themselves. The Germans did not know this, at least until much later, and employed a large staff trying to decode messages which, in fact, were not in code at all; a somewhat arduous and definitely frustrating endeavour.

The B.B.C. Danish section developed the same technique of communicating with the Resistance in Denmark. At first the announcement of an operation in Denmark was made by using different variations in the closing words of the 18.15 broadcast to Denmark. For example: *Vi kommer igen klokken 21.15* or *Lyt igen klokken 21.15* or simply *Paa gensyn* would all mean something to groups in Denmark who had already been briefed about the meaning of the various phrases. For example: *Lyt igen klokken 21.15* might be the signal that a plane would drop arms that night at a prearranged place and time. Or again it might have indicated that the planned operation was cancelled because the weather was bad.

However, with the rising number of arms-dropping operations, the variations of this system became quite inadequate. Flemming Muus, while he was in London, went to the B.B.C. for discussions about the special messages, and it was then proposed to try a new system. From then on it was decided to give each operation a name. To announce a specific operation only meant mentioning that one name, usually among several dummies. For those who were responsible for receptions in Denmark that one name meant that arms or a parachutist were to be dropped on a certain date, at a certain place and time. The meaning of the message was previously transmitted by direct radio link with the Resistance in Denmark. All that the

[1] In his book, *They Fought Alone*.

reception group had to do, after it received its instructions from S.O.E. by radio transmitter, was to listen at 18.15 to the B.B.C. each evening for its special code word.

After discussions with the B.B.C. about this Muus left England to return to Denmark. His arrival was announced over the B.B.C. by the old method, however. The B.B.C. signal *Paa genhør* ('you will be hearing from us') was a variation of the normal closing words of the Danish service, and in this case it signified that 'Jørgen arrives tonight at 21.00'.[1]

Shortly afterwards the new plan was adopted and instructions to the Resistance began to be added to the regular personal messages to Denmark from Danes in Britain. The last special message broadcast to the Danish Resistance on 4 May 1945 has been preserved, and will serve as an example:[2] it was: *Hilsen til Kennedy Oliver Morits Rikke Sebastian Peggy Larry Elgin Gertrude Duncan Dagmar Arnold Bruce Fatima Sally Tristan Pam Samuel Elly Dora Signe Edmund og Axel.*

Twenty-three names were mentioned, but only a few meant anything at all.[3] Those which meant something would indicate that arms would be dropped that night, according to a prearranged plan, and that the reception group should be there to receive them. Arms dropped by canister were received by a group, so that they could be hidden quickly and distributed as soon as possible.

The B.B.C. personal and special messages were used for other purposes too, for example as a receipt for money paid to the Resistance. Muus thought that the whole idea of using personal names arose from a man in Denmark lending the Resistance 10,000 kroner.[4] He wanted the money credited in London and returned after the war, and for a receipt he asked the Danish section of the B.B.C. to give a birthday greeting to his wife. The greeting was transmitted, and the man accepted it as his re-

[1] See Flemming Muus's book, *The Spark and the Flame*, ch. 16.

[2] B.B.C. Archives.

[3] It is difficult to estimate how many names in the B.B.C.'s special messages were dummies and how many meant that parachuting of arms would in fact take place. In 1943 probably only one name in 24 meant action. Certainly by 1944–5, when arms-dropping was rapidly increasing, the proportion was much higher.

[4] See *The Spark and the Flame*, ch. 16.

ceipt. The French section of S.O.E. also used the B.B.C. to guarantee repayment of loans. Buckmaster's agents sometimes needed the help of the B.B.C. in establishing their identity, when, for example, they approached factory owners about sabotaging machinery being used by the Germans in their factories. If the factory owner doubted the identity of the agent, he would be asked to request a personal message over the B.B.C. in French. If that message came two or three days later then the agent was *bona fide* and, in at least one instance, was allowed to proceed to sabotage a factory under the owner's very nose.[1]

In December 1943 *The Times*, in an article headed 'Economic Warfare by Broadcasting—Guiding Sabotage Abroad', described how sabotage operations in German-occupied countries had become an 'organized campaign'. The article read:

Since the early days of the war close contact [with resistance groups] has been maintained by the B.B.C. and the Ministry of Economic Warfare, which promptly realized the potentialities of broadcasting in connection with the economic side of the struggle. The Foreign Services of the B.B.C., combined with other means of communicating with the oppressed peoples of Europe, have done much to encourage and guide sabotage. By this method the enemy has been hindered from utilizing the resources of the occupied countries, and a weapon of no little importance has been added to the blockade. The sabotage of enemy transport has developed into an organized campaign which has been synchronized to a useful extent with the bombing of locomotives—not only those in operation but also those under construction or repair. Traffic on inland waterways in France, Belgium and Holland has been interrupted by the jamming of lock gates for long periods and by interference with bridges so that they cannot be swung or lifted when barges or other craft want to pass through. On highways and viaducts frequent mining and demolitions have forced the Germans to station guards at important points in many areas of Europe. Unaccountable numbers of collisions have taken place and ships in Norwegian and Danish ports have been damaged.

Two weeks before this report reached *The Times*, news had come through of extensive rail sabotage in Denmark. There had

[1] See *They Fought Alone*.

been sabotage 'apparently committed by well-trained experts, on both the main lines running northward from Germany through South Jutland'.[1]

Reports of similar attacks on railways in Denmark were received in increasing numbers in London during 1943 and 1944. Between 1943 and 1945 there were 1,804 attacks against railways alone.[2] These attacks against the railways were aimed at stopping the flow of German troops through Denmark. The main route for troop trains was southwards from Norway through Jutland and into North Germany.

The B.B.C. played a major role in encouraging sabotage against German troop movements. The campaign was heightened after D-day and especially in the remaining months of 1944, when it was vital to prevent the successful and quick withdrawal of German troops from Norway to take part in the battle for France. The very successful and numerous attacks made by Danish patriots against the railways were without doubt the most important single contribution of the Danish Resistance to the defeat of the Germans. This was a tactical campaign aimed at a specific military target—prevention of German troop movements. The B.B.C.'s part in this campaign was, first, to give all possible encouragement to Danish patriots and, secondly, to tell them that their work was of the utmost strategic importance to the Allies.

The campaign began in earnest on the day of the invasion of France, when the B.B.C. broadcast in Danish General Eisenhower's message to the underground armies of Western Europe in which he asked them to be ready for action, and to wait for further instructions.[3] This was followed by the order to the 'Chair Organization' previously quoted, 'to carry out harassing and delaying tactics against enemy troop movements to and from Denmark'. Communications became the main objective of Danish saboteurs, and throughout the autumn of 1944 the B.B.C. broadcast regular messages of encouragement. The B.B.C.

[1] *The Times*, 13 December 1943.
[2] Figures quoted in *Panorama Denmark*.
[3] B.B.C. broadcast, 6 June 1944.

was once again playing one of its most effective roles, as a support for military operations, and as the best means of contacting Europe's invisible armies.

In a broadcast during September Ole Kiilerich warned that

> the Germans have to prepare themselves for a guerilla war on their own soil and in the countries which they are still occupying, but which they never succeeded in suppressing. Denmark may perhaps be the country which they will not leave until the very last moment, and our country is providing the most outstanding proof that the Germans were at no time capable of suppressing the occupied countries.[1]

During September too the B.B.C.'s naval correspondent again impressed on listeners the strategic importance of Denmark as the main route for German troops returning from Norway and eventually Finland.

He also warned Denmark of another possibility. 'It is important', he said, 'that from an Allied strategic point of view the Danes do everything possible to prevent the Germans from using Jutland as a pierhead stretching out from their mainland, where they may harbour hopes of securing their retreat northwards.'[2] There was every possibility, at this stage, of the battle being carried into Danish territory.

In October the B.B.C. announced to the whole of Denmark that the Germans were now placing hostages in German troop trains:[3] 'The Danish Radio last night [7 October 1944] broadcast an announcement from the German authorities that in future arrested Danish saboteurs will be carried in all German troop trains in Denmark. This step, the announcement says, is because of the repeated derailing of such trains by explosions with consequent deaths among the German soldiers.'

This German step did not deter the campaign. Ole Kiilerich, speaking over the B.B.C. on 2 November, discussed the R.A.F.

[1] Talk by Ole Kiilerich, 5 September 1944 (B.B.C. Archives).

[2] The exact date of this broadcast is unknown. It is quoted in part in Jørgensen, *London Kalder*, p. 193.

The naval correspondent was Brian Tunstall.

[3] Announced 8 October 1944 (B.B.C. Archives).

attack on Aarhus, and then made a further direct appeal for sabotage.[1]

The traffic system is the most vulnerable German point now when the Allies press forward in the direction of the base of the Jutland Peninsula, and the liberation of Norway has begun from the North. The Danish patriots must now, with the same precision that we admired in the R.A.F., show their British pilot friends that they wholly understand how to utilize the support which the British flyers so willingly and so incredibly skilfully afforded the Danish Home Front last Tuesday.[2]

T. M. Terkelsen, on 27 November, gave a talk over the B.B.C. entitled 'Transport Sabotage':[3]

It is no longer a rare occurrence to see German divisions on their way from Norway to the front delayed for four or five days, or supplies for the sorely tried German troops in Norway seriously delayed on their way through Denmark, if they get through at all. The Danish patriots now do a share similar to that of the French freedom fighters in June and July, with the difference that the Danish saboteurs do their work alone, while the French Maquis were strongly supported by Allied tactical bombers.

On 5 March 1945 the following communiqué, an appreciation of the work of Danish saboteurs, was released from General Eisenhower's headquarters:[4]

News has been received of the success achieved by Danish saboteurs against German troop movements through Denmark.

Repeated attacks have been made by Danish patriots on all railway lines in the country, with the result that not one train arrives in Germany without having been delayed, either by direct attacks or by the necessity of its having to be diverted because of sabotage.

As well, the problem has been made more difficult for the Germans by the destruction of factories making rails and junction points, by the sabotage of water towers and by the blowing up of electric points, turntables and railway stations.

[1] Talk by Ole Kiilerich called 'R.A.F. Help Danish Patriots' on 2 November 1944 (B.B.C. Archives).

[2] This referred to the R.A.F. attack on the Gestapo headquarters at Aarhus.

[3] Talk by T. M. Terkelsen called 'Transport Sabotage' on 27 November 1944 (B.B.C. Archives).

[4] Quoted in *The Times*, 6 March 1945

This action by Danish saboteurs is an effective contribution to current military operations on both the western and eastern fronts.

On 5 May *The Times* printed an article which summed up the achievements of Danish sabotage in Jutland.[1] It was estimated that after the withdrawal of troops from Finland, the Germans had about nineteen divisions in Norway. They had great difficulty in getting these troops back to Germany. Convoys hugging the Norwegian coast were subject to allied attack by both sea and air. Also there was successful sabotage of Norwegian railways by Norwegian saboteurs.

From Norway the troops were usually shipped to the Danish ports of Frederikshavn and Aarhus, from where they proceeded to Germany by rail. Danish sabotage was extensive as the allied communiqué indicated. Not only did Danish saboteurs prevent troop movements, but it was estimated that they were also responsible for keeping some 200,000 German soldiers pinned down in Denmark in the spring of 1945 when they were needed on other fronts.[2]

It was largely this campaign in Jutland which led Churchill himself to add his appreciation to that of allied headquarters for the work of the Danish Resistance. The following message from Churchill was broadcast in Danish by the B.B.C. on 31 December 1944.[3]

At the beginning of the New Year I cannot promise you that the end is near; but I can say that the Nazi beast is cornered and that its destruction is inevitable. The wounds inflicted by the armed might of the Grand Alliance are mortal. And when we in Britain speak of the Grand Alliance, we mean not only the armies, navies, and air forces of the United Nations; we mean also the Resistance movements throughout Europe whose members have played so gallant a part in this total war against a brutal and unscrupulous enemy.

To you in the Danish Resistance movement, under the war leadership of the Freedom Council, I say this: we know what price you have paid and are paying, for refusing to be tempted by Nazi threats;

[1] 'Withdrawal of German troops from Norway', *ibid.* 5 May 1945.

[2] This was the estimated number given by Hæstrup in *Panorama Denmark*.

[3] Quoted in *The Times*, 1 January 1945.

we know something of your achievements in harrying and wrecking the German war machine which rolled across your defenceless frontiers nearly five years ago. We admire your steadfastness and your skill. Your performance is a valuable contribution both to the Allied cause, and to the future prosperity of a free Denmark. Now, as the enemy is near defeat and becomes more violent, we must all stand firm—we must strengthen our grip to hasten the end with cool heads and stout hearts. Let us march together to the victory which will restore the ancient liberties of the Danish people.

There is no doubt that the Jutland sabotage campaign was a Danish victory, an action carried out and led by the Danish Resistance. The part played by the B.B.C. in this success was small but nevertheless important. There were a few resistance groups which had direct telegraphic contact with London, but the B.B.C. was the main link between the Allies and the underground armies in the field. Because of this contact through the B.B.C. it was possible to plan, co-ordinate and execute sabotage attacks from Trondheim to the Danish-German border. In every case the B.B.C. played a vital part in the communication of plans and orders. Perhaps even more important, the B.B.C. was an instrument of encouragement to these resistance groups. It provided the means of showing Danish saboteurs how important their campaign was to allied strategy.

CHAPTER 16

BLACK PROPAGANDA

> You must hate propaganda to do it well, and we British did hate it, and therefore took more trouble to conceal what we were doing.
>
> R. H. S. Crossman, 'Psychological Warfare', in the *Journal of the Royal United Service Institution*, 1952

During wartime, the British government was ultimately responsible for the European Services of the B.B.C. It advised on policy and took responsibility for what was broadcast. The Minister of Information was responsible to Parliament for the European Services and could if necessary be questioned about the B.B.C. by members of Parliament.[1] To this extent the Danish section of the B.B.C. spoke with the authority of the British government on Danish affairs. Although the B.B.C. was during the war, as it is today, an independent corporate body, it was also in wartime a part of foreign policy. As such it was ultimately responsible to a government minister, in this case the Foreign Secretary. The broadcasts to Denmark, as well as to other European countries, were the chief means of spreading British propaganda abroad. This was recognized by the government.

Harold Nicolson, M.P., parliamentary secretary to the Ministry of Information, wrote in the *B.B.C. Handbook* for 1941 that 'the British public have a healthy dislike of all forms of governmental propaganda', and that they 'do not want to be told what they ought to think or feel'. For this reason he thought that the Ministry of Information was 'the most unpopular department in the whole British Commonwealth of Nations'.

This may well have been so, and perhaps explains why it was never desired—nor probably would it have been possible—to set up a propaganda ministry in Britain, similar to that of

[1] See Bruce Lockhart, *Comes the Reckoning*, p. 126.

Goebbels in Germany. Public opinion would not have tolerated it. There was also no real need for the British government to set up such an institution. British wartime politics did not depend for their success on the same mass thinking as Nazi politics did. The British government was right in not trying to inject a mass standardization of thought into its own people and into the peoples of Europe.

Yet the fight against the Nazis was partly a fight for the mind. It was also a propaganda war against both the enemy and the neutrals. If this had not been recognized there would have been no Political Warfare Executive set up in Britain. Political warfare, or psychological warfare, as the Americans called it, was aimed at influencing the mind, and sometimes the nerves. The Nazis used every technique possible in this battle. The British government felt that it could not adopt similar techniques officially, and yet the realists amongst the British propagandists felt that Britain could not enter the propaganda battle with one arm bound. The answer was black propaganda.

During the war the public was not allowed to know anything about black propaganda. Not only was the work secret, it was not even recognized by the government. The government was not responsible for it, and yet it was carried out by a government department.

R. H. S. Crossman, who during the war worked for both the B.B.C. and in secret propaganda work, defined the two terms, 'white' and 'black' propaganda. White propaganda was quite simply 'activity which is openly sponsored by one's Government, that is activity which purports to be British'.[1]

Black propaganda came in two forms, by radio and by leaflet. This type of propaganda, wrote Crossman, 'purports to come from organizations inside the enemy country (for instance from some illegal organization)'. It included 'leaflets which the British Government would not be very proud to publish'. Crossman explained that 'if for instance one is trying

[1] R. H. S. Crossman in an essay called 'Psychological Warfare' in the *Journal of the Royal United Service Institution* (1952).

to persuade a German that while he is abroad his wife is being seduced by a foreign worker, it may be necessary to have the leaflet so designed that no one can say that it comes from the British Government'.[1]

There were also varying shades of grey propaganda: 'For instance one may run a radio station which is not a black station —because no Germans would be so foolish as to believe that a medium-wave station could be a secret station in Germany— but which certainly is not a B.B.C. station. Certain things can be said by such a station for which no British Government could take the responsibility.'[2]

There were therefore two chief reasons why nobody mentioned black propaganda in wartime. First, because any element of surprise would be lost if it became generally known that the British were responsible for broadcasts which were supposed to come from behind the enemy lines. Secondly, the type of leaflets and broadcasts which no British government would be prepared to recognize openly as its own could be spread abroad anonymously. Black propaganda was Britain's unofficial answer to all Goebbels' techniques.

The headquarters of black propaganda was, for most of the war, at Woburn on the estate of the Duke of Bedford. There, and in particular at Wavendon Park Farm on the estate, black propagandists worked on the same regional basis as the European Services of the B.B.C.

Sefton Delmer, in a book entitled *Black Boomerang*, revealed a great deal of the workings of black propaganda to Germany. In this book he described how he was instructed to produce ideas for broadcasts for his R.U. (Research Unit). This was a cover name for the black broadcasting groups. His job involved trickery and deception, and this, he wrote, 'was a task which lay right outside what it was possible or desirable for the B.B.C. to undertake'.[3]

[1] *Ibid.* [2] *Ibid.*

[3] Sefton Delmer led the group which was responsible for black propaganda to Germany.

Delmer's group was responsible for setting up a radio station which the Germans were to think came from within Germany itself. His plan was to take a patriotic German line, and under cover of this, to spread all kinds of subversive rumours and lies. He hoped that the listeners would think that it was a dissident group of German patriots who controlled the radio and through it showed their dissatisfaction with the Nazi régime. To succeed in this it was very necessary to build up as much detailed information of German affairs as possible so that the broadcasts would have a truly German flavour. Information was gathered by all conceivable means, from secret microphones hidden in prisoner of war cages, from the interception of letters from Germany to neutral countries and from other secret sources. The Admiralty was the best official source of information.

Delmer's view was that 'carefully selected news items skilfully presented' were the best subversive propaganda. The name of the black station broadcasting to Germany was changed on more than one occasion but perhaps *Soldatensender Calais* was the best known. This station, originating from Woburn, but often genuinely thought to be operating from the Continent, developed definite objectives and characteristics. The main objective was to break the morale of the Germans throughout Europe. This was done partly by suggestions, for example, that while German soldiers fought and suffered miseries, the Nazi party officials were living in luxury at home, and partly by inventing and publicizing an anti-Nazi resistance within Germany. 'We want Hitler and the Gestapo', Delmer wrote,[1] 'to believe that they are faced not only with a Polish or a French underground, but with a German anti-Nazi resistance as well.' Black broadcasters to Germany were delighted when in fact the army generals revolted against Hitler in 1944, as it was exactly this kind of subversion which they had encouraged from the start.

Black propaganda worked very closely with S.O.E. Delmer had been advised at the outset when he submitted his ideas for his 'R.U.' to state that his work would fit in very closely with

[1] In *Black Boomerang*.

S.O.E.'s operational plans. Delmer benefited by this S.O.E. connection in his attempt to sabotage German morale. He had one request to S.O.E. men in Germany: 'Whenever they killed a German I wanted them to do their best to make it look as if he had been killed by Germans.'

Clearly this type of propaganda differed from country to country. The German black broadcasts were directed at the centre of the Nazi empire. Their work, as it was aimed at the heart of Nazism, was of the blackest black. Delmer's book gives some idea of the fabrications, lies and rumours which were circulated in Germany as a result of black broadcasts and leaflets, and it also gives a certain amount of evidence of their effect. To what extent the broadcasts went in their invention of lies will probably never be known as most of the documents were burnt after the war. Denmark was on the periphery of the Nazi empire. It received black propaganda in its characteristic form, but certainly with neither the intensity nor in the quantity with which it was directed at Germany. There was, too, another problem for those involved in Danish propaganda—that Denmark was German-occupied, but not at war with Germany, and therefore the attitude of its people had to be considered too. Radio Denmark, as the secret station broadcasting from Britain to Denmark was called, was involved in a lighter shade of black propaganda than, for example, *Soldatensender Calais*. It gave, however, more extreme and more detailed broadcasts than the B.B.C. could. It interfered in Danish internal politics more than the B.B.C. could, and it spoke with a voice for which the British government had no official responsibility.

There is little documentary evidence about this type of broadcasting to Denmark. Most of it, like the German material, was burnt after the war. There is, however, enough to piece together a bare outline.

Sten Gudme, a Danish journalist, was asked to go to England by Ebbe Munck, and he arrived in London in May 1941.[1] He

[1] Sten Gudme wrote an account of his activities in Britain, and this is now deposited in the Danish Archives.

was introduced to Commander Hollingworth of the Danish section of S.O.E. and was then taken down to Wavendon Park Farm on the Woburn estate. The Political Intelligence Department had its headquarters at Woburn. Here Gudme met Terkelsen, Jens Gielstrup, who later joined the R.A.F., and Captain Fischer. They were working on the Radio Denmark broadcasts. He also met Thomas Barman, head of the Northern Department of P.I.D., who had originally asked for him. Barman told Gudme that his work was to be in black propaganda.

At this time Gudme recalled that activity in Danish affairs was restricted to broadcasts only. No pamphlets were written or sent then. Gudme's particular job was to write talks for Radio Denmark, and to act as a speaker and announcer. He was soon put in charge of this radio station.

He had to be very 'secret and mystical'. For the first six months he had a false name, Stone (which was not very original as his Christian name was Sten, Danish for Stone), and he was told not to go near London. In addition to his job with Radio Denmark he was asked to write a report on Denmark which was sent to the Foreign Office and the Ministry of Information. He later heard that this was the first full account of the political situation in Denmark which the British had received since the German occupation.[1] Rodney Gallop of the Foreign Office also admitted that, until the Foreign Office had received Gudme's full report, the only information of value about the situation in Denmark had come from a letter written by Gudme to Tillge-Rasmussen, a Danish journalist in London.[2]

Gudme's contacts with S.O.E. were also close. He briefed the two S.O.E. men, C. J. Bruhn and Mogens Hammer, on conditions in Denmark before they went in by parachute in December 1941.[3]

As he was directly concerned with propaganda to Denmark,

[1] This demonstrates how little information about Danish affairs was received in Britain during the first year of the German occupation of Denmark.

[2] Sten Gudme's account (Danish Archives).

[3] See chapter 4. Mogens Hammer of the Danish section of S.O.E. was parachuted into Denmark with C. J. Bruhn in December 1941.

Gudme received guidance from British propaganda advisers.[1] He maintained that he was able to guess the vacillations in British foreign policy towards Denmark from the information he received.

Soon after his arrival in May 1941 he was told by Barman of P.I.D. that Britain wanted more action in Denmark.[2] The invitation sent to various Danes in the autumn of 1941 which resulted in Christmas Møller's coming to Britain was proof of the desire for a stronger line from Britain. This is also confirmed by the B.B.C. Danish broadcasts at this time, and by Barman's letter to Robert Jørgensen of 1 November 1941 previously quoted.[3]

At this point Gudme's account of his work at Woburn finishes. He gives no indication, for example, of the kind of broadcasts he was making, and naturally no scripts of these broadcasts are available, even if they still exist. However, one vital document still remains which shows there was a change in black broadcasting to Denmark during 1942. Radio Denmark I was discontinued and Radio Denmark II, to be called *Frihedssenderen* [Freedom Station], was started. The following document headed 'Most Secret', and quoted in full, shows the aims and the methods of Radio Denmark II.[4]

MEMORANDUM

Most Secret

To: Mr Barman,
Mr Brinley Thomas,
Mr Terkelsen.

From: W.P.F. [Wavendon Park Farm]

Date: June 14th 1942.

Please find some suggestions for R.D.2.

[1] Sten Gudme's account (Danish Archives).
[2] *Ibid.* [3] In chapter 4.
[4] Amongst the papers of Christmas Møller (Danish Archives).

A. General Remarks

1. NAME: *Frihedssenderen.* It should be the same station that gives the ordinary daily transmissions as the weekly Newspaper in dictating speed.

2. TRANSMISSION-HOURS: (agreed with Simpsons)

(*a*) 7–7.15 a.m. (B.B.C. 6.20) Devote some minutes every day to the children in this transmission. Give them some questions they can put to their teachers, give them small rhymes etc. This early transmission should not take place Sundays and holidays. Once a week fully dedicated to children completing their history-lessons in current affairs by thrilling but factual stories of the new world's heroes: Michailovitch,[1] Norway's resistance etc.
(*b*) 7–7.15 p.m. (Kalundborg 6.35)
(*c*) 23–23.15
(*d*) Weekly Newspaper dictate Tuesday 23.15–23.45

3. RECORDING-TIME: 10.30 a.m.

In the first week it is suggested that there should be only one transmission daily (7–7.15 p.m.), then in the next week two, and after some days three, starting on a day we have got a thing of particular interest. As much irregularity as possible, both in cutting abruptly and cancelling transmissions. Introducing once in a while a 'ghost voice', being a German Nazi speaking Danish in accordance with the famous '*Oprob*'.[2]

4. SIGNAL-TUNE: *I Danmark er jeg født*, repeated three–four times in the beginning of the transmission and repeated between the separate items. Most transmissions should consist of 2–3 talks, and smaller items, intermitted by rhymes, slogans etc., like the French B.B.C.'s *Les Français parlent aux Français.* Every talk to have a headline f.i. *Frihedssenderen giver nu de sidste Oplysninger om Baggrunden for Regerings-erklæringen.*[3] The transmission ends with announcing: *Hermed slutter Frihedssenderen. Vi kommer igen Kl...*

[1] Alternative spelling for Mihailović (see chapter 6).
[2] This refers to the German *Oprop til Danmarks Soldater og Danmarks Folk*, signed by General Kaupisch, and spread amongst the Danish population on 9 April 1940.
[3] (*Frihedssenderen* now gives the latest information on the background for the Government statement.)

5. WAVELENGTH: 31 . . ., 49 . . .

It is in this connection suggested that the new station and its wavelengths should be advertised in Danish papers some days before it is started. Illegal papers published in Denmark should be asked to give publicity to the station. After a fortnight listeners should be asked to give their views on the station in chainletters.

6. LOCALITY: As less as possible should be said about this, but it should be implied that the station might be situated in Denmark itself. Even if the Government and most intelligent people realise that the situation is in England, a good deal of the common men would not know, and are probably inclined to believe that it is in Denmark. And if they are told—by the Government f.i.—that the station is situated outside the country, it might then be useful to drop a hint that it could be situated on the Faroe Islands, in Iceland or on a ship located outside the Danish coast.

To confuse people we might try to get a talk by Aksel Larsen, the communist leader, recorded in Denmark and sent here.

B. Programme and policy

The R/U is not bound to any special political party in Denmark. We are especially talking to the younger people (*Dansk Ungdomssamvirke*), but not in particular to the Communists, as they seem to be quite able to fight their own fight. We are going in for the national solidarity on the basis of the Coalition Government, as they will, for the time being, be preferable to some authoritarian system. But we are showing how men like Erik Scavenius and Gunnar Larsen[1] (specially the latter one) are threatening the fundamental elements for this co-operation by still giving away too much to the Germans. Gunnar Larsen to be attacked as an ambitious, young man who without any scruples is trying to get the leader-post, eventually in co-operation with the Nazis (*Den Kommende Mand*); further attack his negotiations, behind the back of the Government, in Germany. The strongest possible line should be taken here with regard to Gunnar Larsen and his accomplices, Sthyr, Juncker, etc. It may be appropriate soon to warn those people in big business, who, although despising Larsen, are working with him, that they may find themselves and their firms on a blacklist in the coming twenty years of the British-Russian Rule of Europe.

[1] Gunnar Larsen was considered to be one of the most blatant Danish collaborators.

Scavenius should be ridiculed; he is always wrong—he was in the last war, he is even more so now. There may be drawn a useful Scavenius–Laval parallel, which gives the opportunity also to parallelise the growth of the new French spirit (St-Nazaire, Bir Hakeim, etc.) in defiance of the whole bankrupted policy.

As we are going in for the principle of a Coalition Government the spirit of the R/U must be that it is a meeting-place for young national enthusiasts, who are fighting to keep the people's will to resistance alive. And defend Democracy in its broadest sense: trade-unions' rights, appeal for sympathy-strikes if the principle of unemployment-relief is further attacked; warning the Danes against the semi-Fascist tendencies in such economic plans which are sponsored by Larsen and his group. It is no use being always in the defensive, we must try hard to give the Danes the offensive spirit, just like the Sønderjyder before 1920.[1]

The Danes have for two years been successful as far as their defensive fight is concerned. All news from Denmark tends to prove that, alone for psychological reasons, the spirit is clamouring for activity and, maybe, offensiveness. This is in accordance with official B.B.C.-policy, where it is more and more implied that Danes are in the fight (Free Danes, Danish sailors, etc.) and that thereby a path is opened along which Denmark may find its way as an Ally.

I. HOW FAR WILL THE R/U SUPPORT THE GOVERNMENT?

There are five exact limits; we will not support a Government which:

(*a*) introduces anti-Jewish legislation;
(*b*) permits the Gestapo to take over police-power in Denmark;
(*c*) sends Danish soldiers to Russia or against England;
(*d*) adheres to the Three Power Pact;
(*e*) permits conscription of Danish workers to Germany or German-occupied territories.

We must, furthermore, constantly keep the Danes' minds open to what is taking place as regard breaches of our fundamental laws, the Constitution, etc. We are repeating the paragraphs in the Constitutional law which have been violated, so that all people can learn them by heart.

[1] *Sønderjyder*. This refers to the Danes who lived in North Schleswig and were under German rule from 1864–1920. They maintained their nationalistic outlook during the long period they were under foreign domination, and resisted German attempts to suppress them.

II. WHOM ARE WE ATTACKING?

(*a*) The Danes who are working with or dealing with Germany, especially businessmen, engineers (see above about Gunnar Larsen's gang). We must try to get names from the small provincial towns and blacklist them. People advertising in the Nazi-papers. We should mention firms working for Germany; warning the workers in these factories that they will be bombed.

(*b*) The Danish Nazis. This should be one of our most important efforts—and this could be done on the same lines as in the late R/U, where, after all, we had a good deal of reactions on this special point. This line is not taken because we regard the Nazis as the biggest danger in Denmark. But because they present the best opportunity for demonstrations and open expression of hatred towards the German occupation. Supply widest possible material for the nerve-war in Denmark against the Clausenists.

(*c*) The Germans. Close cooperation with Sefton Delmer to get material from Germany. We must be supposed to get lots of news from Danes coming back from journeys to Germany. Attempt a campaign of derision and pity with regard to the decent ones amongst German soldiers in Denmark and stress the importance of telling the German soldiers, one by one, when Danes get in touch with them, how hopeless is their war, and how much Hitlerism is endangering the German people by sowing a hatred against them, all over German-occupied Europe and in the whole world. Refer to sentences from the last war: *Wir siegen uns tot* and 'The position of the German army is splendid—but hopeless' (Ludendorff, 1918).

(*d*) Danish workers going to Germany. They must pay their way back to Denmark through making sabotage in Germany. Take the line that Danes working in Germany—higher paid as skilled workers than thousands of other foreign workers—are endangering their own future within the framework of the workmen's international co-operation, becoming despised by Polish, French, Czech, and—specially—Norwegian workers, because they are now as foremen, skilled gang-leaders in road-building etc. making it possible for the Germans to employ their slaves. A special point should be made of that danger in connection with Danish workers going to Trondheim and thereby threatening the heroic resistance of Norwegian workers themselves. We must have regular contributions of warnings from one of the Danes who went to Trondheim and realised what he had done.

(*e*) The Frikorps Danmark.[1]
(*f*) The Danish Press.
(*g*) Occasionally: B.B.C.

C. Special Campaigns etc.

(*a*) The farmers: They can do harm to Germany by keeping the goods away; all current Danish-German trade agreements are on the basis that the Danish market shall be supplied first; the Germans are only getting the surplus. Keep the livestocks: better feeding your own cow than a German soldier. Tell the farmer that the war may suddenly come to an end—and only if he has got something to offer *at once* can he regain the world market.

(*b*) The workers: Rather appeal indirectly to their will to sabotage by giving stories of sabotage from other countries; create Norwegian, Polish heroes.

(*c*) Norwegian news in a dramatic way.

(*d*) Finland: Discount the ideas of Danish material help to Finland by stressing

(1) that after the Hitler-Mannerheim talk it is now a German responsibility to feed the Finns, and
(2) further cuts in the Danish rations for the sake of Finland would never materialise in any greater help to the Finns but would only be a means for Germany to get more themselves.

Do not disclaim Danish humanitarian help to Finland, but do everything to make this help suspicious in the Germans' and the Finnish Fascists' eyes. It is a very good thing to take Finnish children to Denmark in order to educate them in Anti-Nazism.

(*e*) Give one or two weekly military surveys.

(*f*) The last day in every month most Danish papers give long surveys of the foreign events in the last month. The same day the R/U should bring a survey: how these articles would have been if they had been written in a free country. As a whole, events in the world at large should be commented upon from the point of view, that here is the thing which the Danish press certainly would have written today if they had been free to do so, and that what they are writing is dictated by the Germans.

(*g*) As a regular bi-weekly feature a talk between three men: discussing current events and topical items from the Danish press, f.i. Christmas Møller; one man the hopelessly doubting, the second man who wishes for a strong line but is scared by the risks of damaging

[1] Danes enrolled by the Germans in the *Frikorps Danmark* for service, mainly on the Eastern Front.

the coalition-system, and the third person in a minor role (the boy in Hans Andersen's *Kejserens Nye Klæder*, who realized how naked the Kejser was).

(*h*) Try to make the regular transmission on a fixed day and time to special categories of the population, e.g. soldiers, workers, farmers, the rifle-association-members, children and students.

(*i*) It is very important that we get more Danish news. Is it possible to get direct information from Denmark? Specially for the Newspaper on Tuesdays this will be important.

[signed] Helingboy.[1]

This memorandum was from W.P.F. (Wavendon Park Farm), and was addressed to the three men responsible for formulating propaganda policy to Denmark, Thomas Barman of the Political Intelligence Department, and Brinley Thomas and T. M. Terkelsen of the Political Warfare Executive.

It is clear from this document that Radio Denmark II was to be a Danish Resistance radio, presumed to be operating from Denmark. It was to be a 'meeting place for young national enthusiasts, who are fighting to keep the people's will to resistance alive', and the reason for 'as much irregularity as possible both in cutting abruptly and in cancelling transmissions' was to give the impression that the broadcasters were liable to the risk of being caught by the Germans.

The section on policy is interesting. It confirms that the propaganda policy for Radio Denmark II had also to be in line with the policy of P.W.E. and the Foreign Office. The aim of Radio Denmark II was 'national solidarity on the basis of the Coalition Government...for the time being'. This was precisely the policy the B.B.C. was following in 1942 when it never directly encouraged rebellion against the Danish government, but merely pointed out that men like Scavenius were betraying Danish interests by their pro-German policy. The B.B.C.'s hope, as was undoubtedly also Radio Denmark's, was that the Danish people would eventually see that their government was not

[1] Helingboy was a code name, and it is not certain who Helingboy was. It could have been Sten Gudme. From the odd expressions and grammar used in the directive it is clear that it was written by someone whose native tongue was not English.

acting in the best Danish interests, and would therefore force it out of office. Clearly in the summer of 1942 there was to be no open incitement, by any means, from Britain to encourage Danes to defy their government and the Germans, because it was considered too soon for widespread resistance to take place in Denmark. Direct encouragement from Britain at this point in 1942, when S.O.E. was only able to give very limited material support to the Danish Resistance, might have led to premature and unsuccessful actions by sabotage groups, and perhaps even to a stronger pro-government feeling amongst the population generally.

One of the most common tools of British propaganda was the 'black list'. It was sometimes used by the B.B.C., but was probably most effective in the case of Denmark when mentioned in the broadcasts from the Freedom Station.

The knowledge that their names were known to a Danish broadcasting group, supposedly on Danish soil, was likely to have caused greater fear of reprisals and possible liquidation amongst Danish industrialists working for the Germans than if their names were mentioned only over the British radio. The revenge of the patriots seemed uncomfortably possible. From the directive it can be seen that the first target for attack by Radio Denmark II was 'Danes who are working with or dealing with Germany, especially business men, engineers'. On black radio there was no need to disguise threats.

The other main objective of Radio Denmark was to break the morale of the German troops in Denmark. The broadcasters on the Freedom Station were to co-operate closely with Sefton Delmer in getting material from Germany. Their task was to use the Danish listeners for spreading anti-German rumours in Denmark. The listener's job was, if he had any contact with the Germans at all, to spread alarm and despondency amongst the soldiers as much as possible. The task of demoralization was much more effectively done by pamphlet than by radio, except where, as with Sefton Delmer's group, the broadcasts were spoken in German and were aimed directly at German listeners.

The B.B.C. was to be attacked to give Radio Denmark an air of independence and to show that it did not necessarily follow British policy.

The B.B.C. Intelligence report of November 1941 gave some idea of Radio Denmark I's reception in Denmark, and also an amusing story.[1] In a paragraph headed 'Radio Denmark—Freedom Station', it was stated that a considerable number of Danes listened in. It was generally believed at this time that the station operated either from the Faroe Islands or from Sweden. There had, however, been a report in a Danish newspaper that the announcer over Radio Denmark closed down on 7 October with the words 'We are now closing down from London for tonight'!

The report contained another story, which illustrated the attitude of the Danes to Scavenius, then foreign minister in the government. He had announced a few months previously that the Freedom Station, Radio Denmark, had been located somewhere in the south of England. The reaction of the Danes was that if Scavenius said that the Freedom Station was in England, then England was the one place it could not possibly be.

It was later reported by B.B.C. Intelligence that:

> The Danish Freedom Station can be received only poorly in this country [Sweden] but is apparently heard fairly well in Denmark, and in various outlying parts of the world. Its announcers are excellent, and its topics, usually political or economic, show an intimate knowledge of Danish internal problems. Danish politicians such as the anti-German Hedtoft-Hansen and Christmas Møller and the pro-German Stauning and Gunnar Larsen have occasionally been mentioned by name. The Freedom Station shows a tendency to specialize in themes which would be awkward for the B.B.C. to handle but constitutes an admirable addition to our own output. No further guesses at the whereabouts of this station appear to have been made by the Germans.[2]

There are two main reasons why more evidence exists today about the infiltration of pamphlets into Denmark than about

[1] 17 November 1941 (Danish Archives).
[2] In an undated report (*ibid.*).

Radio Denmark. First, many of the pamphlets were kept and can be examined. Secondly, the success of the infiltration depended very largely on Danes organizing the distribution of leaflets in German-occupied Denmark. Those Danes who took part in this were not bound by the same rules of secrecy and silence as were Gudme and others who worked with the British-controlled Freedom Station at Woburn.

Sten Gudme confirmed in his account that it was at Wavendon Park Farm that the pamphlets which were distributed in Denmark were written.[1] The group responsible for the pamphlets began first with a series called *Vi Danske*, which was sent partly by parachute and partly via Sweden. Later they produced a booklet called *Vi Vil Vinde*—the title taken from the B.B.C.'s *V* signal to Denmark. Gudme kept in close contact with S.O.E. over the problem of transporting these leaflets to Denmark and distributing them. Reginald Spink of S.O.E.'s Danish section in Baker Street was later put in charge of organizing the distribution of S.O.E.'s black propaganda in Denmark. By late 1944 Spink was feeding all kinds of propaganda material into Denmark. For example he sent films, on 16 mm. spools, of the Normandy landings 'which we think will interest a Danish audience',[2] also miniature negatives, war photographs and copies of books which were in great demand by the illegal Danish press.

The sending of photographs from Britain was an important part of this propaganda work. Its main purpose was to provide the illegal newspapers in Denmark with up-to-date photographs of general war events which they were unable to obtain elsewhere. A common practice was to send out press photographs, with a brief description of the facts recorded in the photographs. For example in October 1943 a press photograph was sent to Denmark, showing extensive bomb damage in Germany with the following description:

On October 9th 1943 Flying Fortresses of the U.S. attacked the huge Focke Wulf aircraft factory at Marienburg, south east of Danzig, and two hundred miles beyond Berlin. This plant covering

[1] Sten Gudme's account (*ibid.*).

[2] Undated letter (*ibid.*).

more than a hundred acres was believed to assemble approximately half of all the Focke Wulf 190 fighter planes produced. It was announced after the raid that the plant was 'virtually destroyed'. The German defences were taken unawares by this raid. The picture shows the height of attack when the factory had been fired by incendiary and high explosive bombs.[1]

Films sent over by S.O.E. were a popular accessory to British propaganda in Denmark. Ronald Seth in a chapter on the Danish Resistance in his book *The Undaunted* has a vivid if slightly popularized description of this:

For cool audacity nothing can surpass the showing of English films in Copenhagen. An armed and organized group would suddenly descend on a cinema, and the Germans present would be given the opportunity of either watching the film or being temporarily detained elsewhere. The English film was then put through the projector. In this way Danish audiences saw 'The Moon Is Down', 'In Which We Serve', 'The Fight For Stalingrad', 'Donald Duck In Germany', and 'The Lambeth Walk'. The performance over, the Resistance retreated as they had come.

The organization for distributing British propaganda material, mainly leaflets, was set up in Denmark during 1943. A Dane, Sven Seehusen, had been picked out in Britain to lead the work of distribution in Denmark. He was a journalist who was involved with the Danish underground press, and he had cooperated with parachutists during the previous year. Seehusen first heard that he had been picked out to organize this work in Denmark, in March 1943, when he received a letter from Turnbull, from the British Legation in Stockholm.[2]At the same time he received a batch of propaganda leaflets from the British Consul in Gothenburg, Albert Christensen.[3]

In this letter Seehusen was told that he had been recommended

[1] Text in Danish Archives.

[2] Sven Seehusen's account (*ibid.*).

[3] Most of the black propaganda pamphlets distributed in Denmark were sent through Albert Christensen (code name Matros). Some containers of pamphlets were also parachuted in. On one occasion an S.O.E. agent Peter Carlsen drowned a whole container of pamphlets in the Kattegat because he had received instructions not to deal with propaganda material (see Hæstrup, *Kontakt med England*, p. 254).

for this work by Christmas Møller. He was instructed not to contact any of the other parachutists from England, especially Muus, and he was given instructions on how to arrange receptions of propaganda material by parachute.

During the summer of 1943 Turnbull also contacted an army officer, Captain Rantzau, and asked him to join Seehusen in the work of distribution. The idea was that they should work as a team. It was hoped that Seehusen could use his wide contacts amongst illegal newspapermen to help infiltrate propaganda leaflets amongst the German soldiers. Rantzau, who was able to make regular journeys to Stockholm, was to keep the channels open between Sweden and Denmark for the reception of propaganda material.

On 30 July 1943 Rantzau wrote to Spink in London and in this letter he described his work.[1] He thought his job had three main objectives, which were:

(*a*) the reception and distribution of mass droppings of pamphlets;

(*b*) to ensure the quickest and most effective utilization of individual propaganda articles such as books, periodicals and films;

(*c*) organizing propaganda operations in Denmark to ensure the maximum amount of infiltration.

This propaganda drive met with a certain amount of opposition from S.O.E.'s leader in the field, Flemming Muus, who considered propaganda work to be only of minor importance. This explains the warning in the original letter from Turnbull to Seehusen, that he should not get involved with Muus. In fact it was clear from a letter which Turnbull wrote to Muus in July 1943 that Muus had protested that the organization of propaganda in Denmark was separate and did not come under his command, and he had asked why this was so.

Turnbull's reply was:

> Chop [code name for Hollingworth] and I have purposely kept this propaganda operation from your notice since we do not wish to endanger you in what is after all only a second-rate operation.

[1] Letter from Rantzau to Spink, 30 July 1943 (Danish Archives).

You have a vital job to do but your mandate does not cover propaganda and the authority for arranging such operations resides at headquarters and in this office. It is precisely because we know that this propaganda work is exposed and liable to be 'blown' that we have kept you and Table [S.O.E. operations] entirely separate from it, and will continue to do so.

These were fairly harsh words to Muus designed to stop his interference with propaganda work. Muus had clearly objected to the choice of Rantzau, because the final part of Turnbull's letter defended this choice, and explained that the kind of work which Rantzau was expected to do was purely operational: 'He [Rantzau] is however not meant to be a propaganda expert in the sense of a journalist or publicity expert. This is not necessary, since he is linked up with those illegal propaganda departments with which we have chosen to collaborate. Prop [Rantzau's code name] is simply a technical carrying agent.'[1]

Rantzau shortly afterwards took over the leadership of the work when Seehusen was forced to flee to Sweden on 29 August 1943.[2] London, however, soon appointed Aage Schoch to take over the whole organization, but he was immediately forced to go underground and was not able to take an active part in propaganda work until January 1944. Rantzau led the work through a difficult five months, and was withdrawn by S.O.E. when Schoch was able to take over active leadership.[3]

During 1944 it was decided in London that propaganda work in Denmark should be increased further. In February, Hollingworth warned Schoch that S.O.E. was about to send in two more parachutists who were specially trained in propaganda work. The two men, Herschend and Hecht Johansen, were parachuted in during March, and had strict orders to do nothing but propaganda work. Despite instructions from London, Muus's opposition to propaganda work continued. As soon as Hecht Johansen arrived in Denmark on 31 March, Muus ordered him to Fyn where he was told to replace an S.O.E. parachutist, Peter Carlsen.[4]

[1] Letter from Turnbull to Muus, July 1943 (*ibid.*).
[2] Sven Seehusen's account (*ibid.*).
[3] See Hæstrup, *Hemmelig Alliance*, vol. 1, p. 234.
[4] *Ibid.*

The two parachutists had been ordered to make all possible contacts with the Danish illegal press, and to co-ordinate its work with British propaganda.[1] With the help of the illegal press they were to take opinion polls in Denmark. It was the illegal press and reports from S.O.E. men in the field that provided the basis for the comments which reached the Danish section of the B.B.C. about the broadcasts to Denmark. Schoch, leader of propaganda distribution in Denmark, corresponded with Brinley Thomas of P.W.E. about these opinion polls in June 1944.[2] The propaganda parachutists were to have their own radio operator so that news could be sent to and from England more effectively, and better and quicker propaganda could be put out by both the B.B.C. and the Danish illegal press. From other telegrams at this time it can be seen that the parachutists were instructed to listen in regularly to both the B.B.C. and Radio Denmark, and were to send back any comments and criticisms which they could gather about these broadcasts. They were also to distribute English films, and record interviews with Danish people on gramophone records, so that these could be played back over the B.B.C. Clearly during 1944 S.O.E. laid great emphasis on propaganda work.

Rantzau's letter of July 1943 to S.O.E.[3] showed the type of material which he was receiving from England for distribution in Denmark. He was asked to distribute British pamphlets and films to Danes, particularly to those in the Resistance, and also pamphlets written in German to the German soldiers. Spink was then sending over a pamphlet called *Krigen Som Vore Venner Ser Den* ('The war as our friends see it'), and *Vi Vil Vinde*, which were written at Woburn.

In addition Rantzau was to circulate minute editions of the *Times Weekly* on India paper. As this was written in English and the print was so small as to be almost illegible, its value, as far as propaganda was concerned, must have been suspect. *Vi Vil Vinde*, however, seemed to be much more effective. Spink

[1] See *Hemmelig Alliance*, vol. 1, p. 234.
[2] *Ibid.* p. 336, n. 32.
[3] Letter from Rantzau to Spink, 30 July 1943.

hoped to be able to send a thirty-two side edition regularly every month.[1]

The two main categories of British pamphlets sent from London for distribution in Denmark, were, first, those directed at Danish readers and, secondly, those at the German soldiers. The first category was again subdivided. Some of the pamphlets intended for Danish readers openly acknowledged their British origin with the words *Med R.A.F.* ('from the R.A.F.') on the front page. Others, although their allied origin could probably be guessed from the news content, gave no open indication of where they came from. It was this latter category which it was intended should circulate with the underground newspapers in Denmark.[2]

Vi Danske was the first pamphlet which Sten Gudme worked on. It appears to have been issued monthly, and was certainly circulated in Denmark during 1942. It was published on India paper and was written in Danish. It was intended to be a newsletter which put forward the allied point of view, but did not neglect to recount how many Danes were taking part in the allied struggle.

For example, edition no. 10 in June 1942 devoted its front page to an article which claimed that 'every second a bomb falls on a German town'. Inside was a long article on Christmas Møller's activities in London. This was followed on page 3 with an attack on Gunnar Larsen and a reproduction of a *Daily Express* cartoon ridiculing Goering. The final page showed two aerial photographs of factories in Cologne, before and after an R.A.F. bombing attack.

The next month's edition followed a similar pattern. A full-page picture of Molotov, Churchill and Eden was intended to show how united the Allies were. The inside pages carried a warning to Danish workers who decided to go to Germany, reproduced a picture of corpses swinging from gallows to

[1] *Ibid.*

[2] The following observations are made after a study of a number of black pamphlets, which were collected during the German occupation and are now kept in a private collection in Copenhagen.

illustrate German bestiality in Poland, and reprinted an article from the *Manchester Guardian* on Denmark. The final page carried technical instructions on how to fit anti-interference gadgets on radios. The article explained that Scavenius had ordered jamming apparatus to be set up to prevent the B.B.C. being heard in Denmark. These instructions were to counter the effect of jamming.

Pamphlets devoted to specific issues were also infiltrated. One released during the early years of the war was called *Den Tomme Stol i London* ('The empty chair in London'). This was patriotic and anti-German and devoted much space to the example of the Danish seamen who sailed with the Allies. Clearly, this and a similar one called *Med Norge i Vore Hjerter* ('With Norway in our hearts') were intended to make the Danish population feel that they should themselves take part in the fight, and not remain passive. Reminding Denmark of the courage shown by the Norwegians was a popular wartime method of stirring Danish consciences.

None of these pamphlets gave any definite indication of their origin, though many would have guessed from the news content that they were compiled in Britain. Probably it was a deliberate policy that these pamphlets were anonymous. It was felt in the early stages of the war that the Danish population had first to show itself to be anti-Nazi before it received direct and open encouragement from Britain.

By 1943 when the Danish population had shown openly where its feelings lay, most of the pamphlets which came from Britain were marked with the R.A.F. roundel and the words *Med R.A.F.*

Vi Vil Vinde, which Rantzau had mentioned in his letter to Spink of 30 July 1943, was probably the most elaborate of the pamphlets which openly indicated their allied origin. The first number was issued in November 1942, and it was this, according to Gudme, which followed the anonymous *Vi Danske*. *Vi Vil Vinde* was totally different. It was in the form of a small magazine, and each edition had between thirty and fifty pages. It was intended mainly as a news letter, and therefore devoted space to allied war news. However, there was also a strongly Danish flavour to it. T. M. Terkelsen, Christmas Møller and Sven Tillge-Rasmussen all wrote articles at various times for this pamphlet. Also articles from the leaders of the Home Front in Denmark, like Professor Mogens Fog, were often included. All of the editions were liberally supplied with photographs, illustrations, and reproductions of cartoons, mainly from the English newspapers.

Not only did *Vi Vil Vinde* print news, but it was also of some practical importance. It certainly helped the B.B.C. by reproducing the full texts of various broadcasts. *Vi Danske* had given instructions on how to fit anti-interference gadgets to radios so that the B.B.C. could be heard clearly. *Vi Vil Vinde* followed this tradition. In the February–March 1944 edition an article entitled *Lav Selv en Rammeantenne* gave technical instructions on how to build an aerial to ensure better reception of broadcasts. There was also, usually on the final page, a list of the Danish programmes from London with transmission times. In January 1944 these were daily at 7.15–7.30, 12.15–12.30, 18.15–18.30, 21.15–21.30, four programmes of a quarter of an hour each.

Apart from helping the B.B.C. by giving it publicity, *Vi Vil Vinde* also made Danish people aware of the importance to the Germans of the railways and ports in Jutland. In an article in the March–April 1943 edition it was pointed out that these communications were vital for German troop movements. Coloured diagrams showed the exact routes used by the Germans. The article ended with the warning that, because of the strategic importance of these communications, the R.A.F. would probably have to bomb them as it had bombed Burmeister and Wain in January 1943. The implications of this article were obvious. As a result of Danish sabotage the R.A.F. never found it necessary to make any special bombing raids on railways or ports in Denmark.

Leaflets on specific subjects were continually infiltrated during 1943 and 1944. There was a special leaflet brought out for the Danish students called *Hilsen fra England til Mødet i Gerløv*, with a long article by Christmas Møller.[1] The *Hilsen Fra England* series continued with a special edition on Churchill's appreciation of 'Fighting Denmark'. One edition gave a Danish translation of Air Marshal Harris's warning to the German people at the onset of the allied bombing offensive. Norway continued to be a subject for pamphlets. One was devoted entirely to describing how Norwegian school teachers had been treated when seven hundred of their number had been deported from a concentration camp and put to forced labour.[2]

All these pamphlets were aimed at Danish targets. They were intended at first to encourage anti-German feeling in the Danish population, and later, when this became less necessary, to give as much war news and information about Danish activities abroad as possible.

The second kind of pamphlets infiltrated into Denmark were written in German and were designed to break the morale of the German troops. They were very largely pictorial pamphlets, and almost all showed pictures of German corpses lying in snow-covered battlefields. They were crude, basic, but to the point. They were quickly read, and were designed to make the maximum impact in a few seconds. There was little text, but what there was seemed only to describe photographs which really needed little explanation. They were intended to make the German soldier lose faith in the leadership of his country. These pamphlets were circulated in Denmark and followed the general pattern of all black pamphlets sent to German troops throughout Europe.

There were several techniques of deception which were characteristic of this type of black pamphlet warfare. Sefton Delmer wrote that

> one leaflet, designed to stimulate desertion to Sweden and Switzerland, was got up to look exactly like a propaganda hand-out

[1] British propagandists, as well as Christmas Møller, were well aware that students were a good 'target' for propaganda. An article called 'Education in Democracy 1944', written by Christmas Møller and K. Watson as a contribution to a book *Higher Education in German-occupied Countries* laid great emphasis on the part played by schools and the universities in keeping the spirit of resistance alive amongst their students.

[2] Pamphlet *Saadan blev Norges Lærere Behandlet.*

issued to officers by the O.K.W. under the title *Mitteilungen für die Truppe*. Our leaflet discussed the problem of the increasing number of desertions to neutral countries and called on officers to instruct their men not to leave the hunt for deserters to the overburdened and by no means numerous Field Police, but to watch out for themselves for these treacherous cowards and prevent them from giving neutral countries a poor impression of the *Wehrmacht's* fighting spirit. The plan was for members of the Resistance to leave this leaflet somewhere where a German officer might have dropped it, and where it could be picked up by a German soldier.[1]

R. H. S. Crossman wrote that defeat was a good time to start propaganda.[2] This principle was employed in a slightly different way in British pamphlets to German troops. These pamphlets continually reminded the German soldier of past victories, and then drew the contrast with present defeats. They gave the impression that the German army was slowly but surely being destroyed. Pictures of headless corpses in German uniforms seemed to confirm this. Effective pictorial contrasts were made, for example, between the triumphant way the Germans marched into Holland and the far from triumphant way they retreated from Russia. One pamphlet, on the subject of Stalingrad, and suitably illustrated with photographs of slaughtered Germans, contrasted Hitler's promises with reality. It was a favourite trick of British black propagandists to quote from Hitler's earlier speeches promising a quick victory, and then to compare them with events in 1943 and 1944. It was much easier to make good propaganda from a military position which passed from the defensive to the offensive, than vice versa.

Hitler was caricatured in these pamphlets by photographs which made him out to be a raving madman. His leadership was continually criticized, either by comparing promises with facts or in photographs contrasting the swaggering German army in 1940 with the defeated and dejected army in 1944. A leaflet with the title *Hitler Kann den Krieg nicht mehr Gewinnen*, with four good reasons why this was so, was typical of the campaign to

[1] *Black Boomerang*.
[2] In the *Journal of the Royal United Service Institution* (1952).

denigrate Hitler as a leader in the eyes of his soldiers. A series of photographs showing Hitler with the gleam of victory in his eye and German troops marching into Poland, and ending with Hitler wide-eyed and sweating, superimposed on photographs of German prisoners of war in Russia, or upon the ruins of Hamburg, gave just the impression of incompetent leadership which the British propagandists wanted to implant in the German army.

The technique of picture stories was used to exploit the German love of the family and the home. One such leaflet showed in pictures the story of a young German who left his trade as a carpenter to serve in a German U-boat. The first half of the story showed the glory of recruitment to Hitler's navy. The second showed the young German, Günther Hartmuth, drowning with the wreck of his U-boat, and his young and pretty wife collapsing when she read the news of his death in a telegram. The final picture showed Hitler urging more men to their deaths in U-boats.

These were only a few of the methods used by the British black propagandists to demoralize German troops in Europe. Their leaflets showed a combination of the worst qualities of horrific press photography with those of the horror comic. However, included in these pamphlets was enough factual evidence to make them seem credible and not entirely imaginary. None of them gave any open indication that they were of British origin.

It was the duty of Rantzau and others involved in distributing these pamphlets to spread them wherever it was possible that Germans would read them. Members of the Resistance and the underground press had their own methods of infiltration amongst German troops stationed in Denmark.

From letters and telegrams it is known that S.O.E. was intimately involved in organizing the distribution of propaganda. A letter from Hollingworth to Muus showed the precise degree to which S.O.E. was concerned in spreading subversive propaganda.[1]

[1] Hollingworth to Muus, undated (Danish Archives).

This letter discussed the possibility of S.O.E. agents encouraging all forms of subversive activities amongst Danish workers, and contained a general directive to foreign workers going into Germany. Danish workers were clearly able not only to infiltrate anti-Nazi leaflets into Germany, but also to do greater damage. S.O.E. was aware of this, as the following directive addressed to foreign workers in Germany indicated.

Therefore do not miss any opportunity of:

1. (*a*) Expressing fear of heavy U.S.A. and British bombing in Germany.

(*b*) Pointing out hopelessly inadequate protection against air-raids.

(*c*) Spreading stories of appalling damage that you have heard of in other parts of Germany.

(*d*) Expressing amazement that the Party Bigwigs have their luxuries and orgies at home, while German soldiers die in thousands on the Russian and other fronts, and German workers are being worked to death and bombed to death like slaves. [The theme of the vile Nazi party official and the good, honest German soldier and worker was frequently stressed by British black propagandists.]

2. Subtly encouraging all forms of malingering, going slow and passive resistance.

3. Hindering.

(*a*) Wasting time. Pay frequent and long visits to the lavatories. Waste time when obtaining tools and materials.

(*b*) Waste oil, rags and all materials.

(*c*) In your own particular trade do whatever you know will cause trouble with the least detection. If you are employed in some other trade find out from your fellow workers what most frequently causes normal stoppages.

It seems that Goebbels's propaganda was met, at least as far as black pamphlets were concerned, with some competition from the supposedly straightforward and overt British propaganda.

CHAPTER 17

RADIO AND RESISTANCE

In his book *Black Boomerang* Sefton Delmer compared the virtue of black and white propaganda:

Nor am I in any way disparaging Carleton Greene[1] [head of the German section of the B.B.C.'s European Service] and his men when I say that the spinsterish insistence of the B.B.C. on its freedom from government control made it inevitable that the services would look around for an alternative medium without these virginal complexes. The whole of our white radio output suffered under the system of divided responsibility by which the B.B.C., an independent corporation, controlled what was broadcast to Germany in the name of Britain, while the government's planners and policy makers, sitting in my department were merely considered by the B.B.C. as advisers. This meant that it was never possible to gear B.B.C. output to operational requirements as perfectly as could be done with a unit where policy making, planning, intelligence and production were all under one hat. That alone made black and grey [propaganda] a necessity.

Delmer wrote here with particular reference to propaganda to Germany. His view that black propaganda was in many ways more effective than the B.B.C. broadcasts was not correct in the case of Denmark. The reason for this was simply that Denmark never became a theatre of war and therefore there was never any necessity for propaganda to be co-ordinated with military operations to such an extent as in France and Germany, where every broadcast and every pamphlet, particularly as the allied armies fought their way across Europe to the German frontier, had to be strictly in line with operational policy.

Delmer recounted how the Admiralty used black propaganda to suit its operational needs in a way in which the B.B.C. could never be used. 'What the Admiralty liked about black', he wrote, 'was its ability to make statements about sinkings, for

[1] Sir Hugh Carleton Greene is at present director-general of the B.B.C.

instance, without the Admiralty being held responsible. Had they been broadcast by the B.B.C. on the other hand, these would have been quoted as official Admiralty statements.' As a result, with the backing of the Admiralty, black propaganda 'intruded into the most sacred preserves of the B.B.C. with a live news broadcast of its own'.

The B.B.C. was not prepared to allow itself to be used by the service ministries in this way. All B.B.C. news bulletins were written by a member of the B.B.C. staff, and facts could not therefore be altered to suit any strategic requirement. Therefore there were clearly advantages in the service ministries using black propaganda for news items. There was no need for the strict regard for the truth or the quoting of sources which was the usual B.B.C. custom.

The B.B.C. provided first and foremost a news service, and news had to be accurate. The B.B.C. could not therefore allow itself to be subjected to the will of a service ministry as a propaganda tool, for some short-term advantage, which might in the end prejudice the reputation for accuracy which it had gradually built up.

The independence of the B.B.C., or its 'virginal complex' as Delmer termed it, may have been a disadvantage to the government in its attempt to co-ordinate propaganda and military operations in Germany and other theatres of war. In broadcasting to Denmark, the independence of the B.B.C. was the most vitally important factor, and it was in countries such as Denmark and Norway that the B.B.C. made its greatest impact. As far as these two countries were concerned, there was no need for the service ministries to try and subject the B.B.C. to their demands. Apart from the abortive expedition to Norway in 1940, these two countries were never areas where allied and German armies met and fought. Therefore propaganda to them never required the high degree of co-ordination with military strategy which was needed in any battle area. Had the Allies fought in Denmark, there would probably have been the same rivalries between those responsible for sending black and white propaganda to Denmark as there were between those responsible for propaganda to Germany. Danish black propaganda would have occupied an equal, perhaps even a greater, position of importance than the B.B.C.

From this it appears that the B.B.C. broadcasts were more important to those countries which were not combat areas, because the competition from black propaganda was less, and the B.B.C. was subject to less pressure from Britain's military strategists. B.B.C. broadcasts could be used for operational purposes to a certain extent only. The limit was when the independent nature of the B.B.C. was considered to be violated by service ministry demands. For example the B.B.C. co-operated wholeheartedly with S.O.E. in helping to send parachutists into enemy-occupied countries by the use of special messages. On the other hand the B.B.C. was not prepared to state in a news bulletin that there were fewer British ships sunk than there really were, so that the Admiralty could conceal a temporary disadvantage.

The history of British propaganda to German-occupied Denmark illustrates this fact clearly. At no time during the war was black propaganda ever as important to Denmark as the B.B.C. broadcasts. It was not competitive but complementary to the B.B.C. The later editions of *Vi Vil Vinde* gave the times of B.B.C. broadcasts and reproduced word for word several of the more important talks given in Danish over the B.B.C. Many Danes who took part in the Resistance are today unaware that there was any propaganda carried out from Britain except by the B.B.C. Radio Denmark is not mentioned now as frequently as the Danish section of the B.B.C., and most Danes did not know of its existence. The only way in which British black propaganda was able to affect Denmark, in a way in which the B.B.C. Danish Service could not, was by spreading pamphlets written in German and intended for the German soldiers stationed in Denmark.

The B.B.C. therefore undertook the major part of British propaganda to Denmark. The independence of the B.B.C. was not, as far as it can be seen from existing documents, violated by demands from service ministries which could not be met. The navy, the army and the R.A.F. did not need to put pressure on the Danish section of the B.B.C. as Denmark was not a battle area.

Policy was a different matter. Policy directives from government departments did not conflict with the ideas of the B.B.C. to such a degree as operational needs sometimes did. The Foreign Office did not ask the B.B.C. to put out broadcasts which prejudiced its reputation for reliability as the service ministries were inclined to do. The B.B.C. and the Foreign Office, through P.W.E., were together able to work out a policy for broadcasting to Denmark. Through P.W.E., the Foreign Office exercised control in propaganda policy over the broadcasts to Denmark. The only effective external control of the Danish section was exercised in policy matters. The degree of outside policy control varied from section to section in the B.B.C.'s European Service. As far as Denmark was concerned it seems that the Foreign Office and P.W.E. were responsible for most of the major changes in broadcasting policy. The B.B.C. exercised complete control of programme content, but in policy-making it was not independent of the Foreign Office. The control by the Foreign Office of the Danish section was maintained throughout the war. During 1940 and 1941 it seems to have been fairly slight but, after P.W.E. was formed, control was increased and regular directives sent.

The existing documents confirm that the Danish section was subject to external control. Instances have been quoted where Robert Jørgensen received directives and letters from P.W.E. and P.I.D. (both responsible to the Foreign Office) and from the Foreign Office itself. Jørgensen's reprimand from the Foreign Office in December 1943 for allowing it to be announced over the B.B.C. that Denmark had been recognized as an ally was indicative of the close eye the Foreign Office kept on broadcasts to Denmark.[1]

A typical Foreign Office directive on broadcasting policy

[1] See chapter 12.

can be quoted as an example. This was dated 24 March 1942 and was on the subject of Sweden.[1] It was sent to the editors of the B.B.C.'s Scandinavian Services, and began:

> There is abundant evidence that Germany is at present waging a war of nerves against Sweden. [The Germans had created expectation of a German invasion of Sweden, and the directive continued with a warning that the B.B.C. had to be very careful how it presented news about Sweden, so that it did not help the German war of nerves.] Where an item which suits the German purpose, such as the announcement of the suspension of German-Swedish trade negotiations, or the confiscation of fifteen Swedish newspapers for printing atrocity stories, must be broadcast because of its obvious news value, our aim should be either to put it in as innocuous a way as possible, or to supplement it with a parallel item which serves as an antidote.
>
> Those responsible for broadcasting to Scandinavia must consult with the Swedish team but this is not enough, as statements put out on the Home, Empire and other programmes are liable to have a damaging effect, since it is known that the people of the Northern Countries listen a great deal to bulletins directed to non-Scandinavian countries.

This was a detailed instruction on the policy to be carried out. Normally directives were acted upon by the Danish section, as there was no alternative. Policy control of the Danish section was probably greater than over other European sections of the B.B.C., because of Denmark's complex political status after the German occupation. There was no other country which had been occupied by the Germans, but which was allowed to carry on with the appearances at least of constitutional government. Policy towards Denmark after April 1940 was a political problem, which only the Foreign Office was competent to solve. The cautious attitude towards Denmark of the Foreign Office compared with that of S.O.E. has already been noted.[2] The Northern Department of the Foreign Office had to think not only in terms of the war but also of future Anglo-Danish relations. In this situation their caution was perhaps understandable. Sir John Anderson had said in the House of Commons

[1] Draft Foreign Office directive for Sweden, 24 March 1942 (Danish Archives).
[2] See chapter 12 and notes.

in July 1941 that foreign propaganda had to be in line with foreign policy.[1] So the Danish broadcasts had to be in line with Foreign Office policy towards Denmark.

Obviously a certain amount of flexibility was allowed to the Danish section within the terms of the directives. Robert Jørgensen was not forced to obey the directives to the letter. At times clearly he did not. At other times broadcasts were put out which contravened official policy, as was the case with the 'North Sea Powers' broadcast.[2]

N. F. Newsome's directive to all editors of the European Service in June 1942, which said, 'Not only do some editors follow their own line without reference to any instructions, but they actually adopt a line directly contrary to that which has been laid down',[3] shows that despite the official chain of control, many editors in the European Service did at times follow their own intuition.

It was precisely to avoid situations such as Newsome complained about that the weekly directive meetings between P.W.E. and the B.B.C. editors were held. Here it was possible to thrash out policy matters, each member present having the opportunity to say what he thought. The idea was that disagreement should show itself before the policy was decided upon and not after. On the whole this system seems to have been successful and from the evidence available most policy decisions made at these meetings and incorporated in directives seem to have been followed. It is quite certain, however, that as P.W.E. was responsible to the Foreign Office, no policy decision of which the Foreign Office did not approve was ever written into a P.W.E. directive.

It appears then that the Danish section of the B.B.C. reflected as accurate a picture as it is possible to obtain of British foreign policy towards Denmark during the Second World War, that it was the major weapon of British propaganda to Denmark, that it was comparatively free from any pressure from British service ministries because Denmark was not a combat

[1] See chapter 3. [2] See chapter 12. [3] See chapter 7.

area, and that as a result black propaganda played only a very small part.

How successful was the B.B.C. in the role assigned to it?

The two main purposes of the B.B.C.'s broadcasts to Denmark were to provide an objective and comprehensive news service and to give active support whenever possible to the Danish Resistance movement.

It was vital to give news to Denmark for, deprived of news, an enemy-occupied country does not know which way to turn. Without fact, it has nothing upon which to base its decisions. In Denmark it became apparent soon after the occupation that part of the German policy was to starve the Danish people of all news from the outside world. The Germans hoped that the Danes would be content with their mild treatment and would not wish to take part in the war. To prevent news freely circulating in Denmark became of prime importance to the Germans.

Without news the Danish people had little to help them understand the real nature of the struggle. A Dane might read an article in a newspaper and know that it was only half the truth as a result of German censorship. If it remained impossible for him to know the truth, then it was unlikely that he would take action against the Germans. Few men will risk their lives against overwhelming force, unless they understand something of the real situation and know that there are others who believe as they do.

It was vital, therefore, to build up a news service to keep Denmark informed of events both outside and inside Denmark, and to counteract the oppressive effect of German propaganda. The German press attaché, Meisner, was efficient at his job but he ultimately failed. Instructions were given to all Danish newspaper editors that they should maintain their cheerful pre-invasion tone.[1] British communiqués and Churchill's speeches were not to be printed. German newspapers were brought by plane every day from Germany, but they were left in heaps, unsold, all over Copenhagen.

[1] For a description of German methods of censorship in Denmark, see *Denmark —Hitler's Model Protectorate* by Sten Gudme.

The Danish underground press and the B.B.C. counteracted the menace of German censorship and propaganda within Denmark. This was the first victory of the Danish Resistance—to get uncensored news freely circulating round Denmark. The underground press grew rapidly. By the end of the war a total of 538 different underground papers were published. In 1940 their combined circulation was estimated at 1,200, in 1943 at 2,600,000 and in the first four months of 1945 at 10,131,000. The largest paper reached a circulation of 150,000 copies in the spring of 1945.[1] From 1943 the illegal news agency *Information* supplied every major newspaper with news, and had daily contact with Stockholm, from where the news was transmitted to the free world.[2]

The B.B.C. broadcast news bulletins in Danish from the day of the German occupation to the day of liberation. Most of the B.B.C.'s news of Danish events came from underground sources in Denmark, and after 1943 mainly from the *Information* news agency.[3] The one advantage which the B.B.C. had over the illegal newspapers was that it was able to relay news more quickly. By 1944 there were four broadcasts daily from the B.B.C. to Denmark, and urgent news items could be, and were, included in the programmes as soon as they were received. This provided a quicker method of disseminating news than the illegal papers, which had to be passed secretly from one person to another. Furthermore, Denmark had proportionately the second highest number of radio owners in the whole of Europe.

Despite occasional mistakes, the B.B.C. built up in Denmark the reputation for reliability and objectivity which it has so carefully guarded ever since. This was a deliberate policy which worked with great advantage in Denmark, where the real need was for reliable news of both general war events and Danish affairs.

R. H. S. Crossman, one of Britain's chief wartime propagandists, gave one example of how it paid to tell the truth: 'I shall never forget', he wrote, 'the first really big raid on Berlin.

[1] Figures quoted in Hæstrup, *Panorama Denmark*.

[2] See *Panorama Denmark*.

[3] See chapter 13.

It was a terrible disaster. We announced the losses of the R.A.F., before the German Communiqué came out, and our admission of our losses was larger than the German claim. This was the greatest psychological warfare triumph of the year.'[1]

On the subject of the truth he wrote:

> We discovered, after many experiments in Dr Goebbels' technique, that the truth pays. It is a complete delusion to think of the brilliant propagandist as being a professional liar. The brilliant propagandist is the man who tells the truth, or that selection of the truth which is requisite for his purpose, and tells it in such a way that the recipient does not realize that he is receiving any propaganda...From what I am saying there arises this conclusion—if the art of propaganda is to conceal that you are doing propaganda then the central substance of propaganda is hard, correct information.[2]

To give hard, correct information was the aim of the B.B.C. broadcasts to Denmark.

The other prime purpose of the B.B.C. Danish Service was to give support whenever possible to the Danish Resistance. This was the less easy of the two objectives because it was both tactical and political, and in giving support to the Resistance the B.B.C. was, throughout, subject to control and restraint by the Foreign Office.

Spreading news was in itself supporting the Resistance, because the dissemination of true and objective information made it easier for the Danes to decide whether or not to fight. The neutralizing of German propaganda in Denmark, and the spreading of British and allied news, helped to create an atmosphere where more and more Danes decided to join the active fight against the Germans. The B.B.C. was, however, able to help the Danish Resistance in a more positive way than merely by the spreading of news.

First, it helped to create a climate of opinion which was firmly against any form of collaboration by Danish politicians. It has been noted that it was not until the early summer of

[1] R. H. S. Crossman in the *Journal of the Royal United Service Institution* (1952).

[2] *Ibid.*

1943 that the Danish section of the B.B.C. came out fully against the continuation of a Danish government. This was because it was some time before Denmark showed itself ready for the crisis which would involve the collapse of the government and the taking over of control by the Germans. The first subject of attack was Scavenius and other pro-German figures. When Scavenius became prime minister, the attack became more general. The aim was to show the Danish people that their government, because of German pressure, could act no longer in Danish interests. The third and final phase, after the elections of March 1943 and the end of the negotiations between S.O.E. and the League, was to encourage active resistance and sabotage, in the hope that the Danish government would fall, and the Germans would be forced to take over control of the country.

At no time during the war could it be claimed that the B.B.C. broadcasts *created* an atmosphere of unrest which directly led to action. Nor could it be claimed that the B.B.C. broadcasts caused demonstrations against the Germans amongst the Danish population. Propaganda is rarely the direct cause of action. It is most effective as a probe when events proclaim that a tense and inflammable situation exists. Denmark was no exception to this general rule.

The B.B.C., however, can claim that its broadcasts supported active resistance by stirring any unrest that existed. It put salt into Danish wounds, and punctured German and Danish Nazi propaganda. If feeling ran high amongst the Danish population, the B.B.C. immediately broadcast talks which were designed to inflame those feelings. The most obvious example was the rioting in Copenhagen when Scavenius signed the Anti-Comintern Pact in 1941.[1] Christmas Møller admitted that, although the outburst was a genuine expression of Danish feelings, the effect of the rioting was considerably increased by broadcasts from London.[2] The riots were not caused, but encouraged, by the B.B.C.

The broadcasts during the summer of 1943 showed the B.B.C.'s

[1] See chapter 4. [2] See chapter 4.

propaganda at its best. Here a policy decision was taken to increase the tension that already existed amongst the Danish working population and add to their resentment against the Scavenius government and the Germans. It would be wrong to say that these broadcasts caused the outbreaks of strikes during August, but these broadcasts week after week must have helped many Danish men decide that some action had to be taken. There were many other factors involved, but the B.B.C. can claim a share of the credit for helping the Danish Resistance precipitate the crisis of August 1943.

If it is asked whether the B.B.C. could have helped the Resistance more than it did, the answer must be yes. In the early months of 1944, which were critical for the Danish Home Front, the B.B.C. could and should have included far more Danish local news in its broadcasts. The criticisms from Stockholm were justified. In the last days of June, when rioting and sabotage in Copenhagen reached a peak, *Information* relayed page after page of news to Stockholm where it was transmitted immediately to London. Yet at this time the B.B.C. devoted only a minimal portion of its news bulletins to Danish events, and failed to broadcast the Freedom Council's orders. As a result, Danes in other parts of the country did not know of the events in Copenhagen as soon as they might have done. At this time the amount of general war news, supplied by the Central News Desk of the B.B.C., should have been cut drastically, in favour of Danish news.

The amount of Danish news allowed in the B.B.C. broadcasts was initially very small. It is difficult to be certain who was responsible for this policy—the existing documents do not prove it one way or the other—but the decision must have been reached jointly by the Foreign Office, P.W.E., and the B.B.C. It was probably on Foreign Office initiative, and the reason for it was that Denmark was not an ally and could not therefore be accorded the same privileges as other countries who were officially recognized as allies. Therefore projection of British views had, in Denmark, to be on a larger scale than in other German-occupied countries with allied governments in London. These allied countries were allowed much greater time for local news.

Although the situation had changed by the end of 1944 as a result of a complete cessation of D.P.T. news from Stockholm, the B.B.C. should have acted before such drastic moves by Danes in Stockholm were necessary. There was enough evidence from Stockholm to show how damaging the lack of local news in the B.B.C. broadcasts was to the Danish Resistance. A man from Esbjerg had said that the only means by which he could hear about sabotage was over the B.B.C.[1] If the B.B.C. cut local news to a minimum, one part of the country did not know what was happening in the other, and unity was lost.

By November 1944 the amount of Danish local news had increased to the proportion allowed to other countries. The Foreign Office and P.W.E. had altered their views. This was the one occasion in the history of broadcasting to Denmark where the B.B.C. could perhaps have asserted its independence of P.W.E. and the Foreign Office. The Editor of the Danish section was well aware of the need, and so was the Central News Desk. There was ample reason for an increase in Danish local news but the opportunity was not grasped. The result was that for a short time the Danish Resistance suffered until action from Stockholm forced a change of policy. P.W.E. answered the criticisms and the B.B.C. increased the amount of Danish local news.

This is the picture of events suggested by the available documents.

Apart from this one instance in the first half of 1944, the Danish section of the B.B.C. acted as a valuable support for the Danish Resistance, giving talks, commentaries, encouragement and appeals—all designed to swing public opinion more and more against the Germans.

As Dr Hæstrup has shown, S.O.E. played a major part in the Danish fight for freedom. The B.B.C. was able to help S.O.E. operations in a limited but, nevertheless, regular and important

[1] See chapter 14.

way. The special message system of giving signals to underground groups to announce the arrival of parachutists or containers was the most effective way possible of maintaining operational contact between Britain and the Resistance. The military importance of the B.B.C. would have increased greatly had S.H.A.E.F. mounted a campaign in Denmark. This is borne out by S.H.A.E.F.'s operational order to the Danish Resistance of 14 June 1944.[1] Had this plan been put into general operation the chief method of communicating with the resistance groups would have been through the B.B.C. As there was no S.H.A.E.F. campaign in Denmark the B.B.C.'s role was limited to assisting S.O.E. with parachuting arms and men to the Resistance.

Throughout the war the nature of the B.B.C.'s work was that of support—support for British foreign policy, support for S.O.E. operations, and support for the Danish Resistance with news and propaganda broadcasts. No propaganda body could ever *create* a resistance movement and throughout the war P.W.E. and the B.B.C. realized that the inspiration and determination to resist had first to become widespread amongst the Danish people. When the will to resist had become evident then the B.B.C. was able to give valuable propaganda support to Danish actions and ideals. The B.B.C. could never claim to have played more than a minor part in the success of the vast organization which was the Danish Resistance by 1945. To be a member of that Resistance meant a decision on the part of each individual, and that decision meant sacrifice and possibly death. The B.B.C. could not make this decision. It could only support and encourage it, once it was made.

The Danish section of the B.B.C. realized that this decision had to be made by each individual. On 27 December 1944 T. M. Terkelsen read out a letter over the B.B.C. which had been written by the daughter of Marius Fiil, the innkeeper at Hvidsten, to Dr Werner Best, the German plenipotentiary, on the day when eight people from her village were executed.

[1] Quoted in chapter 15.

Marius Fiil was one of the many who decided that his duty was to resist. His sacrifice was his own life.

His daughter wrote:

The sabotage our men have done was not undertaken out of hatred for Germany, but because Denmark is at war: for Denmark is at war. I myself have a little daughter who today lost her father, her grandfather and her uncle. She fortunately does not understand, but if she could understand it she would be proud of them. They had one aim in life and were not afraid to die for it. Every single person who gave his life for Denmark is a witness that even a small country like Denmark has a right to think independently. I have no more to say, but I would like to add that I am proud to have had a husband, a father and a brother who were deemed worthy to die for Denmark.[1]

[1] Quoted in a B.B.C. talk by T. M. Terkelsen called 'The Nature of Resistance', 27 December 1944 (B.B.C. Archives).

SOURCE MATERIAL AND BIBLIOGRAPHY

UNPUBLISHED

IN ENGLISH

Transcripts of the broadcasts of the Danish section of the B.B.C. 1940–5 (B.B.C. Archives).

General directives to the editors of the European Service of the B.B.C. from the Director of European Broadcasts 1941–4 (B.B.C. Archives).

Reports of the Foreign Research and Press Service 1940–5 (Foreign Office Library).

Some Notes on the B.B.C. Danish Service (B.B.C. Archives).

Papers written for the Conference on European Resistance Movements held at St Antony's College, Oxford, in December 1962, especially:

Denmark and Britain by Dr Jørgen Hæstrup.
Britain and Denmark by Major-General Sir Colin Gubbins.
Norway and Britain by Professor M. Skodvin.
Britain and Norway by Lt.-Colonel C. S. Hampton.
Yugoslavia and Britain by Professor J. Marjanović.
Britain and Yugoslavia by F. W. Deakin.
Holland and Britain by Dr. L. de Jong.

Copies of intelligence reports, in private possession in Denmark, which were sent to S.O.E. headquarters in London.

Civil Defence Discussion Group pamphlet, *The Nazis in Scandinavia*, by K. Kenney and T. M. Terkelsen, London 1944 (not for general publication).

IN DANISH

The personal papers, deposited in the Royal Archives in Copenhagen, of the following:

Foss, Erling
Gudme, Sten
Gundel, Leif
Hansen, Arne Duus
Jørgensen, Robert
Munck, Ebbe
Møller, J. Christmas
Seehusen, Sven
Seidenfaden, Erik

Also the papers of the Danish Press Service deposited in the Royal Archives.

SOURCE MATERIAL AND BIBLIOGRAPHY

PUBLISHED

IN ENGLISH

Beachcroft, T. O. *British Broadcasting*. London, 1946.

B.B.C. *The European Service of the B.B.C.—Two Decades of Broadcasting to Europe, 1938–1959*. London, 1957.

Buckmaster, Maurice. *They Fought Alone*. London, 1958.

Bullock, Alan. *Hitler—A Study in Tyranny*. London, 1960.

Butler, J. R. M. *Grand Strategy*, vol. II of *The History of the Second World War*. London, 1957.

Crossman, R. H. S. 'Psychological Warfare', *Journal of the Royal United Service Institution*. London, August 1952.

Dalton, Hugh. *The Fateful Years*. London, 1957.

Dancy, Eric. *Danes Stand to for Zero*. London, 1943.

Delmer, D. Sefton. *Trail Sinister*. London, 1961.

—— *Black Boomerang*. London, 1962.

Ehrman, John. *Grand Strategy*, vol. V of *The History of the Second World War*. London, 1956.

Ellis, L. F. *Victory in the West*. London, 1962.

European Resistance Movements 1939–45. Oxford, 1964 (Pergamon Press).

Europe under the Nazi Scourge. London, 1940 (Times Publishing Company).

Flender, Harold. *Rescue in Denmark*. London, 1963.

Fraser, Lindley. *Propaganda*. London, 1957.

Gubbins, Sir Colin. 'Resistance Movements in the War', *Journal of the Royal United Service Institution*. London, May 1948.

Gudme, Sten. *Denmark—Hitler's Model Protectorate*, 3rd rev. ed. London, 1942.

Hæstrup, Jørgen. *Panorama Denmark* (From Occupied to Ally—Danish Resistance Movement 1940–45). Danish Ministry of Foreign Affairs, Copenhagen, 1963.

Krabbe, Henning. *Voices from Britain*. London, 1947.

Lampe, David. *The Savage Canary*. London, 1957.

Lean, E. Tangye. *Voices in the Darkness*. London, 1943.

Lerner, Daniel. *Sykewar*. New York, 1949.

Lockhart, Sir Robert Bruce. *Comes the Reckoning*. London, 1947.

Maclean, Fitzroy. *Eastern Approaches*. London, 1949.

Muus, Flemming. *The Spark and the Flame*. London, 1957.

Rolo, C. J. *Radio Goes to War*. London, 1943.

Royal Institute of International Affairs. *Survey of International Affairs 1939–46—Hitler's Europe*. London, 1954.

Royal Institute of International Affairs. *Documents on International Affairs 1939–46*, vol. I, London, 1951; vol. II, London, 1954.
Seth, Ronald. *The Undaunted*. London, 1956.
Sweet-Escott, Bickham. *Baker Street Irregular*. London, 1965.
Terkelsen, T. M. *Denmark—Fight Follows Surrender*, 4th rev. ed. London, 1943.
—— *Front Line in Denmark*. London, 1944.
Thomas, Ivor. *Warfare by Words*. Harmondsworth, 1942.
Woodward, Sir Llewellyn. *British Foreign Policy in the Second World War*. London, 1962.

Also useful were copies of the magazine *Denmark*, published by the Anglo-Danish Society, London, the *B.B.C. Handbooks* for 1939–45, and the British press. Indexed books of wartime newspaper cuttings can be found in London at the Royal Institute of International Affairs, at the Wiener Library and in the B.B.C. Archives.

IN DANISH

B.B.C. Publication. *De Hører B.B.C.* London, 1946.
Foss, Erling. *Fra Passiv til Aktiv Modstand*. Copenhagen, 1946.
—— *På Eget Ansvar*. Copenhagen, 1958.
Gundel, Leif. *Her er London*. Copenhagen, 1945.
Hæstrup, Jørgen. *Kontakt med England*. Copenhagen, 1954.
—— *Hemmelig Alliance*, vols. I and II. Copenhagen, 1959.
—— *Table Top Jyske Samlinger*, vol. V, part 4. Aarhus, 1961.
Jørgensen, Robert. *London Kalder*. Copenhagen, 1945.
Kirchoff, Hans, Nissen, Henrik S. and Poulsen, Henning. *Besættelsestidens Historie*. Copenhagen, 1964.
Nissen, Henrik and Poulsen, Henning. *På Dansk Friheds Grund*. Copenhagen, 1963.
Politiken Press. *Besættelsens Hvem—Hvad—Hvor*. Copenhagen, 1965.
Røder, H. C. *De Seljede Bare*. Copenhagen, 1957.

PERSONAL INTERVIEWS

Foss, Erling
Gundel, Leif
Jørgensen, Robert
Krabbe, Henning
Muus, Flemming
Rush, F. A.
Seehusen, Sven
Seidenfaden, Erik
Terkelsen, T. M.
Tillge-Rasmussen, Sven
Truelsen, Svend

INDEX

For EU product safety concerns, contact us at Calle de José Abascal, 56–1°,
28003 Madrid, Spain or eugpsr@cambridge.org.

www.ingramcontent.com/pod-product-compliance
Ingram Content Group UK Ltd.
Pitfield, Milton Keynes, MK11 3LW, UK
UKHW010346140625
459647UK00010B/855

* 9 7 8 0 5 2 1 1 5 8 4 4 2 *